The Place of Thought

THE MIDDLE AGES SERIES

Ruth Mazo Karras, Series Editor

Edward Peters, Founding Editor

A complete list of books in the series
is available from the publisher.

The Place of Thought

The Complexity of One in Late Medieval French Didactic Poetry

Sarah Kay

PENN

UNIVERSITY OF PENNSYLVANIA PRESS

Philadelphia

10 9 8 7 6 5 4 3 2 1

Published by
University of Pennsylvania Press
Philadelphia, Pennsylvania 19104-4112

Library of Congress Cataloging-in-Publication Data
Kay, Sarah.
    The place of thought : the complexity of one in late medieval French didactic poetry /
Sarah Kay.
        p.   cm. — (Middle ages series)
    Includes bibliographical references (p.   ) and index.
    ISBN-13: 978-0-8122-4007-8
    ISBN-10: 0-8122-4007-3 (cloth : alk. paper)
    1. French poetry—To 1500—History and criticism.   2. Didactic poetry, French—
History and criticism.   I. Title.
PQ216.K38   2007
841.209   22

                                                            2006051055

Contents

Illustrations

Abbreviations, References, and Other Conventions

Abbreviations for Principal Medieval Texts

BA   *Breviari d'amor*
CLE   *Chemin de long estude*
JBJ   *Le Joli buisson de Jonece*
JRB   *Le Jugement du roy de Behaigne*
JRN   *Le Jugement dou roy de Navarre*
OM   *Ovide moralisé*
PVH   *Le Pèlerinage de vie humaine*
RR   *Le Roman de la rose*

References

References to the *Breviari d'amor* follow Ricketts's convention of distinguishing verse, prose, and rubrics. A number alone refers to a line of verse, a number prefaced by P refers to prose, and one prefaced by T designates a rubric.

The works of Aristotle are cited by Bekker reference; Aquinas's *Summa theologiae* is cited by question and article; Augustine's works are cited in the form *Work*, Book, chapter, and section; e.g., *On the Trinity*, V, vi, §10.

Secondary works are referenced using a shortened form of the title; full bibliographical references can be found in the Bibliography.

Translations and Quotations

Works in medieval French and Occitan are cited in English translation and the original in the text; all translations are my own. Works in Latin and modern foreign languages are cited in English in the text and in the original in the notes; the source of translations is indicated; in some cases, even where published translations exist, I have opted to use my own.

Spellings

I have respected the spellings used by the authors or editors in all texts cited, except for the *Pèlerinage de vie humaine,* where I have supplied acute accents on words that are otherwise ambiguous. I have standardized the punctuation of direct speech in quotations from all medieval texts in conformity with modern usage and have used lowercase forms at the beginnings of lines except where uppercase is required by the syntax.

All through this book I have been faced with the problem of whether to write "one" or "One." Sometimes the answer is clear: a particular individual is a lowercase one, God gets the divine majuscule. But there is a gray area where what is being conceived is some abstracted unity whose rights to the big *O* are less clear cut. Since the whole point of my argument is that the concept of one/One is problematic, it is not surprising that I have not found an unambiguous criterion to decide by. Readers are most welcome to entertain the possibility of spelling otherwise than in the form eventually chosen.

Preface

WHEN I BEGAN WRITING this book several years ago, interest in didacticism, and in monologic discourse more generally, seemed to me a valid way of questioning what had become a critical orthodoxy that privileged playfulness, irony, multiplicity, and indeterminacy. This conviction was fed, in particular, by the recent writings of Slavoj Žižek, such as his book *Did Somebody Say Totalitarianism?* which uncovers the repressive tendencies at work in liberal critical practice. As my project developed, though, I became concerned that, in resisting the current liberal orthodoxy, I ran the risk of being associated with a tradition I knew to be conservative. Was my sympathy toward this poetry, which I saw as both advancing and reflecting on some kind of "oneness" of meaning, in fact repeating the reductiveness of Robertsonian criticism, or playing into the hands of conservatism? In Europe, Žižek was far from alone, since left-leaning thinkers had been interested in notions of oneness (singularity, community, universality) for some time, but in the United States progressive thinking (as well as some reactionary thinking, of course) remained unabashedly liberal.

By way of preface to this book, then, I would like to make it clear that its argument is intended to be antihegemonic. Its aim is to remind critics, especially but not only of medieval literature, that multiplicity is not inherently more radical than oneness. Although some of the texts I include have a pious agenda, the desire to transmit a unified message leads them to realize that "oneness" is problematic, and "one" meaning difficult if not impossible to assign. It is because of this difficulty that "placing" thought is both so attractive to the poets I discuss—it offers them the hope of fixing or determining meaning in the visual field—and ultimately so elusive, as the place itself retreats into invisibility. What I have called the "complexity of one" is a poetic practice that, at once intellectually and aesthetically challenging, is not to be confused with dogmatism or intolerance.

Introduction

Another and More Perfect World

I SHALL LET THE SYBIL introduce this book for me, since her words to Christine de Pizan while escorting her on her journey in the *Livre du Chemin de long estude* epitomize what I see as the ambition of didactic poetry:

> But if you will follow my banner/pen, I believe I can lead you indeed into another and more perfect world, where you will truly be able to learn far more than you could comprehend in this one, about things more worthy of note, more delightful or more beneficial, and where there is nothing base or sorrowful. If you will make me your teacher, I will show you the source of all the misfortune that befalls the world.

> Mais se veulx suivre mon penon
> je te cuid conduire de fait
> en autre monde plus parfaict,
> ou tu pourras trop plus apprendre
> que tu ne peus en cestui comprendre,
> voire de choses plus nottables,
> plus plaisans et plus prouffitables,
> et ou n'a vilté ne destrece.
> Et se de moy fais ta mestrece,
> je te monstreray dont tout vient
> le meschief qui au monde avient. (*CLE*, 648–56)

The Sybil's pun on *penon* (meaning both "banner" and "pen") makes writing a heroic mission, but one that can be invested if need be with powers of coercion. Readers are to have their minds enlarged, their worth increased, and their enjoyment enhanced, but to do so they must submit to its teaching and follow its lead. This place to which they will be taken if they do so, this "other and more perfect world," is an example of the "place of thought" in my title.

The urge to "place" thought in this way is typical of writing in France in what can be called "the long fourteenth century"—the period that extends from Jean de Meun's continuation of the *Roman de la rose* in the 1270s to the works of Christine de Pizan in the early fifteenth century. This is the time span within which all of the works discussed in this book fall. They are a late thirteenth-century Occitan encyclopedia, the *Breviari d'amor* by Matfre Ermengaud; a series of works that range through the fourteenth century—the *Ovide moralisé* (between 1316 and 1325), Guillaume de Deguileville's *Pèlerinage de vie humaine* (1330–31), Machaut's *Jugement dou roy de Navarre* (1349 or 1350, or later), and Froissart's *Joli buisson de Jonece* (usually dated 1373); and the text from which my opening quotation is taken, Christine de Pizan's *Livre du Chemin de long estude* of 1402. In the Conclusion I return to the beginning of the period and the *Roman de la rose*, which both makes and breaks the mold for many of the intellectual "places" in these subsequent works.

In this period of the long fourteenth century, didacticism is everywhere perceptible. Vernacular writers compose or translate treatises to incite their readers to excellence in a variety of fields. The *exemplum* becomes a staple of composition of works of all kinds. The influence of ancient ethical writings, especially those of Boethius, is pervasive. Literary works throng with personified abstractions that make explicit a concern not only with moral or social defects or qualities but also with theological and philosophical schemes. Even predominantly courtly literature betrays an overwhelming urge to be improving. In texts of this kind, metaphors of place are omnipresent. Readers are forever being invited to locate themselves on a path somewhere, by some fountain, in some study, or within some garden, castle, or city.

Typically, these metaphors have a deliberately banal quality; that is, the place in question is in more than one sense a common place, a *locus communis*. First, these *loci* are traditional, aligning the text that contains them with its predecessors. Some of them are knowingly adapted from late antique texts, like the image of the city, taken up by Christine de Pizan from Augustine in the *Cité des dames*, or of the prison cell adapted in various ways by Machaut, Froissart, and others from Boethius. Others are harder to ascribe a source to, like the ubiquitous courts and palaces of courtly poetry. The *Roman de la rose* clearly provided a rich repertoire of spatial images that was consciously reworked to produce whole shrubberies of *dits*.

Second, the explicit function of these *loci* is to group together sets of characters, typically either personified abstractions or else the historical or mythical figures of classical *exempla*, and thereby to situate the text's argument in an identifiably common ground. The common place is thus one that is shared both between texts, and by various elements within the text. This use of the term *locus communis* as a place of argument is found in Quintilian—even though, as Mary Carruthers points out, he "warns his readers that he is using the word in an unusual sense."[1] Carruthers goes on: "It seems to me that the basic notion of a memory-place as a common-place into which one 'gathers' a variety of material is essential to understanding how the process of ethical valorizing [of reading] occurs."[2] It is from this usage that the collections of *sententiae*, which in the Middle Ages were gathered into *florilegia*, became known in the early modern period as "commonplace books."[3]

Carruthers's comment points to a third sense in which the "place of thought" is a common place. Marshaling its figures together not only provides a location for arguments inside the text, it also anticipates the moral or intellectual consensus that the text sets out to forge. Its readers are being enticed, lured, exhorted, summoned, and if necessary dragooned into this *locus communis*, which will thereby become an expression of their *community* of outlook. The "places" of didactic poetry—paths, temples, gardens, courtrooms, and so on—both assume a degree of homogeneity and aspire to forge one; or, to put it less benignly, they set out to impose one.

Thus at the basis of this book is the perception that many of the didactic poems of the long fourteenth century work by "placing" thought within a recognizable location. The spatial image serves to unify both the expression and reception of this thought; that is, it is a prop of didacticism, broadly understood as an attempt to articulate, convey, and if necessary enforce unity of meaning and interpretation. Didactic texts, in the sense that I am using the term here, thereby belong in the domain of what has been called "monologism." The concept of monologism was coined by Bakhtin in opposition to what he called "dialogism," the unresolved proliferation of discourses that he sees as characterizing the nineteenth-century novel.[4] By comparison with dialogism, monologism, or the convergence of discourses in unity, did not interest him. It was not just the inferior pole of the dichotomy but also went largely unexplored in a theory whose entire attention was directed in the opposing direction. And since Bakhtin, "monologic" has been used primarily as a term of disparagement. For example, when Terence Cave writes of late medieval allegories that "the range of signification is trapped within what is essentially a monologic discourse," there is no doubt that he intends to criticize these texts for operating within a limited and restrictive framework.[5] Yet didactic poetry has always found a receptive readership, which suggests that monologism is not without the power to charm. Moreover, for much of the history of thought, where the "problem of the one and the many" has held sway, it has by no means been the case that "one" can be regarded as intellectually inferior to "many." Indeed, recent years have seen renewed philosophical interest in concepts of oneness, such as singularity, universality, and community, among writers as prominent as Agamben, Deleuze, Derrida, Lacan, Levinas, Nancy, and Žižek.

My contention in this book is that when didactic texts promote some "one" of thought, this inevitably commits them to thinking, at some level, about the meaning of "one," and that this commitment has aesthetic as well as intellectual consequences. Aristotle said, "Without an image thinking is impossible," and this was confirmed by Aquinas, for whom "understanding never takes place without images and there are no images apart from the body."[6] The inherent difficulty or complexity of this "one" is realized in the *loci* in which it is "placed," since although these are in some ways familiar and strongly visual in their appeal, they frequently also defy our capacity to visualize them. The descriptions of places found in didactic works, and indeed the illuminations in the manuscripts that contain them, often testify to the challenge of conceptualizing the unity of thought that the text promotes. This fusion of the intellectual with the aesthetic is what founds the appeal of such works.

The remainder of this Introduction contains four sections in which I elaborate on my central terms of "place," "thought," "the complexity of one," and "poetry" and a final section sketching the argument of the chapters that follow.

Place

The places of didactic poetry—from landscapes and gardens to palaces and temples, and including Christine's travels through the cosmos—have been the object of considerable study. However, they have tended to be approached within a perspective shaped by rhetoric. Attention has been paid to the metaphorical or thematic value of particular places—how a garden might evoke paradise, for example—or to the way place founds proximity and thus makes it easier to recall how one idea may be articulated with another.[7] This bias toward rhetoric in the analysis of the didactic place means that individual poetic *loci* have been seen as part of a range of places rather than as instances of place as such. Given that many of the didactic works that use spatial images are quite philosophically sophisticated, it is worth also taking into account the philosophical understanding of place that Aristotle advances in his *Physics*, a text extensively taught and commented on from the thirteenth century onward. Its canonical status is attested, for example, in the *Roman de la rose* when Nature defers to the authority of Aristotle as the most qualified observer of her workings:

And he should take care to learn from Aristotle who observed Nature better than anyone since the days of Cain.

> Et li convandroit prandre cure
> d'estre deciples Aristote,
> qui mieuz mist natures en note
> que nus hon puis le tans Caÿn. (*RR*, 18000–18003)

Aristotle starts off from the general assumption that everything is somewhere, and that this somewhere is what we would call "place." Place would thus play a foundational role toward all other things: "Hesiod . . . thought, with most people, that everything is somewhere, and in place. If this is its nature, the power of place must be a marvellous thing, and be prior to all other things" (*Physics*, 208b28–35).[8] As the ground on which reality is determined, place is, however, decidedly difficult to determine in itself. We have here an instance where, if thinking always takes place with reference to the visual, then some things are decidedly less easy to envision than others. Aristotle argues that place needs to be distinguished on the one hand from void and on the other hand from body. Place cannot be a void, because the whole of physics (i.e., nature), Aristotle thinks, is dependent upon motion, with every body following some inherent trajectory; for example, fire moves upward and earth downward. Given that a vacuum cannot serve to articulate movement, he implicitly rejects the concept of "space" in favor of that of "place."[9] (Indeed, historians of ideas have gone so far as to contend that there is no notion of space in the Middle Ages, only one of place.)[10] If things are in a place, for Aristotle, they are in something that is ordered and possesses the basic orientations of up, down, left, right, front, and back. Place, unlike void, would thus guarantee the possibility of motion. A body also possesses these same dimensions of up, down, back, front, left, and right. Does this mean that place can be identified with a body? On the contrary, Aristotle argues, the two must be distinct, since the reason for wanting to know what place is, is to know what a body is *in*. If a place were a body, then "there would be two bodies in the same place" (*Physics*, 209a6–7).[11]

Aristotle's conclusion is that place is not itself a body but the limit of a body: "place . . . is . . . the boundary of the containing body at which it is in contact with the contained body" (*Physics*, 212a5–7), "the place of a thing is the innermost motionless boundary of what contains it" (*Physics*, 212a20).[12] Benjamin Morison comments helpfully on these passages when he glosses Aristotle's notion of containment here as "circumscriptive": "Circumscriptive containing is when x is in its surroundings in the sense that x's surroundings are moulded to x; they impinge on x and stop at x's borders. In this sense, for instance, liquid is in a vessel; this is indeed Aristotle's favoured illustration of the locative sense of 'in.' In this sense too I am in the air in this room, or a fish is in the sea."[13] This is different from what Morrison calls "receptive" containment, which does not define a border in the same way. As I move around a room I displace the air as I go; however, "suppose I am in France; I do not make a me-shaped hole in France, nor do I displace parts of France when I travel round in it."[14] I am contained *receptively* in France but *circumscriptively* in the air in France.

The essential features of place, as Aristotle understands it, then, are that it is internally differentiated or ordered; and that it circumscribes or defines the limit of a body. Without wanting to set excessive store on the Sybil's pun on *penon*, we can see, I think, that it responds directly to both these features. Insofar as the *penon* denotes the act of writing, the "place" to which we will follow it can be seen as internally differentiated, ordered, intelligible, definable; and insofar as the implications of the *penon* are military, the "place" in question is also subject to containment, to limitation, to regulation, to constraint. The philosophical concept of place is especially appropriate to the didactic enterprise because it confers on thought an "outline" that enables it to be transmitted intelligibly and, if necessary, imposed.[15]

In this book I do not always approach the places deployed in didactic texts solely from this Aristotelian standpoint. These *loci* undoubtedly belong in the rhetorical texture of the poetic works that contain them. However, they are also always considered in relation to the way they serve to locate and structure thought, because of the way they serve to order and circumscribe the unity of meaning to which the didactic text aspires.

Thought

As Aristotle's argument in the *Physics* progresses, it becomes clear that he doesn't himself associate thought with place. His account of place is entirely concerned with physical bodies and does not apply to abstract qualities or ideas. As Morison puts it, "Aristotle believes that everything is somewhere, but that *not* all things have places. Wisdom, for instance, although *somewhere*, is not in a place; it is rather that the thing in which wisdom 'resides' . . . is in a place. So wisdom may be somewhere, namely in Socrates, but it is Socrates who is in a place" (*On Location*, 5; emphasis in the original). Thus Aristotle would never seek to locate thought in a place or direct readers to a place to find it. Place is sensible (that is, belonging to the order of the senses) and subject to motion; thought is intellectual and motionless; the first cannot therefore be *in* the second in a literal sense.

Nevertheless, in the period addressed in this book—the period I have called "the long fourteenth century"—philosophers reflected with quite especial intensity on Aristotle's teaching (e.g., in his *Metaphysics*) according to which only individual instances really exist; abstract ideas or qualities may be said to exist in a secondary sense, but Plato's view that existence resides in disembodied Forms is no longer widely upheld. Place, then, is what orders, disposes, bounds, a body in the physical world, while thought is what renders it intelligible in the mental one. The mutable and the physical, that is, provide both the means and the model by which we go on to conceive immutable and metaphysical truths.

An analogy between intellection and physical circumscription is indeed implied in the *Physics* at the point where Aristotle reviews the possible meanings of the word "in." Something may be said to be in something else in the following senses: as a part is in the whole (as a finger in the hand); as the whole is in its parts (no example); as the species is in the genus (as man in animal); as any part of the species is in its definition (as the genus in the species); as form is in the matter (as health is in things); as something is in its primary motive agent (as the affairs of the Greeks are in the king of Persia); as something is in its end (as something in its good); and last, as something is in a place (as a thing in a vessel).[16] What is striking about this list, from my perspective, is that all but the last three are concerned with intellecting unities or forms of oneness. The relation of part to whole in the first two examples involves understanding the complex makeup of particular entities; in the examples following, recognizing species, genera, and their formal properties involves intellecting universals, the basic unities by means of which we know and understand the world.

It is not surprising, then, that medieval didactic poets should have sought to "place" thought. Their didacticism operates against a background of contemporary concern with the relation between (sensible) perception and (intellectual) cognition. Place defines the really existing singular body in the physical realm much as intellection makes sense of it in the mental world. This background informs the poets' own experiments with configurations of bodies and ideas as they seek to mold, form, or coerce the thinking of their readers. It also conditions the places they choose to represent, which, overwhelmingly, are ones that can be measured in relation to the human body. The didactic paths, cities, towers, gardens, and so on, are all places of human habitation, relaxation, or labor. When thinking about human nature in universal terms, it seems obvious to begin from an individual body and to locate that body in a place appropriate to to its dimensions. A telling example is the prison cell in Boethius's *Consolation of Philosophy*, which is repeatedly recast as a study by Christine de Pizan.[17] The place where a person's thinking body sits in philosophical contemplation provides the means of outlining, authorizing, and communicating the thoughts that are produced in that place. Although thought does not, in its nature, belong in place, to associate it with place is a way of grounding it in individual experience and of implying that it is orderly and rational.

At the same time, the fact that thought as such is not in a place contributes to the paradoxicality of didactic places. Given that the world that lies outside one's thoughts is represented within them, the place of one's own mind is repeatedly found to contain within it infinitely larger places. Dream-vision poetry depends on exactly this discovery of an entire landscape within the dreamer's sleeping head; Christine's study in the *Chemin de long estude*, for example, turns out to enclose all of the cosmos. This disproportion between places contributes to making didactic poetry, however graphic, difficult to visualize. Such play between place and thought, between the physical and the metaphysical, is exploited in varying degrees in all the works studied in this book, most explicitly in an uneasy response to Aristotle's *Physics* in the *Pèlerinage de vie humaine* (see Chapter 3).

The One and Its Complexities

"The One is therefore not a simple concept," writes André Green.[18] Although Green's concern is the unity of the self, his words could serve as an epigram to vast swathes of antique and medieval thought. Indeed, in the period I am calling the long fourteenth century, philosophy reached unprecedented heights of subtlety precisely in its investigation of concepts of oneness. It is dominated by the careers and influence of such brilliant and technically sophisticated philosophers as Thomas Aquinas (1225–74), John Duns Scotus (ca. 1265–1308), and William of Ockham (ca. 1285–1347/9), to cite only the best known. Although the poets I discuss here were certainly not professional thinkers, they were all educated people who would have felt, although at a distance, the repercussions of these higher-level academic debates. The complexity of one was, as it were, in the water, even if that meant it reached vernacular writers belatedly and in a diluted form.

All through the Middle Ages (and not only then) the notion of one is first and foremost associated with a God who both is One and wants his creatures to be one with him. His divinity, however, exceeds human understanding, and community with him is beyond words. In deference to him, truth becomes identified with oneness that we can't hope to define. Textual commentary is guided (as Henri de Lubac puts it) by "belief in the universal and definitive truth of the Christian faith, which is made to assimilate everything and unite everything, thereby transforming it."[19] Antoine Compagnon has baptized this impetus "monography": a theological mode of writing that aims to integrate previous texts and authorities in a single tradition in order to gesture toward a transcendental unity that would encompass and found them all.[20] This truth is so utterly unique, however, that—whether despite or because of the accumulation of citations—it comes to seem beyond words. While modeling his term "monography" on Bakhtin's "monologism," Compagnon scrupulously avoids disparaging the discourse that he analyzes with such care. Instead, he documents the hermeneutic ingenuity and intellectual boldness with which the complexity of one is negotiated.[21] The demand to reconcile everything within a unity of meaning is an adventure whose paths are often devious, and whose outcome perpetually shifts.

With its multiplicity of witnesses testifying to a mysterious One of truth, Compagnon's "monography" is a good example of the "complexity of one" within the problematic of "the one and the many." A more strictly philosophical approach to this problematic in the Middle Ages took the form of what is nowadays referred to as "the universals debate": an inquiry into the status of genera and species versus that of individual beings. Genera and species are "universals," or instances of unity ("the one") as compared with the proliferating diversity of particulars or singulars ("the many"). One reason why the one of unity is perceived as more complex than the many is that universals are known by means of the intellect, whereas singulars are primarily experienced by means of the senses.

In the period covered by this book, the universals debate continued to operate within the horizon that had shaped it in the twelfth century, that of the opposition between nominalism and realism. Does a universal term such as "man," which is capable of designating all individual men, derive its validity from some real property common to all men (realism) or is it a term that we apply by convention to what we designate as men (nominalism)? But from the late thirteenth century the debate took new directions that had major implications for poetry as well as philosophy and theology: a definitive shift away from Platonist epistemology, a rise in a subjective psychology, and a new emphasis on the so-called integral one, or one of singularity. Each of these developments calls for brief comment, since all have an impact on the ways "one" is conceived in the vernacular didactic poetry of this period.

A long-standing typology distinguishes between: (a) universals prior to plurality, (b) universals that follow from plurality, and (c) universals in plurality. In the period that concerns me, these three possible "states of the universal" were explored and combined in various ways by all the leading thinkers. The first—that of universals prior to plurality—had, in the twelfth century, overwhelmingly been associated with the Platonic (or Neoplatonic) versions of realism, which held that individual exemplars are mere copies of a preexisting metaphysical Idea or Form. Broadly speaking, this is the approach that underpins Compagnon's "monography"; the view that individual things are manifestations of a divine Idea is found in theologically inspired vernacular texts, such as the *Ovide moralisé*. But where secular thought is concerned, the philosophical tide turns against this version of realism. From the early thirteenth century onward, more of Aristotle's writings had become available; by late in the century, their hold on the philosophical canon had tightened.[22] Leading thinkers scrutinize Aristotle's teaching, which locates being in individuals and then seeks to determine how, from our physical experience of these different beings, we arrive at the intellectual categories of species and genus.[23] Attention tends to be focused principally on the second two ways of conceiving the universal: as following from plurality (the universal *post rem*) or as inhering in it (*in re*). Locating the universal *in re* involves contending that there is some inherent feature that unites all the particulars of a given species—for example, something intrinsically doggy in every dog that leads us to abstract the universal "dog" from all the dogs we encounter—and results in forms of realism. Deriving the universal *post rem* means proposing that the universal is primarily mental, conceptual, or verbal, and so tends toward nominalism. But these are not hard and fast distinctions, as different philosophers all had different ways of evaluating the significance of, and interrelations among, things, words, and thoughts.

Aquinas steered a course as close as possible to his understanding of Aristotle. While things in the world may share in a common nature, this does not make that nature as such universal; rather, this shared nature is what enables the mind to conceptualize it in universal terms. Nor is the universal to be found in individuals, because the universal is by definition the unity that unites individuals together. Hence, nature considered in itself is neither universal nor particular. For Aquinas, then, universals exist only in the mind, but they do so as a result of the mind's capacity to form mental concepts of what things in the world are really like, as a result of their common nature. The mind does this, for Aquinas (following Aristotle), by abstracting "intelligible species" from the "sensible species" or sense perceptions of individual things. Universals are not in themselves the things that we know but the means whereby we can know and talk about those things; they are of an entirely different order from nature. "Reality" thus means different things, since it exists in common nature, in singular things, and in our conceptual apparatus, but only in our conceptual apparatus can it be termed "universal."

Like Aquinas, Duns Scotus argued for the presence in individuals of a common reality that was distinctive of their species.[24] The common nature exists in reality; although not in itself universal, it leads the intellect to formulate universal concepts; universals exist only in the intellect, not in things. Thus, for example, "man of itself is neither universal nor particular but indifferent to each. Man is completely universal only insofar as it exists in the intellect, and numerically one and particular only insofar as it exists in reality."[25] Scotus hoped by these means both to explain how we categorize reality and to safeguard the universal from being nothing but a fictional construct.[26] The universal remains, however, a purely conceptual reality. So it was also for more extreme nominalists like Scotus's opponent William of Ockham, who had no interest in the notion of "common nature" but rather maintained that "everything that exists in reality is essentially singular—i.e., logically incapable of existing in, as a constituent of, numerically many simultaneously"—and that "universals are nothing other than names—naturally significant general concepts primarily, and secondarily the conventional signs corresponding to them."[27]

This movement away from Platonist realism puts the didactic poetry of the long fourteenth century into an intellectual context entirely different from the Platonic-dominated climate of the twelfth. The poets of the later period seek less to raise their sights to disembodied metaphysical essences (Ideas), of which particular creatures are mere shadows, than to reflect on the reality of embodied individuals, on the possibility of a reality vested in common nature, or on the conceptual, internal, mental reality of concepts. In particular, the proximity of universals to fictions, a proximity philosophers are well aware of (and even alarmed by), may have seemed to license poetic manipulation and play. If our ideas about the world are (as it were) "made up," then literature and ideas belong together as never before.

This tendency to define universals as mental realities is symptomatic of the second change that characterizes the long fourteenth century by contrast with the preceding era, namely, the reorientation of the universals debate away from logic and toward psychology. Instead of focusing on language and predication, philosophers investigated the nature of perception, cognition, and desire. They asked how, from really existing individuals, we could arrive at the categories necessary for knowledge, the universal levels of species and genus. The Boethian answer had been that we observe similarities between individuals, on the basis of which we abstract their common features. But with the irruption of the Arab Aristotelian tradition in the thirteenth century this solution was discarded, since it did not explain how we perceived similarity in the first place. Efforts were concentrated instead on theorizing how universals—whatever they were—were arrived at from our experience of particular bodies—whatever that meant. How was generic unity made perceptible to the intellect? Through images that are impressed on the mind by the senses and thus are akin to vision or imagination, or through some formal property that causes the mind to respond with cognition?[28]

For Aquinas (as for Aristotle), perception of the sensible remains the model on which to understand intellection. Sensation requires an act combining an agent that can sense (the sentient) with something that can be sensed (the sensible); intellection likewise is a synergy of intellect with the intelligible; "in this way, the process culminating in the formation of the image becomes the structural model for the process leading from the image to the concept."[29] Subsequently, the theory of knowledge developed by William of Ockham is based on a new account of perception that enables universals to be formed on the basis of encounters with singular things. The universal is not arrived at on the basis of resemblance; rather, the opposite is the case: it is because of "cospecificity" (the fact of belonging to a common species) that resemblance is perceptible in the first place.[30]

The earlier focus on language and predication had approached the question of ontology in what we might term an "objective" way. Putting emphasis instead on perception and the individual's will to know insinuates the subject into the heart of philosophical inquiry, and has immediate and obvious implications for literature. It helps to explain, for example, why didactic poetry is so often cast as first-person reminiscence, and why poets should associate their thought with experiences of vision (including pictures and dreams, for example) as well as with formal patterns of language. Interest in the dependence of intellectual processes on the individual's will and memory saw a return of Augustinian psychology, the vernacular effects of which are especially clear in the *Pèlerinage de vie humaine*, but which also affect poets like Machaut and Froissart, whose preoccupations lie in the field of human love, desire, and memory.

A final development that is of major importance for the poetic works discussed in this book is the new interest in, and anxiety about, our knowledge of singular beings; that is, of the numerical one as opposed to the generic (or universal) one. The Aristotelian inheritance posits a radical gap between being and knowledge: only singular entities exist, but only universals are intelligible. Within this perspective, the problem of the one and the many is that of somehow bridging this chasm that divides the proliferating things that *are* from the unities (genera and species) we can *know*. The medieval-Aristotelian bridge, as we have seen, was held up by the supporting pillars of sensory perception, the production of "sensible species" from sense data, and the abstraction from sensible species of "intelligible species." However, the Christian faith contended that we might also have some knowledge of entities that had no body (such as God); and it further insisted that God had knowledge of each person in his or her unique singularity. One of the tasks medieval philosophy set itself from the latter thirteenth century onward, therefore, was to find ways of accounting for such knowledge within a properly philosophical framework. This could not be achieved without considerable violence to the Aristotelian legacy.[31]

Toward the end of the thirteenth century, Aquinas argued that "there is knowledge of material singulars at the level of intellect" even though dependency on the senses remains primary, and this position gained widespread official acceptance.[32] The fourteenth century is dedicated to the refining and debating of what came to be known as *cognitio singularis*, "knowledge of singulars." Scotus thought that in each individual the reality common to its species was inflected by a principle of individuation or "thisness" (*haecceitas*) that guaranteed the individual's singularity, its differentiation from other seemingly identical members of the same species.[33] Claims varied among philosophers as to the extent to which it was possible to cognize thisness, Ockham (for example) being confident that some intellectual knowledge of singulars *was* possible in this world, since we can know whether or not a particular individual exists. This controversy raised awareness that the singular one posed problems that were every bit as complex as those of the one of unity (or universal one).

Thus in the philosophical thought of the later thirteenth and the fourteenth centuries debates over forms of oneness were center stage. The didactic texts of this period are influenced by these contemporary philosophical currents. Concern with the uniqueness of God, with the potential for community with God, and with the nature of the individual are manifested in the Christian didactic writings I examine here, while secular authors are also drawn to the problematic of the individual and the universal in exploring themes of the good, desire, and power. The uniqueness and potential inexpressibility both of the divine One and of our individual experience as embodied creatures (always at issue in first-person poetry) was imbued in this period with new intellectual urgency.

We are particularly well placed to engage with these concerns given that the "complexity of one"—singularity, community, and universality—has made a significant return to the philosophical forefront in recent decades. Several authors, including Deleuze and Agamben, cite Duns Scotus and Ockham among their antecedents, while others, like Badiou and Žižek, increasingly ground their arguments about universality in Christian theology. Yet other thinkers—Derrida and Lacan, for example—continue a more strictly Aristotelian vein by reflecting on the antinomy that exists between the unknowable singular and the intelligible generality of language (or the Symbolic Order). I have not hesitated to draw on modern thinkers when I find resonances between their ideas and the reflections of the medieval texts. It is because they are our contemporaries, just as Scotus and Ockham were the contemporaries of the medieval poets, that we are prepared as modern readers to appreciate that the notions of oneness that underlie the didacticism of later medieval texts may, in their way, be as exciting and as taxing as diversity.

Poetry

The immediately preceding sections of this Introduction have placed intellectual and even theological concerns uppermost, while also tracing their impact on vernacular writing. But although this book is about thought, it is also addressed to texts that are not only in verse but also (to varying degrees) self-consciously poetic. From the early thirteenth century, writers had faced a barrage of claims that prose was a form appropriate to truth, that it delivered its content "straight" and did not pander to the artfulness of form. So it is the more remarkable that a treatise on divine love (the *Breviari*), an allegory of incarnation and redemption (the *Ovide moralisé*), an analysis of human fallibility and salvation (the *Pèlerinage de vie humaine*), an inquiry into the nature of happiness (*Le Jugement dou roy de Navarre*), an essay on memory and desire (*Le Joli buisson de Jonece*), and a treatise on political order and disorder (*Le Chemin de long estude*) should have eschewed prose and chosen instead the medium of verse. In this section I reflect briefly on the value of poeticality, which in these poems coexists so strikingly with intellectual aspiration. The texts explored and evaluated here are concerned to give pleasure as well as provoke reflection. Monologism revolves around "one" as an aesthetic as well as a philosophical goal.

In addition to being composed in verse, three of these texts contain insertions of lyric poetry (the *Breviari*, the *Pèlerinage de vie humaine*, and the *Joli buisson de Jonece*), while the *Ovide moralisé* and the *Chemin de long estude* deploy a variety of meters alongside their standard octosyllabic rhyming couplets. Only the *Jugement* poems discussed in Chapter 4 are metrically uniform, and if I had chosen some of Machaut's other *dits* this uniformity could easily have been avoided. When the texts of this period "place" their "thought" they outline its oneness in a form imbued with the sensuality of lyric poetry. The *Consolation of Philosophy* may have served as model for this combination of metrical variety with philosophical ambition, and in my Conclusion I review the divergent ways the texts I discuss respond to its combination of poetry with thought.

Certainly another respect in which these works declare themselves as "poetic" is in their interaction with other poetic texts. The *Ovide moralisé* is a long poem reiterating and reorienting Ovid's *Metamorphoses*; it and the *Metamorphoses* themselves are explicitly recycled within *Le Joli buisson de Jonece* and *Le Chemin de long estude*. Machaut's *dit* reprises an earlier poem by Machaut himself, while also containing a large number of inset narratives, many of which (such as the *Châtelaine de Vergy*) are themselves texts in verse. Most ambitious of all, Christine de Pizan sets her cap at emulating Virgil, Ovid, and Dante, to name only the most celebrated of her models. Jean de Meun's choice of Guillaume de Lorris's *Roman de la rose* as a text worthy of continuation must have had a major impact on the status of verse in the century that followed, since Jean's continuation, in octosyllabic rhyming couplets, was the most widely circulated and imitated vernacular text of the French Middle Ages. If the *Rose* was in verse, who could doubt that intellectual ideas might find their best expression in poetic form? All but one of the texts considered in this book manifest the influence of the *Rose*, the *Chemin de long estude* leaning especially heavily on it, while the *Pèlerinage* presents itself as the *Rose*'s ideological corrective. The sole exception to this influence is the *Breviari*, which, however, is remarkably similar to the *Rose* in being an encyclopedia, or encyclopedic text, on the subject of love. Composed in Occitan and with an inscribed audience of lovers and troubadours, the *Breviari*'s reference is to Occitan court culture, and its diffusion is uniquely meridional.

How does the aesthetic of the monologic work in these texts? The Sybil speaks to Christine of "another and more perfect world," and in this book I shall be exploring this "place" as a place of poetry as well as of thought. The familiar *loci* of didactic poetry are, as I have said, at once and strongly visual and difficult to visualize. The fact that they are traditional means that, when they are cited, poetic models are absorbed into the text that cites them and assimilated to its form. This constant play between *ekphrasis* and intertextuality in the evocation of place contributes to the play between the visible and the invisible that I have already evoked. By "placing" thought, poetry calls it to mind in a way that flickers between vision and the invisibility of language. The "one" that it promises is both seductively present and mysteriously elusive. Didactic poetry has its pleasures ("more delightful and more beneficial," as the Sybil puts it), which, even if they are not immediately apparent to the modern reader acclimatized to multiplicity and play, are worth pursuing.

The Chapters That Follow

This book consists of a series of studies of didactic poems whose common
feature is the way they coordinate a sense of place with a scheme of
thought and a didactic purpose. While the poets concerned often rely on
a spatial image to unify their readers' responses, this image also makes
visible the complexity of the monologism, the oneness of meaning and
interpretation, to which the didactic text aspires. I argue that the texts I
examine, through their investment in some *one* meaning that they wish to
convey, are committed to reflecting on what they mean by "one." The
challenge posed by this reflection is realized in the *loci* in which this oneness is "placed," since these are, at once, strongly visual in their appeal
and yet also, in some degree, unimaginable. The one (or One) inscribes
itself within a spatial image that, in the end, defies our capacity to visualize
it; this intellectual problematic also constitutes the core of the poems' aesthetic appeal.

The first three chapters are devoted to Christian didactic texts. The
Occitan *Breviari d'amor* (Chapter 1) is concerned with the way all creation
is enfolded in the universal principle of love, and how this love unites, via
this unity, a singular God with singular lovers. The place used to articulate
these forms of one is the figure of a tree, but a tree that loses its reassuring
simplicity of outline as it struggles to represent the complexity of these
ideas. In the *Ovide moralisé*, I argue in Chapter 2, landscape is used as
analogy of Eden. It promises to be the setting of a Christian community
where Christian souls will be modeled on the divine Form of Christ;
Ovid's theme of metamorphosis is developed to express the radical and as
yet unimaginable changes that fallen nature needs to undergo before this
can (literally) take "place." Guillaume de Deguileville, in the *Pèlerinage de
vie humaine*, deploys a series of paradoxical places to explore the relation
between divine and secular reality; Chapter 3 concentrates on the path
divided by the Haie de Penitence (Hedge of Penitence) as a means of
exploring how an individual man, as the result of the complex relation
between body and soul, is both one and more than one.

The remaining three chapters have predominantly secular themes.
Machaut's *Jugement dou roy de Navarre*, I argue in Chapter 4, uses Aristotle's *Ethics* to trouble Boethius's vision (in the *Consolation of Philosophy*)
of a single supreme good. Machaut pursues his theme of disintegration to
the point of questioning whether the individual, as a desiring subject, is

ever knowable in universal terms. The place where, as I claim, the universal is "put on trial" is both a court within a manor house and the figure of the prosecutor, Dame Bonneürté (Lady Happiness). Chapter 5 returns to the image of the tree, first found in the *Breviari* and again in the *Ovide moralisé*, which Froissart uses in his *dit amoureux Le Joli buisson de Jonece* to interrogate the nature of memory. Like Machaut, Froissart plays with the possibility that the unities by means of which we think we understand the world are primarily verbal or mental; but in contrast to Machaut, he chooses to renounce his individuality as a subject of desire and espouse instead a unity grounded in the undisputed reality of the One God. The *Chemin de long estude*, which I discuss in the final chapter, presents Christine's travels through a series of *loci*; my analysis centers on the fountain of the Muses as the source of her questioning whether, given the partiality of every individual, the world could be ever be submitted to universal order under an exemplary ruler.

All of these chapters, then, explore how the placing of thought in medieval didactic poems expresses the sheer difficulty of comprehending, and interrelating, various kinds of one: the one of uniqueness (individuality, singularity), the one of universality (genus, species), the one of "a common nature," and the triune One of the Godhead. In the Conclusion, I offer a reading of Genius's sermon in Jean de Meun's continuation of the *Roman de la rose*. Much as the Sybil calls on Christine to follow her to "another and more perfect place," Genius summons his listeners to enter the *parc* of the Lamb; his didactic enterprise is, I argue, comic precisely because it behaves as if these difficulties did not exist. For Genius there is no distinction between the individual and the universal, no ultimate incompatibility between physical and metaphysical, and no problem about envisaging a "place of thought" where all truth and all knowledge are simultaneously visible. This part of the *Rose* reads like a parody of texts that in fact come after it, simplifying and flattening the didactic enterprise as they will understand it. For the phallic Genius, as befits a talking penis, oneness is simply assumed. The true challenge of monologism, however, is to appreciate the complexity of one.

I

Book-Trees
Deleuze, Porphyry, and the *Breviari d'Amor* by Matfre Ermengaud

THE TREE IMAGE is ubiquitous in the Middle Ages. The various structures that it offers—the vertical axis of summit and base, the network of roots and branches, the progression from flower through fruit to seed—seemed to medieval writers ideal for systematizing and unifying thought. In addition, important biblical prototypes put the tree at the heart of moral and religious understanding. The tree of knowledge of good and evil roots human moral understanding in an originary wrong. The branches of the tree of Jesse interlace through biblical history to culminate in the tree of the cross. The tree of wisdom brings enlightenment to all who inhabit its shade. Familiar and memorable, the tree is repeatedly called upon to impress on the memory of the diligent, or the negligent, the numerical sets—seven deadly sins, seven gifts of the Holy Spirit, ten commandments, twelve articles of faith—enumerated by medieval pedagogues.[1]

In *A Thousand Plateaus*, the French philosopher Gilles Deleuze and his coauthor the psychoanalyst Félix Guattari recognize the historical pre-eminence of the tree image. "The tree has dominated Western reality and all of Western thought, from botany to biology and anatomy, but also gnosiology, theology, ontology, all of philosophy."[2] They reprovingly acknowledge its capacity to hierarchize, centralize, and perpetuate: "Arborescent systems are hierarchical systems with centers of significance and subjectification, central automata like organized memories."[3] As a result, they point out, our idea of a book is classically identified as a tree: "A first type of book is the root-book. The tree is already the image of the world, or the root the image of the world-tree. This is the classical book, as noble, signifying, and subjective organic interiority (the strata of the book). The book imitates the world, as art imitates nature; by procedures specific to it

books frequently envisioned as trees;
D·G disapprove

that accomplish what nature cannot or can no longer do" (*A Thousand Plateaus*, 5). But, they continue, the identification is inherently misleading: "The law of the book is the law of reflection, the One that becomes two. How could the law of the book reside in nature, when it is what presides over the very division between world and book, nature and art? One becomes two: . . . what we have before us is the most classical and reflected on, oldest, and weariest kind of thought" (ibid.).[4] The book thus conceived is here reproached with reflecting back upon the world a form that is in reality quite alien to it. The "knowledge" enshrined in such a book is a conceptual straitjacket of artificial, rigidly hierarchical binarisms that purports to be a part of nature but is, in fact, imposed on it. The unity it promotes through the principle of successive subdivision is inherently flawed. To this unified, centralized, and reductive model of the book, Deleuze and Guattari oppose the multiple, rambling, decentered productivity of the rhizome.

In this chapter I show how a medieval didactic text, the *Breviari d'amor*, challenges Deleuze and Guattari's own binary opposition between rhizome and tree. Composed between 1288 and about 1292 by the late Occitan troubadour Matfre Ermengaud, the *Breviari* is a spiritual treatise-cum-encyclopedia conceived as an exposition of a tree of love. Matfre's theme is the oneness of love, and the figure of the tree endorses the unity of that one; it supports Matfre's aspiration to convey a single truth. But, I shall argue, the tree figure also undergoes a paradoxical kind of *disfigurement* that results from the complexity of that one; this will enable me, at the end of the chapter, to call into question Deleuze and Guattari's aspersions on the book-tree. First, though, I shall consider one philosophical tree that their strictures seem particularly to target and which, I believe, determines how Matfre shaped his poem: that evoked by Porphyry in his *Isagoge*.

Porphyry's Tree

A Greek text known to the Middle Ages in Boethius's Latin translation, the *Isagoge* is an introduction to Aristotle's *Categories*. In the Middle Ages it served as an elementary textbook of dialectic that was widely read by schoolboys, but it also attracted commentaries by distinguished medieval philosophers. Porphyry's stated aim is to initiate students to Aristotle's works on logic by explicating the terms "genus," "difference," "species," "property," and "accident." Porphyry explains that a species is something that confers form and that falls under a genus; difference is what divides one species from another within the same genus. A species can also function as a genus under which are ranged lower species until eventually there are no further subspecies, only individuals. His account thus theorizes the relationship between the one and the many in terms of unities (the universals of genera and species) and singulars (individuals).[5] To explain his meaning, he uses as an example the Aristotelian category of substance:

§22 Let us clarify [this] for just one category. Substance itself is a genus. Under this is body, and under body animate body, under which animal, under animal rational animal, under which man. Under man are Socrates and Plato and the particular men.

§23 Of these, substance is the most general and the one that is only a genus. Man is the most specific and the one that is only a species. Body is a species of substance but a genus of animate body. Animate body is a species of body but a genus of animal. Again, animal is a species of animate body but a genus of rational animal. Rational animal is a species of animal but a genus of man. Now man is a species of rational animal, but no longer a genus—of particular men. Instead it is a species only. Everything prior to individuals and predicated immediately of them is a species only, no longer a genus.[6]

Although Porphyry does not call this scheme a "tree," it becomes identified as one from an early date. In the most widely used medieval logical textbook, Peter of Spain's *Tractatus*, the term is used as if it were commonplace: "All this is clear in the figure called the tree of Porphyry"; there follows a tree diagram similar to that in Figure 1.[7] The Porphyrian tree remains a familiar point of reference for logicians and philosophers throughout the medieval and early modern periods.[8]

Porphyry's specifications mean that, unusually for medieval trees, his is organized from the top down. Under each genus there is a point of difference (*differentia*) from which two subgenera or species branch out. Thus the root is, as it were, at the top, with the branches coming off downward like a stemma. Medieval and early modern illustrators clearly experience problems depicting this arrangement. Some opt for a central column of *differentiae* with the branches forking off on either side; others try for something more like a realistic tree, often with bizarre results, since what Porphyry represents as the point of origin is so clearly at the top (Figure 1). While such pictures help to make sense of Deleuze and Guattari's identification of the tree as simultaneously a root, they also suggest that even a very basic conceptual framework, in which successive levels

Figure 1. Porphyrian tree from Ramón Llull, *Logica Nova*, Munich, Bayerische Staatsbibliothek Hs clm, 18446, fol. 44v. Reproduced by permission.

are envisaged as "branching" downward from the one above, could pose problems of visualization.

Confusion about which way up to represent the Porphyrian tree may have arisen because Porphyry's analysis, although an introduction to logic, also strayed into ontology, inaugurating for medieval readers the question of the three possible "states of the universal."[9] Uncertainty over whether to privilege the top or the bottom of the tree can be seen as reflecting hesitation as to whether being resides in the genus (the one of substance) or in the singular individuals that comprise it. The tree's weirdness thus perpetuates the very problem the tree was designed to address, that of the relation of the one and the many.[10] Porphyry's text, however, is quite explicit in speaking of species being grouped *under* a genus and of individuals being grouped *under* a species. Higher up the tree, for Porphyry, means conceptually more abstract and logically prior, because the top of the tree is the genus and thus what Aristotle called a "first principle." Although at one point (*Isagoge* §6, to which I shall return) Porphyry differentiates between generic and genealogical descent, he acknowledges the analogy between genus and ancestry, "for in this way we say that Orestes has his genus from Tantalus, but Hyllus from Heracles, and again that Pindar is Theban by genus, but Plato Athenian."[11]

Matfre Ermengaud's *Breviari d'Amor*

"There is no difference between what a book talks about and how it is made," say Deleuze and Guattari.[12] Valérie Galent-Fasseur says exactly the same of the *Breviari*: "The tree is, at the same time, love and the book."[13] Matfre Ermengaud's work is conceived *as* a tree, the "albre d'amor," whose structure is outlined at the start of the work and provides the framework of all that follows. Beginning with divine love, Matfre surveys the natural and moral orders and concludes with an exhortation to human marital love. This overall trajectory from Creation to procreation reflects the belief that the world of nature results from God's love as personified in the Holy Spirit; infused with this love, the whole of creation is united with God.[14] The central purpose of the tree image, with all its various ramifications, is to map this unifying flow of love between God and his creatures so that we may appreciate the fruits it can bear in human experience.

The *Breviari* is Occitania's major contribution to the medieval tradi-

tion of vernacular religious teaching-cum-encyclopedism.[15] Different critics have made various suggestions about the intellectual framework in
which the *Breviari* should be read; the ubiquity of the tree image in the
Middle Ages means that there are indeed plenty of models on which Matfre might have drawn.[16] A "tree of love" is used in some mystical writings
to detail levels in the soul's ascent to God. For example, the *Arbor amoris*
is a short Latin treatise outlining the ascent to God via successive "distinctions" that raise love ever higher toward the unknowable.[17] But Matfre
presents his central theme of love analytically rather than mystically; his
concern is to analyze the ways by which God's love unites us and all creation with him, not to explore the means whereby we might ascend to
him. The *Breviari*'s religious teaching, supported by frequent citations
from Augustine and Gregory, belongs in the mainstream of medieval theology.[18] Its Scholastic as opposed to mystical stance gives the *Breviari*
common ground with its slightly earlier contemporary, the Anglo-
Norman *Lumiere as lais*. While Matfre alludes to the mystics' "tree of
love," therefore, I think that he combines it with and subordinates it to
another: the "tree of knowledge" (*arbor scientiae*). The world is the manifestation of God's love, and the impulse to anatomize creation from this
perspective is what drives the *Breviari*'s encyclopedic program.[19]

Impeccably orthodox as to his sources, Matfre Ermengaud is unique
among medieval encyclopedists in his sense of audience. He claims to be
writing at the request of his fellow troubadours in order to expound the
truth about love so that they will appreciate what is worthwhile (and what
reprehensible) in the poetry of *fin' amors*.[20] The last part of his treatise
adapts the dialogue form familiar from the *magister-discipulus* exchanges
in other didactic works, with Matfre answering questions from these other
poets. The authorities cited here are no longer Augustine and Gregory but
extracts from troubadour *cansos*.[21] Sexuality, we are taught, has its place
in human behavior so long as it is morally virtuous and oriented toward
reproduction. The broad framework of the *Breviari* is theological, but
within that Matfre's interests are social and ethical, as befits a poet who
describes himself as "doctor of law and servant of love" ("senhers en leis
e d'amor serss," *BA*, 10).[22]

Matfre's *Albre* and the Porphyrian Tree

Medieval encyclopedias are often implicitly organized according to a tree-
like structure that harks back to the Porphyrian tree as a device for map-

ping the category of substance.[23] But Matfre's debt to Porphyry is unusually extensive and significant. He defines his purpose as being to explain to the troubadours the *generologia* of love, its *divizio*, and its *estatio* in individual creatures:

Explaining the correct course of the descent of love, its subdivisions, and its location when it situates itself in created beings.

> declaran la drecha via
> de la generologia
> d'amor e la divizio
> et on fai sa estatio
> quant en creatura se met. (*BA*, 109–12, recapitulated 391–94)

The term *generologia*, which Levy translates as "généalogie," perpetuates the association between "genealogy" and "genus, genera" found in Porphyry.[24] The *Breviari* continues the analogy between a genus and a "family" to which "individuals" belong by describing the *generologia* of love as a family tree in which the descending elements are identified as "sons" and "daughters." Other items of the Scholastic terminology consecrated by Porphyry (or at least by Boethius's translation of it)—*general, especial, comminal, causa, diferentia, substantia,* and *essentia*—recur throughout the *Breviari*.[25]

Also as in Porphyry, the divisions of love's *generologia* in the *Breviari* are always binary. First (*BA*, 262ff.) Matfre draws a distinction between the Creator's love and created love. The Holy Spirit is the eternal source and root ("fons e razitz," *BA*, 265) of divine love that unites the persons of the Trinity and is integral to the divine nature. But God also created the love pertaining to the world of embodied creatures, the love the troubadours are interested in. Although containing a treatise on angels, Matfre's encyclopedia is chiefly concerned with natural (or embodied) substance. Within that he distinguishes inanimate from animate, sentient from insentient (6910ff.), and rational from nonrational. Creatures that lack reason are ruled only by "natural law" ("dregz de natura," *BA*, 300, 313), but rational beings are also subject to "human law" ("dregz de gens," *BA*, 314). Each of these laws presides over a further distinction between types of love. Natural law results in sexual and parental love; human law in love of temporal goods and love of God and one's neighbor.

Like Porphyry's tree, Matfre's tree branches downward from a supreme genus situated at the top:

And because this is the tree of love, it is necessary that we should know the correct course of love, what it is in the first place in general, not descending or speaking of any specific love on its own account.

> E quar est albre es d'amors
> cove que sabcham lo dreg cors
> d'amors quez es premieiramen
> en general, non dichenden
> ni parlan en especial
> de lunh'amor²⁶ per son cabal. (*BA*, 573–78)

Here Matfre is saying that we need to start with the genus love ("amor en general") as primary before working down (*dichenden*) the tree to its subspecies (*especial* means "pertaining to a species"). He underlines that the supreme substance of divine charity is discernible in all of the specific branches of this tree but is at its purest when at its most abstract. The branches descend because this supreme love, like a first principle, does not move but moves everything beneath it (*BA*, 683–94) and because the love determines the true nature of the lower forms but not vice versa—that is, human love is fully itself only when inhabited by holy charity, not when estranged from it (*BA*, 695–702).²⁷ The rubric is categorical: "HERE IT DEMONSTRATES THAT THE TREE OF LOVE HAS TO BE EXPOUNDED FROM THE TOP DOWN BECAUSE LOVE DESCENDS."²⁸ Similarly, for Porphyry substance as the "first principle" is the starting point of the tree; and its various branches represent the accretion of differences whereby successive species and subspecies are distanced from it, until one arrives at actual individuals.

The "albre d'amor" coincides with Porphyry's tree not just in shape and direction but even in its points of differentiation. Matfre's tree differs from Porphyry's only in that Matfre puts God as love (not substance) at the top, and the individuals whom he ranges at the bottom are not philosophers (Plato, Socrates, and so on) but individual troubadours; the parallels between the two trees are shown in Figure 2. Matfre also echoes Porphyry's account of how two species of the same genus differ from one another. Having described the ordering of the cosmos and all the natural creatures within it, he demarcates humankind from other sentient species:

Each one of the aforementioned laws has its origin in nature, but a difference interposes itself between them, from the point of view of law, because the first (natural law) is common, as I have said, to all forms of life, but the second (human law) is given by nature to mankind alone. Through human law, rational creatures have the obligation to love God.

> Quascus dels davan digz dregz pren
> de natura sso naichamen,
> pero pauza.s diferentia
> entr'ells en legal scientia
> quar le premiers es cominals,
> quo ai dig, a toz animals,
> mas le seguons tan solamen
> es datz per natur' a la gen.
> Per dreg de gens ha drechura
> rationals creatura
> d'amar Deu. (*BA*, 9105–15)

The distinction between human and natural law, derived from Justinian, confirms Matfre's practical orientation and legal expertise.[29] But the way it is drawn conforms exactly to the Porphyrian model, where one branch of each node is differentiated from its partner by the addition of a *differentia* (*BA*, 9107), a feature proper to it and lacking to the other side. Knowledge of God, the passage continues, is a "property" in this Porphyrian sense, since it is unique to, and defining of, rational animals (i.e., man). The need to comprehend this property leads to an analysis of man's spiritual, moral, and social nature that occupies the following sixteen thousand or so lines. After this, Matfre returns for his final eight thousand lines to the nature that man shares with other sentient creatures. This common nature justifies troubadour poetry when it promotes heterosexual love as a path to secular virtues. The culminating virtue of this love, matrimony (*BA*, 32644ff.), leads to the other form of love that man shares with the animals, love of children (*BA*, 34540ff.).

Overall, then, Matfre's encyclopedia uses the structure of the Porphyrian tree to display the relationship between human love, the natural order, and the divine love that is their ultimate cause, and thereby to underline the unity between creature and Creator. But given its Christian didactic purpose, the "albre d'amor" also differs from Porphyry's tree, and I want to highlight three differences, the first involving unity, the second singularity, and the third the centrality of love, all of which contribute to the complexity of the one in Matfre's work.

Under the influence of Christian Neoplatonism the unity conveyed by Matfre's tree is absolute. Porphyry flags this divergence between Aristotle and Plato in *Isagoge* §6 when he compares the relation between suc-

cessive species and genera to that between family members descending
from their forebear, "for example, Agememnon, from Atreus, from Pel-
ops, from Tantalus, and in the end from Zeus." But, he continues,

Now as for genealogies, they lead up to one thing—to Zeus, let us say—to the
origin in most cases. But with genera and species this is not so. For being, as
Aristotle says [*Metaphysics*, 988b22], is not one common genus of all things; neither
are all things "homogeneous" in accordance with one highest genus. Instead, let
us posit the ten first genera as ten first principles, as in the *Categories*. If then one
calls all things "beings," he will do so equivocally, Aristotle says, but not univocally. For if being were one genus common to all, all things would be called "beings" univocally. But since there are instead ten first genera, the community
among them is in name only, not at all in a definition that goes with that name.
(§§29, 30)[30]

Porphyry is pointing out that whereas the Platonic tradition conceived the
sensible universe and the world of Ideas as a hierarchy in which all are
subordinate to the supreme Being, the One, Aristotle's *Categories* fracture
this unity into ten independent principles. While they may all *refer* to
"being," they don't *posit* it as a single entity, so their reference to it as
"one" is only equivocal.[31] By proposing Zeus in the position of the highest genus, by contrast, Porphyry raises the possibility that there could be a
single, unequivocal divine origin for all substance.

   In Matfre's day, belief that all being had as its first cause a divine One
was, by contrast, an orthodox position. Augustine drew from Neoplatonic
philosophy a rationale for attributing to the apparently diverse world an
underlying unity that was motivated by, and enabled the world to be integrated with, its unique Creator; Porphyry, a student of the Neoplatonist
scholar Plotinus, himself contributed to this position.[32] Within this Christian worldview the multiplicity of first principles in the *Categories* had to
be explained away or overridden.[33] Aquinas, for example, succeeds in ignoring this aspect of Aristotle's teaching when he argues that God is the
single, supreme source of all existence, an argument that in other respects
relies on the Porphyrian tree even if it is not explicitly mentioned:[34]
"Whenever different things share something in common, there must be
some cause of this sharing: precisely as different, they themselves do not
account for it. Thus it is that whenever some one element is found in
different things, these receive it from one cause, just as different hot bodies
get their heat from fire. Existence, however, is shared by all things, however much they differ. There must therefore be a single source of existence

A. Porphyrian tree

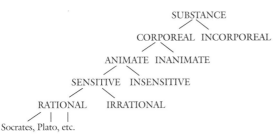

B. Matfre, "albre d'amor"

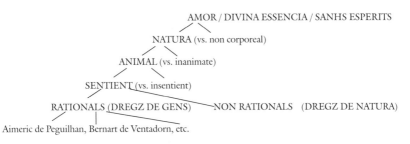

Figure 2. Porphyry's tree and Matfre's "albre d'amor."

from which whatever exists in any manner whatsoever, whether invisible and spiritual or visible and material, obtains its existence."[35] Here Aquinas is grounding all existence (or substance) in its unique point of origin, God, from whom it ramifies in a Porphyrian tree throughout creation.[36] "We are bound to conclude," he says, "that everything that is at all real is from God."[37]

What is remarkable about the *Breviari* is that it accepts the Porphyrian tree as an ontological model while also exploiting its familiarity as an elementary pedagogical device. It takes the theological positions represented by Aquinas, for whom the *Isagoge* is only implicit, and projects them back onto the classroom image of the tree in order to instruct the laity that all of creation exists only by virtue of its participation in the one true being:

In theology God is said to be the divine essence. . . . Only God exists, and nothing else, because no creature has being in the same way as he does. For only the pure godhead is and was without beginning and likewise shall be without end. And moreover the godhead cannot not be otherwise than it is, and nor does the godhead derive its being from any other thing, but all things take their being from God the almighty father.

> Dieus es divina essencia
> digz en la sancta sciencia. . . .
> Sol Dieus es e non es res als
> quar lunhs essers non es aitals
> de neguna creatura;
> quar sol la deitatz pura
> es e fo ses comensamen,
> e ses fi sera eichamen,
> ni pot esser que non sia
> la deitatz, tota via,
> ni esser non pren, so sabchatz,
> d'autra chauza la deitatz,
> mas esser tota cauza pren
> de Dieu lo paire omnipoten. (*BA*, 1363–64, 1373–84)

Here Matfre is asserting that God alone exists and that we have existence only insofar as we derive it from him. For Aristotle there might be ten different trees, but the unity of Matfre's "albre d'amor" derives from an exclusive One.

The second difference between Matfre and Porphyry follows on from this. A genus is a "one" in the sense that it is abstracted from many particulars; but God is not a genus; rather, he is unique. Nor is he a particular, given that a particular is a member of a multitude. Socrates is one man among others, but God is not one of a group. God's singularity is said by Aquinas, as by other theologians, to be not "composite" (as an individual is a combination of substance, specific properties, and accidents) but "simple" or "absolute."[38] This same vocabulary is taken up by Matfre, who repeatedly stresses that God is unique in that his attributes are what constitute his nature, not additions to it:

for every property of God is intrinsic to his divinity, whether it be his love, his wisdom, his justice, or his might.

> quar tota proprietatz
> quez es en Dieu es deitatz,
> sia amors o savieza
> o drechura o grandeza. (*BA*, 275–78)

Thus God is simple [*or*: absolute] unity in which no plurality has any place. For everything that is in the godhead is God and not another thing.

Dieus es donc simpla unitatz
qu'en lui no cass pluralitatz
quar tot sso qu'en deitat es
es Dieus, e res als non es ges. (*BA*, 1029–32)

The unique oneness of God is rendered more enigmatic by his triune nature, invoked at the beginning of the *Breviari* and expounded in its initial section.[39] The persons of the Trinity

are powerful with a single power and loving with a single love and wise with a single wisdom. For no multiplicity of plural being can take place in the godhead, so simple [*or*: absolute] is its nature.

son d'un poder poderos
e d'un' amor son amoros
e son d'una savieza
savi, quar lunha mouteza
d'essencial pluralitat
non pot caber en deitat,
tant es simpla sa natura. (*BA*, 1057–63; cf. *BA*, 1188–91)

The Porphyrian tree is treelike in that it maps the relations between unities (universals) at the top and particulars at the bottom. Matfre's *albre* challenges our conception of a tree by placing singular beings top and bottom, with the unities that are genera and species in between.

The *Breviari* is not alone in turning to the Porphyrian tree when meditating on the Trinity. MS BNF lat. 2802, a collection of short thirteenth-century Latin works on the Trinity, includes a treatise aiming to instruct the simple in the need for faith in the Trinity that likewise emphasizes the absolute simplicity of God.[40] God, it is said, comprises spirituality, rationality, and goodness in his simple substance.[41] At the foot of the folio, apparently as an afterthought, Aristotle's categories following the exposition from Isidore's *Etymologies* are illustrated in the form of a tree. And at the foot of the folio following, Isidore's "five universals" of *species*, *genus*, *differentia*, *proprium*, and *accidens*[42]—the same terms that are explained by Porphyry—are also depicted in a tree diagram (Figure 3).

The third and most obvious difference from Porphyry in Matfre's recasting of the tree is that its subject matter, while it is presented as "essence," is not substance as Aristotle might understand it (it has nothing to do with matter or form, for instance); it is love.[43] Thus, says Matfre, there are two sorts of love. One is natural and creaturely, the other eternal and creative:

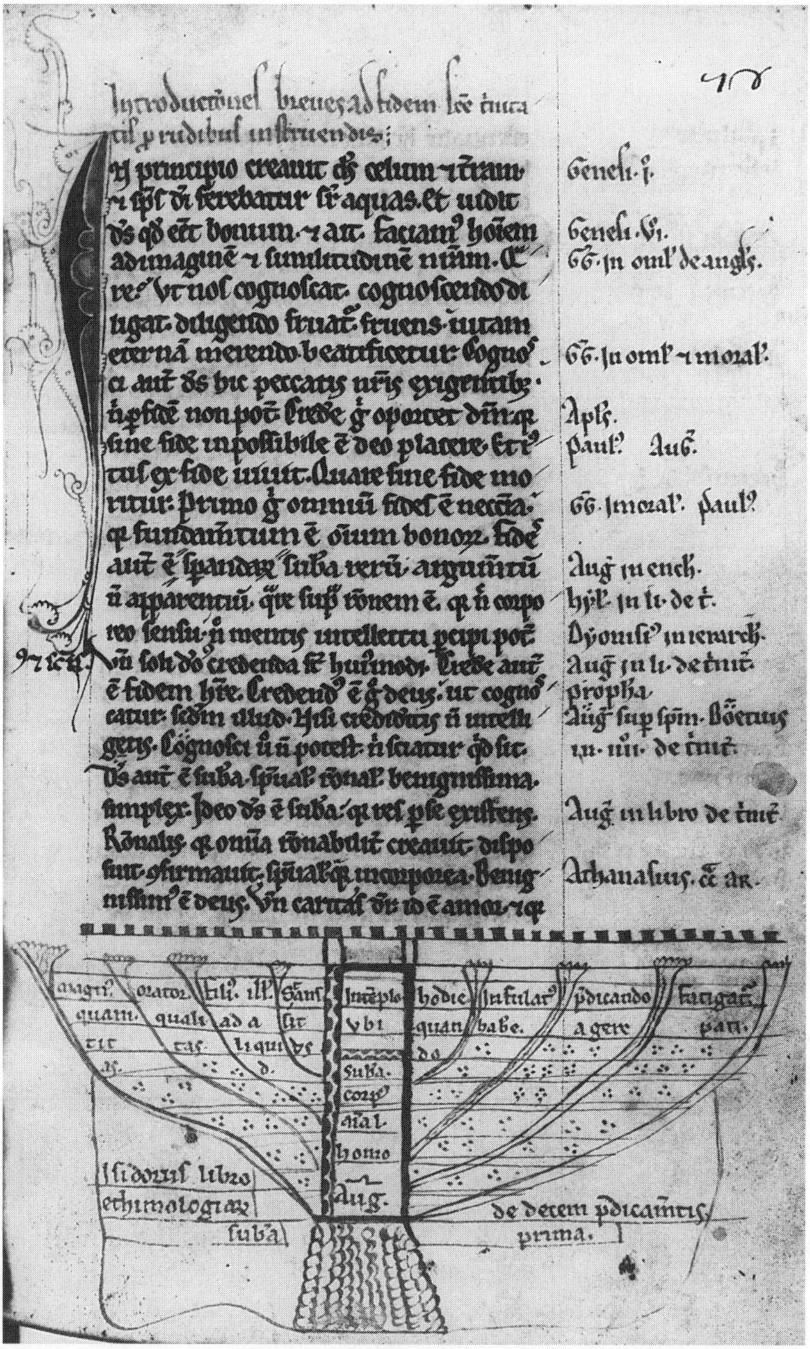

Figure 3. Sketched version of the Porphyrian tree in a Latin treatise on the Trinity, BNF lat. 2802, fol. 78. Reproduced by permission.

This is the Holy Spirit, which is the source and root of love, and the Father and the Son love one another with this love, for it [the Holy Spirit] proceeded from both of them together, from the Father and the Son, outside the world of time; and thus each of them, Father and Son, is both love and lover; for there is no other cause of all three of them, whichever you consider [*lit.* whether the one[44] or the other].

> Aiso es le Sanhs Esperitz
> quez es d'amor fons e razitz;
> et amon se d'aquel amor
> le paires e.l filhs entre lor,
> don prosegigz d'amdos essems
> del paire e del filh, senes temps;
> donc es amors et amaires
> quascus d'els, e.l filhs e.l paires;
> quar ges autra causa non es
> la us que l'autres de totz tres. (*BA*, 265–74)

This difficult passage underlines that the persons of the Trinity are coeternal, and united in their essential nature, which is love. Among creatures, love takes various forms, and Matfre spends a lot of time on the ways in which we should express our love for God. But the love which he flags at the outset as being the main object of his treatise and to which he devotes its final part is sexual love, a "natural movement" (*BA*, 27305) that is inherently good, provided it is used well and isn't concupiscent. Indeed, sexual love, as the ground in which grows the tree of knowledge of good and evil, is the touchstone of ethics. That is why Matfre devotes thousands of lines to defending troubadour love poetry. *Fin' amor*, in particular as hymned by himself, is a true guide to the supreme value of love:

Therefore, since true lovers know the nature of love I should know everything about it because there is no truer lover living who was ever truer in love than me.

> Doncs, pus la natura d'amor
> sabon li verai amador,
> ne dei hieu saber tot quan n'es
> quar plus fis aimans no viu ges
> qui fo anc plus fis en amor
> de me. (*BA*, 27833–38)

This love must be chaste (*BA*, 28518ff.), prefer folly to the wisdom of the world (*BA*, 28638ff.), submit willingly to torment (*BA*, 28802ff.), and defend and praise ladies. The difficulty of articulating love is admitted sympathetically, but troubadours are encouraged to keep trying (*BA*, 31612ff.). This is the only way they can gather the courtly virtues that are the leaves on the tree of knowledge of good and evil, and as a result enjoy its fruit, which are children.

What Matfre has done here is to reconceive substance as dynamizing affect—as an energy or outpouring which is spiritual in the case of divine love and to which we should aspire in our love for God, but which remains fundamentally sexual among creatures. What we take to be the world of reality is the product, or deposit, of this flood of energy between the Holy Spirit and the troubadours. Love, then, is the only true substance. Its nature as an impulse or disposition means that its reality can be located only in singular entities: principally (so far as Matfre is concerned) in the unique Godhead or the individual lover. In consequence, as Valérie Galent-Fasseur acutely observes, the *Breviari*'s account of the cosmos is, at the same time, a mapping of individual interiority.[45]

The Complexity of One in Matfre's Tree-Book

I have said that Matfre's "albre d'amor" differs in three major respects from the tree as Porphyry conceived it: it lays claim to absolute unity, it affirms the singularity of God, and it reconfigures the interconnected identities of this singular God with his individual creatures in terms of the flow of love. What these features have in common is that they all center on the problem of oneness. The monologism of Matfre's project consists in the articulation, in the tree, of the complexity of this one. Concentrating closely now on the "albre d'amor" itself, I shall consider it as a figure of the book before, in the final section, asking what kind of monologistic reading it solicits, and reconsidering Deleuze and Guattari's observations on the book-tree.

So far I have based my account of the *Breviari* on its verse text. However, the work also contains near the beginning an extended passage of prose described as an *abrégé*, which provides an account of the "albre d'amor" rather different from that of the verse,[46] and a program of illustrations.[47] Although in practice illuminations were added to a manuscript *after* the text had been copied, here both verse and prose refer to the images as having existed first. They constantly key their exposition to the pictures; as early as lines 21–22 the verse states as its ambition to "explain the obscure figures of the tree of love" ("declarar las figuras / del albre d'amor obscuras"). Among these images the most important is that of the "albre d'amor" itself, which contains features that are not discussed in either the verse or the prose. It occurs in almost all of the illuminated manuscripts that contain the opening part of the text, with usually only minor variation from one manuscript to another. Reproductions of some of these images are available in modern sources;[48] the one I have given as Figure 4 is from MS *N*, National Library of Russia (formerly St. Petersburg Public Library), Prov. F.v.XIV.1, and is not, to my knowledge, available in print elsewhere. The discrepancies between the three representations of the tree—in verse, prose, and painting—help to explain why no two critics agree on how to summarize the thought of the *Breviari*; each pays heed in varying degree to each of the three divergent schemes. These discrepancies, I shall argue, manifest the complexity of the work's unitary purpose by superimposing different orientations and entry points from which it might be approached.

Although the text insists, as I have said, on the need to understand love as descending from above, there are also times when the "albre d'amor" is organized from the bottom up. In the verse text the poet describes it as having God at its summit ("sima"):

Pointing to the true meaning of this tree you see before you, . . . I shall start at the summit and work down from branch to branch as far as the foot.

> Lo ver entendemen mostran
> d'est albre que.us vezetz denan, . . .
> me penrai sus a la sima,
> dichenden de branqu' em branca,
> tro.l pe. (*BA*, 847–48, 852–54)

Since the Holy Spirit is also said to be the "source and root" of love (*BA*, 266, 660), the tree's root and its summit coincide. The origins of love are further said to lie in the liver of each individual creature (*BA*, 498). In the prose summary, though not in the verse, this origin is elaborated as a set of twelve "roots" that favor the growth of love:

The twelve roots of love are twelve things that are written in the twelve circles at the foot of the tree. And if you can instill these things in the person you intend to love, between them they make love take root very well and grow very firm.

Las .xii. razitz d'amor sso son .xii.causas que son eschrichas en los .xii. cercles del pe del albre, las quals cauzas, qui las fai a la persona en cui vol s'amor pausar, mout fan l'amor enraziguar e fermar entre lor. (*BA*, 108P–12P)

Matfre's tree thus has roots at both top and bottom, superimposing an ascending pattern on the primary one of descent.

This dual orientation is considerably more marked in the pictures, which thus replicate the odd upside-down depictions associated with the Porphyrian tree. It is especially striking in the image in K (BL Harley 4940), which looks more like a tree upside down than right way up. In L (BL Royal 19.C. I) the medallion at the bottom of the tree from which issue the twelve roots of love is inscribed "God source and root of true love" ("dieu fons e razi de veraya amor"), which balances the medallion at the top inscribed "God the beginning of all good without beginning" ("dieus comensamens de tot be ses comensamen"). In the illumination in N (Figure 4), in common with M (Madrid Escurial S. I.3), the medallion at the center of the roots of love, again inscribed "God source and root of true love" ("die*us* fo*ns* e razitz de vera amor"), corresponds instead with a medallion half way up the tree inscribed "God the beginning of all good without beginning" ("die*us* comessame*n* de tot be ses com*en*sam*en*"). Another feature that contributes to the upside-down character of the picture is that several of the elements are depicted twice, once (in conformity with the texts) some way down the tree, and then again at the top. Thus in N again "love of God and one's neighbor," which both verse and prose describe as one of the "daughters" of human law ("dreg de gens"), is located both below the medallion inscribed "dreg de gens" and in the crown of *amors generals*; and love of one's child ("amor de son efan") likewise features twice, once cradled in the hands of *amors generals* and again (where it is situated by the written texts) as a branch issuing from the medallion labeled "dregz de natura."

In the verse and prose texts the "albre d'amor" is described as having four further trees grafted into the main one (*BA*, 501–4). Grafting is an art whereby a plant of one species is made to grow on a stock of a different but related one; the graft is both a separate plant, which continues to produce its own distinctive fruit, and part of the host plant on which it is growing. In the *Breviari*, these grafts (sometimes referred to as "trees" and sometimes as "branches": the equivocation is symptomatic of the point at issue) grow, somewhat surreally, out of each of the four "daughters" of the two forms of law, natural and human. Each bears leaves representing various virtues and its own particular fruit, which results from practicing those virtues. From love of God and one's neighbor issue the theological and cardinal virtues; their fruit is eternal life. From human sexual love grows the tree of knowledge of good and evil. Its leaves are

Figure 4. The "albre d'amor" in the *Breviari d'amor*, National Library of Russia, Prov. F.v.XIV.1, fol. 11v. Reproduced by permission.

fourteen courtly virtues, culminating in matrimony, and its fruit is off-spring. Two smaller branching structures are formed by the tree that grows from the love of temporal goods (whose leaves are care and forethought and whose fruit is pleasure), and the tree grows from love of one's off-spring (whose leaves are education and discipline and whose fruit is joy). The first two trees provide Matfre with the framework for substantial sections of the encyclopedia, but the smaller ones are more or less entirely ignored in it.[49]

In the prose and verse texts it is uncertain whether these grafts within the "albre d'amor" are upward-growing trees or else branches, which would, presumably, be sloping downward, following the Porphyrian model. In the illuminations, however, they are always drawn in the manner of traditional trees of virtues. Their vertical upward growth is superimposed on the more ambiguous orientation of the *albre* overall, as though to suggest that, while God's love flows *down* through creation to us, our love for him can be directed back *up* through the disciplines of the various virtues. This strong upward movement of the inset trees is particularly emphatic in some of the images. In *N*, for example, the larger of the two trees—those of eternal life and of the knowledge of good and evil—project into the frame; in *L* they extend even beyond it.[50]

The distribution of images in the corners of the tree image in *N* and the majority of other manuscripts also raises a question about orientation. Two individual lovers are located in the two top corners when one would surely have expected them to be at the bottom; the verse text, after all, invites lovers to gather *under* the tree (*BA*, 397–98). In the two lower corners, the depiction of Christ overcoming Satan and the victory of the Church over the Synagogue creates an echoing couple, that of Christ and the Church. This symbolic union is not described as such anywhere in the text, either verse or prose; the discussion of matrimony at the end of the encyclopedia does not refer to it; and yet the painting epitomizes Matfre's overall theme that procreation is a way of participating in Creation. In its variant forms of verse, prose and picture, the "albre d'amor" seeks to depict the way all being exists only as a flow of love and desire that binds spiritual and carnal entities together in elaborate oneness.

As well as responding differently to the upward/downward orientation of the *albre*, text and image also diverge in the way it is organized from side to side. The illustrators tend overwhelmingly to make the tree symmetrical around a central vertical axis, whereas both verse and prose texts describe a structure that continually branches sideways in one direction (cf. Figure 2). In general, none of the images I have seen effectively conveys the relation insisted on by the verse that "dreg de gens" (human law) is a subbranch of "dreg de natura" (natural law). Their insistence on symmetry seems rather to suggest that humanity and the natural order are parallel in their dependency on God's love.[51] It is also worth mentioning that the paintings with inscriptions reverse the sides assigned to "natural law" and "human law" by the prose text (the sides are not specified in the verse). The prose situates the natural side on the left and the human on the right, but in the pictorial tradition human law is on the left-hand side.[52]

A final respect in which the illuminations contribute a new orientation to the work is by suggesting that it could be read not from the top down or the bottom up but from the center out. The depiction of the Holy Spirit as a dove at the top of the image is at best unobtrusive, whereas the proportions of some of the pictures—notably those in *M* and *N*—result in the medallion inscribed "God the beginning of all good without beginning" being located almost in the middle.[53] But the element in all of the images that contributes the greatest centralizing impetus is without a doubt the figure of the "lady of the tree."

This "lady Love" barely features in the written texts, and then only in descriptions of the picture (see the prose rubric 114P–27P, and the verse text 611–846). By contrast, she dominates all of the images, dwarfing the "albre d'amor" and certainly making it look much less like a tree. I said that some of the elements in the tree are reiterated in parts of the pictures where, according to the textual accounts, they don't belong. One reason for these repetitions is to situate as many forms of love as possible on or close to the lady. With medallions traversing her body, and radiating outward to her crown, her hands, and her feet, she rather than the tree appears the epitome of the book. In one manuscript the tree has disappeared altogether in favor of the lady.[54] Galent-Fasseur rightly observes that the lady of the tree evokes the Virgin Mary and the courtly *domna* of the troubadours, thus anticipating the content of important future sections of the *Breviari*. But I disagree with her identification of the lady as some kind of "vital force." The name inscribed on her halo, "amors generals" in *N*,[55] makes it clear that she is the genus love, which is why all manifestations of love are gathered within her. Consequently in Matfre's text the "place of thought" is the Porphyrian tree of substance, where substance is identified as "love"; but in the pictorial tradition the substance (or genus) of love is located on this female figure, who seems to address the reader out of the tree. The picture thus concedes what the text does not: that the singularity of God and of individual lovers is only known (and communicated) through the universal, but our understanding of the universal is "placed" with reference to the outline of a body.

"Albre d'Amor" and Rhizome

At the beginning of this chapter I quoted Deleuze and Guattari's denunciation of the tree-book. As they put it, the tree-book reflects on nature, differentiating thought *from* reality, substituting its conceptual framework *for* reality, and "denaturing" it in arid hierarchies. The rhizome, they say, avoids the deadlock of reflection that traps the tree in this reversal of one-into-two and back again. It does not divide and articulate the One, it connects and enacts the multiple in a form that eludes the classical metaphysics of the one and the many: "The rhizome is reducible neither to the One or the multiple. It is not the One that becomes Two or even directly three, four, five, etc. It is not a multiple derived from a One, or to which One is added ($n + 1$). It is composed not of units but of dimensions, or rather directions in motion. It has neither beginning nor end, but always a middle (*milieu*) from which it grows and which it overspills."[56] Now the "albre d'amor" does indeed in some sense "grow from the middle," from the genus "love," and flow with the pulse of love in all directions. It has no single orientation, it has the ambiguous unity of a grafted tree, it has roots or entry points everywhere, and (in the pictorial tradition) it morphs into a vast female figure. Deleuze and Guattari's description of the rhizome as having "neither beginning nor end" is even echoed in N's inscription "God the beginning of all good without beginning" ("die*us* comessame*n* de tot be ses come*nsamen*"). Moreover, the *albre* does not, as I have shown, "derive from the One," or at least not in the way they mean, since Matfre's tree, unlike Porphyry's, does not derive from the unity of a genus. In all these respects, the "albre d'amor" has more in common with what they call the rhizome.

However, the "albre d'amor" *does* proceed from a "One" in another sense, the One in question being not a universal but the simple singularity of God.[57] There is no doubt as to this One's hierarchical supremacy in the figure as a whole; the *albre* certainly conforms to Deleuze and Guattari's definition of trees as "hierarchical systems with centers of significance and subjectification."[58] It is just that this absolutely singular point of origin seems to cause Matfre's tree to ramify indefinitely. The result is that the

Breviari edges toward a form of tree unknown to Deleuze and Guattari: one that celebrates not the multiple (as the rhizome does) but the singular.

The usefulness of Deleuze and Guattari's thought for medieval studies is as yet relatively unexplored. But even this brief comparison enables me to conclude this chapter as follows. Matfre Ermengaud envisions the unity of creation within the singularity of God as a force field of love inspiring desire in individual lovers. His poetic encyclopedia, which is also an encyclopedia of poetry, places its thinking on a version of Porphyry's well-known tree. But the tree image, so basic to medieval didacticism, when used as the place in which to delineate this thought, defies visualization; illuminators end up conflating it with a body. When Matfre confronts the "one" of his own monologism, he uncovers a complexity that prevents it being systematized by the very figure chosen to expound it.

Form in Anamorphosis in the Landscapes
of the *Ovide Moralisé*

AT ONCE SEDUCTIVE AND SHOCKING, Ovid's *Metamorphoses* posed a challenge to medieval readers. Its tenuous story line, in which one tale is often
linked only tangentially to the one that follows, artfully exploits the mechanisms of artificial over natural order and is just as unnatural in its narrative
content, which abounds in hybrid forms (such as centaurs and fauns) and
in all kinds of perverse couplings and grotesque transformations across
species boundaries. It celebrates a richness of creation while also flaunting
what, to Christian orthodoxy, represented a pagan fall from unity into
diversity, whether in its polytheism, its abundance of life forms, natural
and unnatural, or its view of history as fragmented by the rise and fall of
ancient kingdoms.

Successive generations of medieval commentators sought to subdue
Ovid's wild ride in different ways, and so contain his delights within a
framework compatible with Christianity. In *Fabula*, Paule Demats identifies three phases of such activity.[1] In the twelfth and early thirteenth centuries the *Metamorphoses* was read philosophically, with the emphasis being
placed on the first and last books (presenting, respectively, the Creation
of the world and the teachings of Pythagoras). Arnulf of Orléans, for example, drew out the affinities between Ovid's view of transformation (*mutatio*) and that of twelfth-century Platonism.[2] This was followed, in the
thirteenth century, by the mythographic and allegorical readings of such
authors as John of Garland; attention shifts from glossing the *mutatio* of
forms to interpreting the narratives as *fabulae* (fables). Finally, from the
fourteenth century, we have "a properly Christian or 'moralizing' period"
(*Fabula*, 141) where effort is directed to discerning Christian *senefiance* in
these "fables."[3]

The *Ovide moralisé* is the major pioneer of this last phase. It was
probably composed between 1316 and 1325 by a Franciscan friar acting on

commission from Jeanne de Bourgogne (1293–1329), wife of King Philip V.[4] She is the patron to whom we also owe Jean de Vignay's French translations of the *Legenda Aurea* and the *Speculum Historiale*; she clearly liked projects that were both pious and monumental. The first complete translation into French of Ovid's *Metamorphoses*, the *Ovide moralisé* is also the most ambitiously glossed and the most influential.[5] The version edited by de Boer is more than 71,000 lines long; about half of it consists in an expanded translation of Ovid, and the remaining half in "moralizations," some from the existing commentary tradition, but most devised by the French poet;[6] in other manuscripts, however, the amount of moralization and even the number of episodes treated can be much less that this.[7] Following the practice of interpreting non-Christian texts using the multiple levels of reading devised for the Scriptures, which had already been applied to the *Metamorphoses* by Arnulf of Orléans, the *Ovide moralisé* poet offers historical, moral and allegorical glosses on Ovid's tales.[8] If the *Metamorphoses* was troubling on account of its unregulated, ravishing excesses, here was a multistranded discipline powerful enough to tame it.

Unlike some of the other exegetes of the *Metamorphoses*, the *Ovide moralisé* poet does not see his task as being to Christianize Ovid by attributing to him some insight into the Christian revelation. The meanings the moralist claims to find are potentially recoverable from the pagan work itself, provided it is read from the perspective of faith.[9] Typically the glosses begin by discarding or dismissing the elements of pagan supernatural in the stories, salvaging only what can be interpreted as an expression of historical or scientific truth. This preliminary reading exposes human fallibility and the need for redemption; often some element in the pagan text is identified as representing the Jews. (One notices that the pagan elements are used to condemn Judaism more often than polytheism or idolatry; the moralist's assumption of a monotheistic framework abruptly writes out the pagan pantheon.) In a subsequent move, the story is reinfused with a supernatural meaning that is Christian and offers the means of redemption; overwhelmingly the interpretation centers on the person of Christ himself and his Church. The pagan elements in the original narrative are thus both the support and the casualty of the allegorizing process. Viewed through the lens of Christian truth, they are transformed into either unChristian falsehood, or Christianizing fable, or both.

The story of Ino in Book IV (2786ff.) illustrates this process. Ino, daughter of Cadmus of Thebes, marries a rich man who has two children, Phrixus and Hellé, by a previous union. Ino is envious of her stepchildren

and wants to have them exiled. She gives orders that no one in the country
may sow grain unless it has first been cooked. Intimidated, the peasants
obey, and so nothing grows. Ino then wages a campaign of misinforma-
tion to convince the people that the resulting famine has been caused by
Phrixus and his sister, whom the gods can no longer tolerate in their country. The children are driven out, but Jupiter takes pity on them and sends
a golden ram to carry them across the sea. The ram surges into the water
like a ship, but Hellé cannot withstand the waves and drowns, hence the
name Hellespont, "sea of Hellé." The ram carries Phrixus on to Colchis
and is there sacrificed at the temple of Mars.

After the moralist has narrated this story, which is only briefly referred
to in Ovid,[10] he extrapolates its meanings. First comes the historical reading that eliminates the pagan supernatural. The story is true provided that
Jupiter is suppressed and a ship is substituted for the ram. Ino's bribing
her clergy to spread slander about the two children is only too typical of
rulers, as is the gullibility of the people. This comment paves the way for
the second, moral reading: Ino represents a corrupt and dissolute will,
which is widespread as the root of criminality. Sowing cooked grain is "the
work of death, exposing humanity to perdition" ("mortel operacion / qui
met gens a perdicion," *OM*, IV, 2986–87), whereas God sent us his golden
lamb to save us. The third, strictly Christian interpretation gathers
strength from this point on, transforming and displacing Ovid's pagan
merveilleux. The lamb is "virtue and discretion and rational understanding" ("vertus et discretion / et entendement raisonable," *OM*, IV, 2996–
97). Phrixus is "the good soul" ("li bons esperis," *OM*, IV, 3027), which
strives to live cleanly, but Hellé is "the flesh, weak and dissolute" ("la char
frelle et dissolue," *OM*, IV, 3035), which succumbs to temptation. The
sacrifice to Mars marks the victory of the soul in its war against earthly
perils. Ino represents Eve, who caused "the seed of death" to be sown in
the world ("la semence de mort," *OM*, IV, 3059). The sea is hell, and the
golden ram is Jesus, his fleece of gold being from the womb of the Virgin,
"where God, in order to take on human flesh, came down like rain on
wool" ("ou Diex, por prendre char humaine, / descendi comme pluie en
laine," *OM*, IV, 3094–95; this interpretation will be recapitulated à propos
of Jason's quest for the ram's Golden Fleece in Book VII). The two children on the back of the ram represent Christ's dual nature: Hellé frail
humanity, Phrixus the divine Spirit. The sacrifice of the ram is the crucifix-
ion through which the faithful are saved while heretics and infidels are lost.

The moralist's maneuvering out of one supernatural framework and into another has implications for the conception of oneness in his poem. The glossing process takes us from one singular being (an individual with a unique and marvelous history) to another (Christ) via a process of moral generalization, and in this the *Ovide moralisé* resembles the *Breviari* where Matfre Ermengaud sets out to link two singular beings (God and individual troubadour-lovers) via an intermediate universalizing structure (the "tree of love"). But the emphasis on mutation and hybridity in the *Ovide moralisé* also makes it very different from the *Breviari*. Rather than focusing (like Matfre's text) on the differentiated universal forms that are the species within the Porphyrian tree, the *Metamorphoses* assumes a potential continuum between the diverse aspects of creation, which is reflected in the way the stories themselves flow into one another. Creatures are characterized not by generic difference but by the community or *indifference* that enables a human to turn into a bird or tree, a god into an animal, or an animate form into something inanimate like a fountain, a constellation, or a rock. Individual identity is in some degree affirmed by the unique trajectory of every metamorphosis but also undone by the radical instability such metamorphosis implies.

This way of conceiving a singular being as always having the potential to be dislodged into something other than itself can be illumined with reference to Agamben's concept of "whatever" (*qualunque*) in his book *La Comunità che viene* (*The Coming Community*). By "whatever," Agamben designates the singular at its barest and most basic.[11] Merely existent as itself, the whatever is lacking in all attributes apart from its "thisness," that is, the accident of its not being something else. In terms that echo the *Metamorphoses*, Agamben refers to the whatever as "neither generic not individual, neither an image of the divinity nor an animal form."[12] Or again: "whatever singularity" is "freed from the false dilemma that obliges knowledge to choose between the ineffability of the individual and the intelligibility of the universal."[13] Its very rudimentariness, however, endows it with the potential for "being in common" with other things. While itself insignificant and unique, it carries the potential for intelligibility and for relationship. In another passage that calls to mind the *Ovide moralisé*, Agamben suggests that the example is a type of "whatever," since "it is one singularity among others which, however, stands for each of them and serves for all."[14] Agamben derives the term "whatever" from the *quodlibet* of high Scholasticism and aligns it in particular with Duns Scotus's concept of *haecceitas* ("thisness").[15] ("Thisness" is a principle that "contracts" an individual from its common nature and that, thinks

Scotus, might enable us to know it intuitively as a singular, in contrast to
the intellectual operation of "abstraction" by which we arrive at universals.)[16] By putting Agamben's account of "whatever" to work on the
Ovide moralisé, I shall be taking his thinking back to its origins in fourteenth-century culture.

The potential for a relationship to, and thus for the "common," is
the basis of the "coming community" of Agamben's title. Although the
community he invokes is conceived in terms of secular postmodern politics
and ethics, it is fueled by medieval Messianic thinking, both Jewish and
Christian. It is, of course, a version of this same Messianic tradition that
provides the *Ovide moralisé* poet with the rationale for his interpretative
method. From the plethora of secular themes (desire, power, violence, and
so on) that confront the moralist in the pages of Ovid's *Metamorphoses*,
his faith in the Christian revelation draws a tireless consistency of meaning.
Just as in the *Breviari* the Oneness of God provides a point of reference
that unifies Matfre's thought to the point of distortion, so in the *Ovide
moralisé* Christ's incarnation turns out to be the single truth toward which
virtually every exegesis is turned, and which all the poet's readers are exhorted to acknowledge. The unity, or convergence, of all interpretations
in Christ becomes, in this way, the harbinger of the readers' potential
community *with* Christ. So here too we find a medieval antecedent of
Agamben's thinking: a conception of a "coming community" based on
the potential for union with Christ that is not yet realized.

The spatial framework and support for these ideas, which in the *Breviari* is the "albre d'amor," expands in the *Ovide moralisé* to the entire
landscape. Landscape is the place that enables the single to communicate
with the common, since any part of it can become, or may have been,
some other part. As the dust of the ground, the land provides the bodily
matter with which divinely conceived forms are joined. The moralist's ar-
chetypal landscape is that of Eden, also identified as the paradise in which
we all hope to be united. Lured into Ovid's enchanted groves for who
knows what adventures, readers of the *Ovide moralisé* repeatedly discover
in them the traces of the fall and its redemption. It is in this landscape that
the "coming community" will come to be.

Before I consider the importance of place in the poem, however, I
shall look at the concept of "form," which I see as key to this paradoxical
community in which both human and divine singularities participate. At
once the divine Idea, the person of Christ, and the true identity of every
individual, form is revealed thanks to the transformations described in the

text. By means of visible bodily metamorphoses, invisible forms can be discerned via a process comparable with what, in the visual arts, is known as "anamorphosis." This is the technique whereby a distorted perspective is restored to legibility when viewed through an unusual contrivance (such as a cylindrical mirror) or from an unexpected angle. It is a term traditionally associated with early modern painting, but it has been given broader currency by Lacan, and more recently by Žižek.[17] Lacan's favorite example of anamorphosis is Holbein's *The Ambassadors*, in which two incompatible perspectives are juxtaposed. Most of the painting—a portrait of two men in a setting busy with meaningful artifacts—looks right when viewed from the front, but there is a strange, floating object in the foreground that remains completely meaningless from this position. If the viewer moves to the far right of the painting, however, this object is drawn into a normal perspective and becomes recognizable as a skull, while the remainder of the picture recedes into a blur. The discrepancy between the two perspectives enables the viewer to see that what he or she takes for "reality" is one particular take on a "real" that exceeds it.

The relevance of the concept of anamorphosis to the *Ovide moralisé* has already been recognized by James Simpson, who has used it brilliantly to analyze how the moralizer deals with the "real of enjoyment" (or obscene *jouissance*) of the pagan past.[18] My use of the term will be geared to discerning something equally elusive: the form thanks to which individual entities both exist as such and have the potential to meet in community. It because of the way form may be caught in anamorphosis that the "place of thought" in the *Ovide moralisé* is both visual in its appeal and extremely hard to see. The moralist endeavors to glimpse, as though with the gaze of God, truths that lie blurred in the fallen landscape of creation, but that catch our eye when its elements metamorphose.

The Proem and the Meaning of "Form"

Previous scholars have discussed the French poet's handling of the famous proem to the *Metamorphoses*, but there is more to be said about the implications of the way the moralist interprets Ovid's view of "form."[19] Commentators have, he says, misrepresented Ovid by taking the opening lines of the *Metamorphoses*, "in nova fert animus mutatas dicere formas / corpora," to refer to Ovid's intention to speak of "bodies changed into new forms." Downplaying the phrase *mutatas formas* and construing *nova* as

agreeing with *corpora*, the French poet transfers the capacity to mutate
from form to body. The body, he asserts, can only ever be secondary and
subordinate to the unity and immutability of form. The unchanging forms
of the created world exist first as ideas in the mind of God, who then
creates their bodies from nothing (*ex nihilo*):

Ovid said, "My heart wishes to tell of the forms which were changed into new
bodies." Some people whose task was to expound and explain the author set about
corrupting him, reproving and saying the opposite of him, claiming that Ovid
must have said, "the bodies which were changed into new forms." But fables such
as these should not get a hearing; any reasonable man can know that the author
spoke well. Before the Creator created the world there was not yet, nor could
there be, any body that could receive a new form. What body could there be from
which God could, in the beginning, derive a form? There existed nothing apart
from God himself who, in his divine thought, had conceived all form, exactly as
he would bestow it on the bodies he created from nothing, without aid from any
creature, and without present matter.

> Ovides dist: "Mes cuers vieult dire
> les formes qui muees furent
> en nouviaux cors." Aucun qui durent
> l'autour espondre et declairier
> s'entremistrent de l'empirier,
> de l'auteur reprendre et desdire,
> disant que li autours dut dire:
> "Les cors qui en formes noveles
> furent muez"; mais teulz faveles
> ne doivent audience avoir:
> homs raisonables puet savoir
> que bien dist, ce croi, li autours,
> quar, ançois que le Creatours
> creast le monde, il n'iert encors
> ne ne pooit estre nul cors
> qui nove forme receüst.
> Quel cors iert il dont Dieus deüst
> forme traire au comencement?
> Il n'iert riens fors lui seulement,
> qui en sa divine pensee
> avoit toute forme pensee
> tele come il la donneroit
> au cors, que de noient feroit,
> sans aïde de nulle rien,
> sans point de present mairien.[20] (*OM*, I, 72–96)

Demats comments on this passage that "by replacing metamorphosis with
the primordial union of form and matter [the poet] gets rid of the work's

real subject."[21] However, the moralist's point is surely that the mutability (or capacity for metamorphosis) of the *body* is precisely what enables us to see the divinely bestowed identity of its *form*.

This point is amplified with a crucial example: that of God himself. The moralist is at first dismissive of Ovid's appeals to the gods, on the grounds that "there is only one God, one unique Creator" (*OM*, I, 110f.). But then he mitigates his condemnation, conceding that the Trinity was revealed when its persons underwent metamorphosis into three distinct bodies, and so became perceptible to the senses ("sensiblement se muerent," *OM*, I, 120): the Son in Jesus, the Holy Spirit as a dove, and God as a voice pronouncing the words "This is my beloved Son" (*OM*, I, 131). On this analogy, the manifestations that Ovid accepts as gods (in the plural) might be read as revealing the unity of the Godhead. Transformations of the body, however many and various, provided they are read from the right perspective, anamorphically disclose a single divine identity.

Earlier glosses on the *Metamorphoses* illumine what, in the passage just cited, the *Ovide moralisé* poet means by "form" as an idea in the mind of God.[22] The *accessus* "Quidam philosophi," for example, identifies form in this sense as part of a theory of creation that Ovid shares with certain other philosophers: "They said that there had always been three things: namely God, and the four elements mixed together, and the forms of all things existing in the mind of God, that is to say Ideas or Differences, such as rationality and heat and cold, etc., by means of which God would constitute the things that were to come."[23] The existence of such productive forms or underlying archetypes was the object of extensive reflection in the twelfth century, since it formed part of the teaching of Plato in his *Timaeus*. Plato was credited with having intuited the persons of the Trinity because his account of creation distinguished three aspects of God: creative power, wisdom and goodness.[24] The long, composite accessus to the *Metamorphoses* cited by Demats (*Fabula*, Appendix 1, 179–84) alludes to this when it distinguishes three different causes of creation: efficient, formal, and final. These are seen as corresponding with the persons of the Trinity: "And it can be said that by the efficient cause should be understood God the Father who took thought for human nature by creating the visible and invisible realms, and by the formal cause wisdom, that is the Son of God, and by the final cause the Holy Spirit."[25] This idea that God's wisdom personified in his Son is the formal cause of creation was a philosophical commonplace of the twelfth century.[26] When the *Ovide moralisé* poet refers in the proem to an eternal form in the divine mind, he is therefore already thinking of Christ. The Son is the form of God's thinking, the manifestation of his intentions for the created world, the expression of his *devine sapience* ("divine wisdom," *OM*, passim). This identification dominates the allegoresis, as the moralist discerns traces of *devine sapience* throughout the pagan pantheon.[27] In Book II, for example, Phoebus represents divine wisdom (*OM*, II, 2550), so does Pallas when Vulcan attacks her (*OM*, II, 2890–91), Coronea shows how it was forfeit (*OM*, II, 2922), Saturn's love for Philiré figures it (*OM*, II, 3304–5), and Mercury in his eloquence embodies it (*OM*, II, 4534). The French poet thereby fulfills the suggestion made in his prologue that polytheism, correctly interpreted, can lead us to the unity of God's form. It is worth noting, in this respect, that a number of *Ovide moralisé* manuscripts are illustrated with a cycle of pictures of the pagan gods. Rather than representing a "dissociation of text and image," could these be anamorphically soliciting a monothesistic reading?[28]

In short, the concept of form in the reworked proem can be seen as the rationale for the moralist's entire enterprise. His moralizations are so many instances of anamorphosis in which a Christian perspective brings God's redemptive purpose into focus from the distorting blur of the pagan *fabula*. Ovid's text details the fall of humanity in myriad incongruous and shocking ways. But provided we read it awry, it also discloses men's potential for conformity with their divinely conceived form, thanks to its incarnation in God's Son. The more bodies change, the more opportunities they offer of a perspective from which to glimpse the unity of the divine wisdom in whose image we all are formed.

Unity of Interpretation in the *Ovide Moralisé*

Understandably, given its length, most readers consult the *Ovide moralisé* only episodically. They thereby see only the bizarre cocktail of moralizations that follows any one story, at the expense of the work's unity. However, the poet clearly expects his readers to read the poem in its entirety,[29] and, as Renate Blumenfeld-Kosinski has observed, his intention is to provide not so much a series of glosses or even a running commentary on Ovid's poem as "a second text that follows its own logic."[30] The overriding theme of this second text is the incarnation, together with the doctrines most intimately related to it, such as the Virgin Birth, the eclipse of the Synagogue by the Church, the need for redemption, and the hope of obtaining it. Just as the *Metamorphoses* situates itself on the margins of classical epic, construing a history of Rome from the repetitive, the marginalized, and the bizarre,[31] so the glosses work on the edges of Ovid's text to resurrect, from accumulated and disparate moments where the potential for divine revelation is discerned, a vast Christian epic whose subject is none other than salvation. Metamorphosis becomes the vehicle of anamorphosis as every transformation—whether wrought by Ovid on his characters or by the moralist on Ovid—provides a means of seeing Christ incarnate in the very letter of the pagan text.

This is true whether the Ovidian figures that disclose Christ are gods (in Book II, Phoebus, Pallas, Saturn, Aesculapius, Mercury, and Jupiter, as well as Chiron the centaur, are all seen as types of Christ); legendary heroes (in Book VII, Jason, Theseus, Hercules, Pirithoüs, and Minos's son Androgeüz are successively interpreted as models of the incarnation); or transgressors (in Books IX–XI, Hercules's infidelity, the incestuous relationships of Oedipus and Byblis, and the same-sex loves of Iphis, Orpheus, and Ganymede all provide material for the same interpretation). Indeed, unnatural relationships lend themselves especially well to the moralist's double move of condemnation and recuperation, given that the incarnation and the virgin birth likewise flout natural law. Thus, for example, Oedipus invites reading as a figure of the incarnation because he, like God, "entered into his mother's chamber" (*OM*, IX, 1944), and Ganymede, although condemned for his homosexual relations with Jupiter, when borne aloft by him in the form of an eagle is "at the same time true god and true man" (*OM*, X, 3421). Animals too (a ram as we have seen in Book IV, a stag in X, 3220–21, a heifer in XI, 2964–65, or a woodpecker in XIV, 3059–61) can serve as images of Christ and his passion.

The poet can similarly discover the Virgin Mary under a wide variety of disguises. Daphne, fleeing from Apollo's advances in Book I, is transformed into a laurel; Myrrha, guilty of incest with her father in Book X, becomes a myrrh tree. Although one is a model of chastity and the other of transgressive desire, both are figures of the Virgin: Daphne on account of her coldness and virginal resistance, and Myrrha because her incestuous love recalls the fact that Mary was at once daughter, mother, and bride of God (*OM*, X, 3748–809). Thus disparate and often shocking pagan misadventures are united in their capacity to manifest the central tenets of the Christian revelation.

When the commentator is at his best, continuities between episodes in the *Metamorphoses* are matched by a continuous evolution in his own interpretations. So, for example, Bacchus is read as a type of Christ from the end of Book III to the end of Book IV, the gloss weaving a consistent narrative from often fragmentary episodes;[32] the stories surrounding Orpheus are worked together into a single commentary in Books X–XI.[33] Continuity of interpretation is particularly striking from Book XII onward. Here Ovid's account of the Trojan War is supplemented and glossed to represent the confrontation between the Jews (Troy) and Christ and his Church (the Greeks). Figures are found to represent John the Baptist and the first martyrs. As Ovid's narrative gathers momentum with the departure of Aeneas, his journey to Italy, and the founding of Rome (for Ovid, the climactic metamorphosis is the transformation of Caesar into a god), the commentary responds with an interpretation of Aeneas's ship as the Church in whose travels are discerned the vicissitudes of early ecclesiastical history. Dido, for instance, is interpreted as a figure of heresy (*OM*, XIV, 555–96), Circe is the wicked queen of abomination in the Apocalypse (*OM*, XIV, 2563–72), and Turnus figures as Antichrist (*OM*, XIV, 3879–80). These closing books are peppered with satirical attacks on corrupt churchmen and the failure of religious orders in the poet's own day. Thus, just as Ovid brought his historical narrative up to his present, so the moralist gives contemporary color to his own contribution.

I shall return to the way this inclusion of the poem's readership builds the potential for a community founded in the form of Christ. But first I shall go back to the opening sections of the poem to see how the poet develops the notion of form in relation to that of place.

The Creation of "Place" and the Form of Man

After the proem, Book I of the *Metamorphoses* narrates the creation of the world. As Demats has shown, medieval commentators number Ovid among thinkers who envisage creation as beginning when order is first imposed on primal chaos, thus transforming it into place.[34] Following Ovid, the *Ovide moralisé* describes this process. First, chaos is separated into the four elements (*OM*, I, 181–86). Each is then assigned a place (this accords with Aristotle's account of place as internally ordered; see my Introduction), and in turn serves as container to appropriate inhabitants. Ovid's enumeration begins with the stars and demigods and ends with the creation of man. The translator, already adopting biblical phraseology according to which man resembles God (*OM*, I, 317, 327–28), supplements this list with material from Genesis (reptiles in the water, flying creatures in the air, beasts on land, and so on, *OM*, I, 399–402). The parallel he insinuates between the biblical and Ovidian accounts of creation is brought out in a number of illustrations of the *Ovide moralisé*, such as the one in BNF fr. 872 (see Figure 5), on which more below.[35] That the created world results from the conjunction of place (as the receptacle of body) with divinely devised form becomes explicit when God makes man out of earth "in his image and likeness":

From a little clay of the earth God gave form to man, but he did more: for he made man in his image and likeness so that man would know him . . . the matter was base, but the form was most excellent given that man was made in the form of the heavenly King—there could be none finer.

> d'un poi de terre limonee
> a Dieux *forme* a l'homme donee,
> mais tant li fist il d'avantage
> qu'a sa samblance et a s'ymage
> le fist, si qu'homs le conneüst . . .
> mout fu la matire despite,
> mes la *forme* fu tres eslite,
> quant a la *forme* au roi celestre—
> quar nulle meillor ne puet estre—
> fu fais homs. (*OM*, I, 407–11, 415–19, emphasis mine)

Whereas matter is drawn from place (the earth) to provide a body that is liable to change, man's form unites him with God and enables him to participate in "the divine thinking" (*OM*, I, 91). There is potential community between Christ as the form of divine wisdom and man as the likeness of that form.

The significance of the conjunction of form with place (earth) is brought out again in the gloss on Pygmalion in Book X. Pygmalion's creative powers help us understand those of God:

[God] forged our human nature in his form and shape through his divine wisdom, and gave it an ivory form. The matter was clay to which God gave human form. The matter was vile and base on which God set most excellent form and, in his benevolence, filled it with understanding and goodness.

> A sa *forme* et à sa figure
> forga nostre humaine nature
> par sa sapience divine,
> si li dona *forme* eborine.
> La matire fu limonee,

> cui Diex *forme* humaine a donee.
> vilz fu la matire et despite,
> ou Diex mist *forme* tres eslite,
> et par sa bone volenté
> l'empli de sens et de bonté. (*OM*, X, 3590–99, emphasis mine)

The matter of which we are made is mere clay, whereas the radiant clarity of form resides in the imprint on us of God's wisdom, the expression of our likeness to himself that anticipates God's own incarnation as man. In this way, as Agamben observes, the Genesis narrative "rooted the human figure in God, bound it in this way to an invisible archetype, and founded with it the paradoxical concept of an absolutely immaterial resemblance."[36] Bodily change—metamorphosis as the *Ovide moralisé* poet understands it—will prove to be the paradoxical means whereby this form can be perceived and its potential community with the divine form disclosed.

Following immediately after the Creation narrative, the myth of Deucalion and Pyrrha provides a first example of how form emerges anamorphically in the process of material transformation. Deucalion and Pyrrha are summoned by an oracle to repopulate the earth by throwing stones behind them. Gradually the stones turn into human beings, the soft earth becoming soft tissue, while the hard stone expresses man's obduracy:

Just as the statue defines itself, as the sculptor gradually draws it towards its determinate form, in the same way the stones which those two threw took on human likeness.

> Ausi com l'image se trait
> quant li ymagiers la pourtrait
> c'a petit vers *forme* certaine,
> ausi pristrent samblance humaine
> les pierres que cil dui jeterent. (*OM*, I, 2097–2101, emphasis mine)

Comparison with a sculptor at work underlines how form becomes perceptible when matter changes. The "forme certaine" of man emerges in the process of his emergence from stone, the very antithesis of his eventual "semblance humaine." Human form was always already there, within the stone, and when it assumes a human body the stone's hardness can be seen in its true light, as an aspect of human nature. Like the clay with which (according to Genesis) Adam and Eve were made, the rocks that repopulate the earth after the flood point to landscape as the corporeal substance of living forms. The subsequent metamorphoses through which form is disclosed all take place within, and by means of, this landscape.

Metamorphosis, Singularity, and the Coming Community

Metamorphosis in the *Metamorphoses* has a variety of roles that medieval commentators delighted in distinguishing. Caroline Bynum has summarized its various manifestations as "change of body for punishment, escape, or apotheosis, for seduction or betrayal, for discovery or revelation."[37] Rather than pursuing this taxonomy, however, I shall concentrate on just two aspects of metamorphosis in the *Ovide moralisé*: the way it marks out an individual as unique, and yet how, at the same time, it diagnoses in every part of the created world a potential for community. I shall begin with the notion of the common before turning to singularity, and then back again to community.

Mutation is often the initial spur to the moral glosses, and so it acts as a hinge between the career of an individual Ovidian protagonist and the general meaning it can be made to bear. Transformation into an animal, for instance, may be read as a mark of bestiality, or into a plant or inanimate thing as an expression of a desire for insensibility. Human beings are repeatedly exposed as being, in some respects, inhuman. One of the most frequent causes of metamorphosis is an encounter between a mortal and one of the gods. The violent transformations that the mortal undergoes unmask the contingency of "being human" and its contiguity not only with other forms of life but even with the inanimate universe. Incestuous passions are another motif that similarly discloses how to be human is, at the same time, to be capable of being alienated from humanity.

The French poet's moralizations of Pythagoras's teaching in Book XV theorize these happenings by showing how the spiritual and the physical, the living and the inanimate, are all interconnected. Initially, the moralist implies that man has two kinds of form, one of the body and one of the soul. A child's body is formed inside its mother's, and it is also "spirituelment . . . enformez" (*OM*, XV, 3232–33)—this spiritual form being received at baptism (*OM*, XV, 3240). But as the analysis progresses, the distinctness of the two forms wanes. The direction of the commentary is determined by the commonplace that man is a microcosm ("maindre monde," *OM*, XV, 3314). Unpacking this concept leads the moralist to describe how the various elements and humors that constitute the cosmos

are also responsible for the functioning of human beings. The four elements that constitute all body, and hence the human body too, have, as
their spiritual counterparts, the four constituents of the soul ("l'ame ra les
siens elemens," *OM*, XV, 3439), which are understanding, pure thought,
stability, and motion. The humors also have their equivalents ("Ainsi ra
l'ame quatre humors," *OM*, XV, 3484) in the soul's joy, sadness, bitter-
ness, and orderly thinking. Correctly identifying the humors that predominate in the body will serve the purposes of the soul (*OM*, XV, 3539), for
the body's condition impacts directly, not just metaphorically, on its spiritual state.

At the same time, the soul is in communication with other elements
in the cosmos. Thus the cold and moist character of phlegm cools the soul
so as to disincline it to the sins of passion (*OM*, XV, 3574) but can make it
lazy, unrepentant, and unresponsive (*OM*, XV, 3590ff.). Winter and old
age, because they are associated with phlegm, may adversely affect the soul
of the phlegmatic (*OM*, XV, 3639ff.). The heavenly bodies also exert their
influence on the soul, as does diet. The other humors create similar interrelations among body, soul, and cosmos. Indeed, the commentary continues, the whole created order is composed of the four elements (*OM*, XV,
4497–98) and the disposition of creatures among air, earth, and water is
dependent on their makeup. But this disposition, in turn, corresponds
with the range of human qualities and conditions, from the most lofty to
the basest and most sluggish. At times this correspondence appears metaphorical, as when we are told that the large quadrupeds "denote simple
people" (*OM*, XV, 4741). Yet the mapping of moral qualities onto the
physical universe is comprehensive and constantly motivated by such properties as weight, type of appetite, and so on. This analysis of the created
world, that is, operates not in terms of a dualist opposition of body and
soul, but of matter and *form*. It continues to XV, 6248, at which point the
moralist turns back to Ovid's historical narrative.[38]

Pythagoras's teaching as incorporated into the *Moralisé* repeatedly
implies that the whole universe is capable of flux because there is a common being uniting all its various components, including the ones we think
of as "spiritual." Ovid's text is here being inflected toward a perfectly
orthodox Christian position; Aquinas, for example, held that everything
that exists, exists by virtue of its participation in a common being that
stemmed from God.[39] Duns Scotus's views on this common nature are
cited by Agamben as a precedent for his own delineation of "the coming
community."[40] Agamben differentiates himself from Duns Scotus in at-

tributing to him a realist view ("he seems to conceive common nature as an anterior reality"), whereas Agamben's own emphasis is on the virtual nature of community, its "coming" into existence.[41] It would seem, however, that Agamben here misrepresents Duns Scotus, whose position is in reality much closer to Agamben's. The common for Duns Scotus, says de Libera, is not common in the sense that it can truly be predicated of all things; rather, it is "common in the sense that it does not resist being in a subject other than the one in which it is."[42] Community arises thanks to the capacity of all being to be elsewhere than it is. It can be founded in difference, since things that differ resemble one another in the fact they are different.[43] Duns Scotus's concept of the common, then, is not (*pace* Agamben) an "anterior reality" but rather a virtual community held together by difference. It is based not in some preexisting shared substance (such as species) but in the potential for being in some other relation to other things, and in some other place.[44]

I propose that landscape in the *Ovide moralisé* provides a place in which to think about community in this sense. True, it is as a result of the material flux in which all things are caught up that anything whatever (*qualunque*) can potentially assume some other form at some other point in the landscape. But the moralist's reflections on Pythagoras suggest, I think, that he doesn't think this constant potential for change can simply be explained by positing preexisting common properties between individuals that enable any one to mutate into any other. Instead, the convergence that his moralizations effect between physical and moral or spiritual elements points to the potential community, through redemption, of humanity with God—the possibility, that is, that people could be radically transformed from what they have become. But before considering how the *Ovide moralisé* might envisage this "coming community," we need first to look at how it represents singular beings in their fallen and potentially redeemable singularity.

Here too the reflections of Pythagoras in Book XV are illuminating. Pythagoras insists that throughout its bodily mutations the soul remains one and the same. Just as wax can take on different shapes without changing its substance,

Thus I can properly say that the soul is doubtless one, and that the substance proper to it does not change, however it may disguise itself in different shapes.

> Ensi puis je proprement dire
> que l'ame est une, sans doutance,

sans muer sa propre sustance,
ja soit ce qu'elle se desguise
en figures de mainte guise. (*OM*, XV, 488–92)

This unchanging identity is invisible as such, and yet it can be discerned anamorphically in metamorphosis. One index of individual uniqueness is the kind of creature into which an individual mutates. It is noticeable that, as a general rule, no two figures metamorphose into the same thing. There is only one crow, raven, swan, woodpecker, bear, heifer, stag, laurel, pine tree, cypress tree, and so on. Indeed, the plenitude of the Ovidian landscape, to which I shall return, depends on this diversity. Even figures transformed into inanimate things tend to maintain discreteness; they do not simply merge with the sea, the earth, or the heavens in general but become specific fountains, rivers, rocks, or constellations. A second pointer toward the fact that metamorphosis describes a unique being is that it is so commonly triggered by desire. The urge toward union with another creature, especially when it is thwarted, discloses the oneness of each individual. Although dealing with drive rather than desire, James Simpson's account of *jouissance* points to the same conclusion, since each individual has a singular relation to his or her own *jouissance* and is responsible for it. Simpson's approach is perhaps best exemplified by his reading of the story in Book II of Callisto, a nymph who is transformed into a bear by Diana to punish her for getting pregnant after being raped by Jupiter. After her sexual fall, the nymph passes from being a rational creature possessed of a voice to becoming a beast afflicted with a horrified and horrifying muteness, which Simpson sees as the index of the intensity of her *jouissance*. The invisible form of an individual being such as Callisto's is revealed by the process of her becoming other than she was.

Medieval exegetes were already alert to the idea that metamorphosis, while making one other than one was, also makes one more oneself. A familiar example was that of Lycaön in Book I.[45] When this cruel cannibal is metamorphosed into a wolf, his wolfish body manifests what Lycaön in some sense already was: a monster addicted to slaughter and savagery.

When he imagined he was speaking, he howled; and the great wrath that gripped him filled him with a horrifying madness. He is still rabid and hell-bent on devouring simple creatures, and just as he used to slaughter and eat his fellow humans, so now he still slaughters and eats beasts. . . . And he is as full of rage and evil as he was formerly.

Quant cuidoit parler, si ullot,
et de la grant ire qu'il ot
li prist une angoisseuse rage.
Encore angoisse, encore enrage
des simples bestes devourer,
et, si come il seult acorer
les gens et mengier, il acore
les bestes et menjüe encore. . . .
s'est plains de rage et de mauté,
Si come il ot ainçois esté. (*OM*, I, 1373–78, 1387–88)

Similarly, Stephen Murphy has proposed that when Actaeon is transformed as a punishment for coming across Diana and her nymphs bathing,
"the metamorphosis into a deer is no longer simply that which puts an
end to the [profaning] contemplation of divine beauty, but the logical
extension of that ecstatic contemplation."[46] And when Myrrha becomes a
myrrh tree, she nevertheless retains knowledge of sex with her father; the
tree exudes sweetness (myrrh), and the child, Adonis, she conceived with
her father is born from its trunk. I have already shown that the poet's
moralization of Pythagoras resists a simple dualistic account of separation
between body and soul. Such resistance is also borne out in these stories
where the soul's "thinking," whether it be perverse or repentant, intent
or distraught, is manifested in its changing body. Paradoxically, then, the
form of the individual becomes perceptible only when his or her bodily
contours dissolve.

Pythagoras's reflections illumine this point in this passage, where he
hints that behind the concept of birth (*nestre*) lurks that of not being
(*n'estre*):

And by the renewal of its form which it renews it seems to be born anew, and so
people say: "It is born." But what does "being born" mean? Merely beginning to
be other than one was.

Et par le renouvelement
de sa *forme* qu'el renouvele
samble nestre toute nouvele,
si dist l'en "ce nest." Et qu'est "nestre"?
Commencier seulement a estre
la chose autre qu'el n'iert eüe. (*OM*, XV, 702–7)

Non-self-identity is the very form in which identity is disclosed. It is in
becoming other than one was that identity emerges, its true "form"

emerging in the very process of its apparent alteration. The anamorphosis proposed is here is no mere trick of perspective (like the cylindrical mirrors used in early modern art) but has all the metaphysical seriousness it will later assume in the theories of Lacan or Žižek. It offers the means of seeing, as if with the gaze of God, something that is unavailable to the eye in ordinary reality, something that utterly transforms our relationship *to* that reality.

At the same time, the *n'estre* that is inherent to *nestre*, the fissure of nonbeing within being, offers a potential opening into the common and a radical change of form. Indeed, it is only through moral transformation that redemption can take place. With a reminiscence of the story of Callisto, the poet recalls the bestiary tradition that bear cubs were born in a shapeless mass that was then literally "licked into shape" by the parent. Christian teaching can, he maintains, have the same effect on people.

But just as the bear forms and perfects its cubs by licking them, in the same way [people] took on form and perfection from the preaching of the saints who instructed them until they were well formed in the faith and conformed to it.

> Mes si com l'ours *forme* et parfait
> ses faons par son lechement,
> ausi par le precheëment
> des sains, qui les endoctrinoient,
> *forme* et perfection prenoient,
> tant qu'il estoient bien *formé*
> en la creance et *conformeé*. (*OM*, XV, 6030–36)

As the vocabulary of this passage insists, the "form" that is ours is one that is yet to come to us, both as individuals and in relation to the divine model to which we shall "conform." When a person repents, God "renews and reforms him and gives him a new form to follow faithfully and do good works" ("si le renouvele et re*forme* / et li done *nouvele forme* / de bien suivre et de bien ouvrer," *OM*, IV, 4850–52). The author of the *Ovide moralisé* anticipates this potential for radical change in his readers by predicating it of his characters. Lycaön, it is true, is not afforded a redemptive reading. But Callisto is Judea, who, visited by God, conceives in the Virgin Mary and has the possibility of baptism even if she refuses it; Myrrha is also, as I have said, a figure of the Virgin; and Actaeon implies the incarnation because, like God hidden "in the form of a servant" ("sous forme de serf"), he too was hidden from sight, "transformed into a stag" ("muez en cerf," *OM*, III, 629–30). As with the pun on *nestre/*

n'estre, the play on *serf/cerf* offers the chance of radical transformation. Redemption is potentially universal provided all embrace the coming community:

God created the souls of Jews or pagans as much as of Christians in order that they should live and reside in heaven in his heavenly glory.

> L'ame au Juif, l'ame au paien,
> ausi com l'ame au crestien
> cria Dieux por vivre et por estre
> aus cieulz en sa gloire celestre. (*OM*, XV, 2925–28)

The argument of this section has been complex, but its conclusions can be easily summarized. I am proposing that the metamorphosis which characters undergo in Ovid's text often only makes them more the same; read anamorphically by the Christian poet, it confirms their inherent fault and their fallen nature; it discloses their sinful form, which is what we can expect to find recorded in a pagan text. But a further shift of perspective in the moralist's reading also imagines that these errant beings might be transformed, by redemption, into something completely other than they have been, and be enabled thereby to participate in community with God. This second anamorphosis relies not on a preexisting common ground but rather on the capacity for every individual to "take place" otherwise. The mobile landscapes of the *Ovide moralisé* enable the form of each individual to take his or her place in this coming community, and this is the idea I shall develop in the next section.

Displacements of Eden

Right from the beginning of the poem we are told that the proper place for human form to inhabit is the place from which it has been banished, Eden (*OM*, I, 451–53). This lost landscape is what the allegoresis of the *Ovide moralisé* looks awry at the *Metamorphoses* to discover. This, I believe, is why the French poet echoes and reaffirms Ovid's predilection for rural or garden settings—a preference palpable in the *Ovide moralisé*'s descriptions of the Age of Gold, of Thessaly, Arcadia, and Parnassus, and which extends to cases where the historical subject matter (such as the stories of Thebes and Troy) seems rather to lend itself to urban ones.[47]

Even here natural settings predominate, thanks to the long voyages of
Aeneas and Ulysses and the stories (Pomona, Ceyx and Alcyone, Circe,
Glaucus, Picus, Polyphemus) intercalated in them. Ovidian protagonists
can always be found to occupy a place to the side of Eden, a displaced
place that points to an Other place where we may have been but are not
yet.[48]

In the biblical Eden invoked by the moralist in Book I of the *Ovide
moralisé*, God's creation methodically unfolds an orderly progression from
one category of being to the next. Ovid's landscapes, by contrast, result
from the constant confusion of evolved creatures with lower ones as his
tales reiterate the violent transmutation of gods or men into earlier forms
of creation. The Ovidian landscape, as a result, is never what it seems.
There is no feature of it that might not be the metamorphosis of some
previous inhabitant, with his or her own tale of horror. If you encounter
a domestic animal, a heifer, mare, or bull, it is all too likely the changed
aspect of some hapless girl, or else a cover for some wily seducer. All forms
of wildlife—from snakes and weasels to stags and bears—may, in some
former existence, have been humans, nymphs, or gods. Birds too—the
nightingale, swallow, and halcyon—were formerly creatures with human
forms. A tree might formerly have been Daphne or Myrrha, a flower Narcissus or Jacinthus. Even rivers and springs, rocks and stones, and the stars
above were once sentient, rational beings.

As we know from the start of Book I, place provides the material that
creation needs in order to embody divinely conceived form. In moralizing
the *Metamorphoses*, the French poet is faced with this heaving, inconstant
landscape, which he sets out to recuperate to a single place. Ovid's eroti-
cized landscapes enable the moralist to see place itself as involved in the
fall from the divine Idea, but also as potentially contributing to the resto-
ration of paradisal conformity. Indeed, as the commentary on Pythagoras
in Book XV has shown, the interrelation between the elements that make
up our landscape is the key to understanding man's potential for spiritual
renewal. By reading Ovid's pagan landscapes anamorphically, the moralist
can find, virtually traced within them, the outlines of Eden.

This capacity of Ovidian scenarios to echo and anticipate Eden is represented pictorially in group *y* of the *Ovide moralisé* manuscripts, which
open with a picture of God creating Eden. Bizarre as this choice of image
may seem at first sight, it shows an understanding that the whole text
needs to be situated in a virtual landscape, one that is both lost and yet
to come. Its presence in BNF fr. 872 is particularly emphatic, since this

manuscript contains only one picture (Figure 5); God's creation of place (in the upper curve of the *S*) and its inhabitants, most conspicuously Eve (in the lower curve), has been chosen to preface the entire work, placing the pagan text within the theological frame of the fall and its ensuing redemption. The full-page opening illustration of another member of this group, BNF fr. 871, with its division into four scenes, reflects this more elaborately. The two upper images depict on the left Ovid's pagan account of the separation of chaos into landscape and, on the right, the creation of everything except man as recounted in Genesis. In the lower register, the landscape has been refined into a garden, with the pagan scene, again on the left, depicting Prometheus, while on the right God creates Eve. The

Figure 5. The creation of place and the creation of Eve, from the opening of the *Ovide moralisé*, BNF fr. 872, fol. 1. Reproduced by permission.

moralist's program of glimpsing the eternal Christian truths of fall and redemption in the upheavals of a pagan landscape is successfully captured in this complex and beautiful picture. (In this same manuscript, the Orpheus story in Book X inspires an image in which landscape becomes community; see Figure 6, discussed below). A third manuscript of this group, Rouen, Bibliothèque Municipale, o.11 bis, also begins with a picture of the Creation. Depictions of Eden are found here and there in the Arsenal manuscript (Ars. 5069), while Rouen MS o.4 contains numerous typological pictures juxtaposing scenes from Ovid with scenes from the Bible.[49] The "whatever" singular that undergoes metamorphosis is seen anamorphically, in the juxtaposed perspectives of these pictures, as part of the "coming community" necessitated and enabled by the fall.

Orpheus and Landscape

The links between landscape and community, metamorphosis and anamorphosis, are well exemplified by the Orpheus narrative in Book X of the *Ovide moralisé*. In the *Metamorphoses*, Orpheus, who can summon the landscape with his song and so bring it to life, is a deliberate reflection of Ovid's own metamorphosing powers.[50] The Old French poet seems to have appreciated this. He exploits the plasticity of landscape in the Orpheus story, adding further readings of his own that transform it into (and thus reconceive it as) a Christian community grounded in the incarnation.

Book X briefly narrates Eurydice's death as a preface to Orpheus's infernal journey. A moralizing passage identifies the hell into which she has fallen as the hell we discover within ourselves when the "the soul's sensuality" ("la sensualité de l'ame," *OM*, X, 223) treads on the serpent of "mortal vice" lurking under the surface of the grassy landscape of worldly pleasures:

Then the soul falls dolorously into the gloomy darkness of deep misery. This hell is within it, for an evil heart is an abyss full of torment and full of affliction that torments and afflicts the sinner.

> Lors chiet l'ame dolentement
> en la tenebreuse obscurté
> de parfonde maleürté.
> Cil enfers est en lui meïsmes,
> quar mauves cuers est uns abismes

plains de tormens et plains de paine,
qui pecheor torment et paine. (*OM*, X, 247–53)

Orpheus is glossed as "reasonable understanding" (*regnable entendement*, *OM*, X, 221) calling the heart back from vice with the aid of divine inspiration (*OM*, X, 407). His marriage to Eurydice bears other interpretations: the union of the body with the soul and of man with woman, but also, and above all, of divinity with humanity. The story of the fall from Eden resonates in the retelling of Eurydice succumbing to the serpent. Like her, men died (*morurent*) from the serpent's bite (*mors*, *OM*, X, 490). But Orpheus/Christ descended into the pit of hell "in order to draw human nature away from its infernal prison" (*OM*, X, 483–84). When Eurydice/humanity is called, many turn back and are damned without remission. Orpheus's subsequent homosexuality, while literally a sin, is metaphorically justified since his rejection of women confirms God's hatred of the "feminine nature" of worldly pleasures (*OM*, X, 558).

The translator returns at this point to the *Metamorphoses* description of Orpheus with his harp bringing the forest to life. The retentive reader will not need reminding that some of the trees mentioned here (such as the laurel and the peach tree) were once characters in earlier books. For the less observant, explicit reference is made to the transformations that resulted in the pine tree and, in a longer narrative, the cypress. More metamorphoses into plants follow as the book unfolds: Hyacinth, Myrrha, Adonis. These tales are interwoven with those of Pygmalion and Atalanta, which also involve metamorphoses (the statue becoming a woman, Atalanta and her lover lions). All these metamorphoses are, as it were, put into reverse when Orpheus reendows plants and animals with human attributes.

From line 2494 the poet returns to his moralizations. Harking back to his earlier gloss on events following the death of Eurydice, he repeats his condemnation of Orpheus's homosexuality (*OM*, X, 2519–31). Now it is implied that such men are "wild" in the same way as the landscape Orpheus brings to life: his harp summons "a great company of trees, birds, and wild animals" ("une grant compaigne / d'arbres, d'oisiaux, de sauvecine," *OM*, X, 2507–8), while the "fools" who participate in homosexual activities "had harsher natures than trees or wild animals" ("furent de dure orine / plus que arbre ne sauvecine," *OM*, X, 2538–39). However, the commentary continues, Orpheus's summoning of this landscape can also be interpreted allegorically to refer to how Christ peopled the Church with his saints. After the harrowing of hell, God returned "onto the high plain, full of eternal greenery" ("en la haute plaine / de verdour pardurable plaine," *OM*, X, 2552–53), and entrusted his harp to the Church. The "trees, birds, and wild animals" (*OM*, X, 2572) that the Church then summons to this plain by means of the harp are an exact verbal echo of those condemned for "vice" only a few lines earlier.

At that time there were not a lot of people on the plain of the Church, which soon after was filled with trees, birds, and wild animals on account of the sweetness of its teaching.

> Adont n'avoit pas grant planté
> de gent en l'eclesial plaine,
> qui puis en brief terme fu plaine
> d'arbres, d'oisiaux, de sauvecine
> pour la douçour le lor doctrine. (*OM*, X, 2569–73)

In a further echo, the creatures of this wilderness are instructed to ascend "onto the high plain, full of eternal greenery" (*OM*, X, 2576–77, cf. 2552–53).

The subsequent lengthy allegoresis of the harp and its strings multiplies the complexities of this landscape. Orpheus with his harp could reanimate all the animals and birds, and make the trees gather round. Similarly, the preaching of Holy Church, says the poet, can people a landscape with figures of saintliness. The line "trees, birds, and wild animals" occurs again (*OM*, X, 2944) to designate the diverse origins of the saints. The wild animals are holy hermits who embrace the wilderness in order to serve God unencumbered by worldly ties. Birds are those who devote their intellects to understanding God. And trees represent the laity who bear fruit for God in various ways (*OM*, X, 2964–66). However, now the Church is so corrupt that those who "harp" in it orchestrate the same landscape in quite a different guise. The clergy include wild animals that are full of cruelty; other Church leaders are as gluttonous as birds; a wide variety of different kinds of moral character are represented as the trees (*OM*, X, 3031–46). A protracted *exposicion* (beginning *OM*, X, 3047) reviews many species of trees. Among them are many familiar ones resulting from metamorphosis: pine, cypress, laurel, myrrh. The individuals who were transformed in the past into landscape, and were reanimated by sympathy with Orpheus, are now interpreted into a different and contemporary humanity by the moralist.

sympathetic author
pacing

This sequence powerfully illustrates the French poet's anamorphic treatment of Ovid's text. First we see Orpheus in the landscape where Ovid presented him. Looked at from one angle, this landscape is composed of characters from earlier books; from another, it reveals the saints of the early Church summoned into existence by Orpheus/Christ with his harp of doctrine; from yet another, its lineaments are transformed to betray the corruption that nowadays dogs its institutions. And as the commentary goes on, further transformations show how, among the creatures in this landscape, many offer further perspectives on Christ's incarnation. The story of Cyparisus can be viewed in such a way as to discover in his beloved stag that was killed the sacrifice of the incarnate Savior and in Cyparisus himself the sinner saved by penitence. Ganymede borne aloft by the eagle can be seen as "true man and true god at the same time" (*OM*, X, 3421). Hyacinth is an anamorphosis of the saints and martyrs who shed their blood; their bodies died on earth, but their souls flowered in paradise. The nakedness of Pygmalion's statue shows forth Adam and Eve. Myrrha, as well as being read as the Virgin, signifies the sinful soul and its capacity for repentance. Adonis is the sweetness of good works that come from the reformed sinner, Atalanta is the Church, and Persephone's transforming women into mint reveals the good odor attaching to the saints and to good works. The work of salvation from the fall to redemption flickers through every feature of the landscape. Divine form and the material cause of place combine to unite all its inhabitants in potential community with Christ, a community confirmed by the illumination in BNF fr. 871 (fol. 196v) where Orpheus and his listeners are clearly encircled in one place (Figure 6).

Monologism and Community

The harp with which Orpheus/Christ calls people to him is an image of monologism born of a community that is as yet unrealized. The harp can produce harmony even from dissonance, much as the poet of the *Ovide moralisé* reconciles un-Christian materials with Christianity:

For even if the sound is dissimilar, yet it can be harmonized together without discord in it.

> Quar tous soit li sons dessamblables
> doit il estre ensamble acordables
> sans avoir discordance en soi. (*OM*, X, 2584–86)

Figure 6. Orpheus in a monologic circle, surrounded by beasts and birds and trees, in the *Ovide moralisé,* BNF fr. 871, fol. 196v. Reproduced by permission.

Its uniting principle is faith, which has the anamorphic function of turning landscape into community:

His harp is the shared faith that Christians and all those who wish to come into the fullness of the Church, which then was empty, should have: now it is occupied by trees of various natures.

> Sa harpe est la comune foi
> que crestien doivent tenir
> et tuit cil qu vuelent venir
> a la planecse de l'iglise
> qui ja fu wide: hore est porprise
> d'arbres de diverses natures. (*OM*, X, 2587–92)

I do not claim that this community is the same as Agamben's. For Agamben the belonging that will mark the coming community is not a belonging-to but a belonging-as-such that does not depend on shared content but, indeed, excludes it, since the singular beings whose potentiality it is lack all properties, all identity. Thus Agamben insists that " *Whatever* is a resemblance without archetype—in other words, [without] an Idea."[51] In the *Ovide moralisé,* by contrast, there is most certainly an archetype, an Idea that exists in God's mind, in his *sapience devine,* and that is imprinted on mankind before the fall. But this archetype is inaccessible, given that it is lost to us in our present state and can be regained only through redemption. In the *Ovide moralisé* monologism is a striving after this unique form, which is at the same time the promise of community.

The effect of anamorphosis, then, is to enable us to glimpse this invisible form that God originally intended us to have. Although only one form is sought, seeing it depends upon antitheses of perspective. Eternal form is legible in dissolving bodily shapes; the form of God is made visible through his adoption of a series of mortal bodies; the truth of Christianity emerges as an epic from the margins of the pagan text. By looking awry the French poet discerns both the uniqueness of beings and their potential for community with the divine, a community mediated by the inevitable dependence of being on place and hence, in the *Ovide moralisé*, on landscape.

3

The Divided Path in Guillaume de Deguileville's *Pèlerinage de Vie Humaine* Separation and Identity

GUILLAUME DE DEGUILEVILLE'S *Pèlerinage de vie humaine* is a dream-vision poem that was first composed in 1330–1331 but later revised and supplemented by two further poems, the *Pèlerinage de l'âme* and the *Pèlerinage de Jésus Christ*. The second redaction of the *Vie humaine* was the one adapted into English by Lydgate, and thus ultimately the source of John Bunyan's *Pilgrim's Progress*, but it has not been edited and can be read only in manuscript. Among French readers, however, the original *Vie humaine* seems to have been much the more popular, since it survives in fifty-three copies as compared to only nine; it is even found grouped with the *Pèlerinage de l'âme* and the *Pèlerinage de Jésus Christ*, works that were conceived as sequels to the revised text.[1] This chapter is based on this more successful first version, but I indicate how some of its themes were recast in the expanded cycle, citing the second recension of the *Vie humaine* from BNF fr. 829.[2]

Explicitly reworking the narrative of the *Romance of the Rose*, the *Pèlerinage de vie humaine* is premised on the idea that life is a journey the purpose of which is to prepare oneself for death and the afterlife; it thus expands into a long vernacular poem the Latin cliché that, so long as he is in this world, man is but a traveler (*homo viator*).[3] The pilgrim, protagonist of the dream, must learn to turn aside from what is mortal and corporeal, and direct himself toward God and his immortal soul. Grace Dieu figures centrally among the personifications whom Guillaume introduces to accompany the pilgrim along his way, in order to stress that this journey cannot be brought to a successful conclusion without God's grace. The dream begins with the pilgrim's birth and ends with his being on the point of death. In between, he pursues life's journey, in the course of which,

despite the admonishments of Grace Dieu and Raison (Reason), the benefits of the sacraments, the tenets of the creed, and the armor of the cardinal
virtues, he is overwhelmed by the seven deadly sins. Having thus conspicuously failed as an armed pilgrim or crusader-knight, the pilgrim finds salvation from the effects of sin only by appealing to the Virgin and,
subsequently, by finding refuge on the Ship of Religion, where he is received into the order of Cîteau; the life of a contemplative is the one best
suited to the pilgrim's needs.[4] This choice by the pilgrim of the cloistered
over the secular life reflects the fact that Guillaume de Deguileville was, in
reality, a Cistercian monk.[5] The Ship of Religion is one of the best-defined
loci in the poem, both textually and pictorially.[6] With its cast of personifications representing the discipline of the monastic rule, the Ship transports
him across the Sea of the World and prepares him for the final encounter
with his Death.[7]

Although ostensibly the narrative of a journey, this poem does not
have a dynamic relationship to space. Experience may be conveyed as turmoil, frequently violent, but it is not really conceived as movement, and
such progression as it contains is expressed statically through a series of
stations, not dynamically as a constantly unfolding track. Only at one
point, when the pilgrim reaches the Haie de Penitence (Hedge of Penitence), does a choice between alternative routes feature as a way of representing a moral dilemma (*PVH*, 6505ff.). This is another *locus* that inspires
some fine illuminations like the one in Figure 7 (from BNF fr. 12465, fol.
41). Inevitably the pilgrim makes the wrong choice, taking what seems the
easier but is in fact the more perilous path. Separated by the Hedge from
the personifications Raison and Grace Dieu, the pilgrim finds himself de-
fenseless against the onslaught of the sins and is repeatedly floored by
them. The division, whereby most of "him" is on one side of the Hedge
but some of what is arguably "him" is on the other, offers a spatial framework in which Deguileville can explore his principal theme: the imperative
that one should know oneself.

This imperative is spelled out in a dialogue between the pilgrim and
Raison:[8]

It is better to know yourself than to be an emperor, a count or a king, or to know
all there is to be known and possess all the wealth in the world.

> Miex vaut assez connoistre soy
> qu'estre empereur, conte ne roy,
> que toutes sciences savoir,
> et tout l'avoir du monde avoir. (*PVH*, 5937–40)

Figure 7. The pilgrim at the separation of the paths in the *Pèlerinage de vie humaine*, BNF fr. 12465, fol. 41. Reproduced by permission.

What is man's nature? Is it single or double, *seul* or *doubles* (*PVH*, 5733–34)? The core of the problem, it emerges, is the complex relation between body and soul. The pilgrim appeals to Raison:

Lady, I said to her, now I beg you to tell me, who am I? Given that I am not my body, tell me who I am!

> Dame, dis jë, or vous pri je
> que vous me dites, qui sui je?
> Puis que mon cors pas je ne suy
> si me dites donc qui je suy! (*PVH*, 5929–32)

The divided path, with the Hedge of Penitence down the middle, is a "place of thought" in which this problem is explored. I shall contend that it represents the pilgrim's nature as both single and double, since the role of the Hedge is both to separate and connect what lies on either side of it. The illuminations make this point in visual terms, since they depict the pilgrim as almost but not yet actually on the divided path. Figure 7, for example, presents the mat mender (*natier*) with his life of toil on one side of the path and the beautiful figure of Huiseuse (Leisure) on the other. Thus far the pilgrim has not made the "wrong" choice, as he is depicted talking to the *natier*.[9]

This chapter concentrates on the sequence of the Hedge in order to argue that, in its complex reflection on singularity and duality, the *Pèlerinage de vie humaine* forms a part of the Western history of the *cogito*, the inquiry into the relationship between thought and existence most famously epitomized in Descartes' "I think, therefore I am." Foucault sees the problems raised by the *cogito* as diagnostic of the modern subject: "What must I be, I who think and who am my thought, in order to be what I do not think, in order for my thought to be what I am not?"[10] It is well known, however, that much of Descartes' argument is already articulated by Augustine—a fact that Descartes' own contemporaries were not slow to point out.[11] In examining the divided unity of the self in the *Vie humaine* within the broader frame of the Western *cogito* it is therefore first to Augustine that I shall look.[12] Like Augustine before him, and Descartes and others after him, Deguileville's dreamer seeks to know himself as an agency through his inner division and the potential that it creates for self-deception.

Augustine's influence is acknowledged at the very beginning of the *Pèlerinage de vie humaine*, since Augustine is accorded pride of place among those who help souls enter the heavenly Jerusalem (*PVH*, 99–102). Not only is the poem's central image of the "pilgrim soul" Augustinian, its narrative of life's pilgrimage closely recalls *On Christian Teaching*, I, especially §§8, 21–22, and 34, where Augustine compares the soul with a traveler who is exiled from his homeland to which he longs to return, but who is instead constantly ensnared by thorny hedgerows.[13] Deguileville's pilgrim, when he strays from the right path and gets bound hand and foot by various sins, graphically realizes these words from Augustine's *On the Trinity*: "And, therefore, the series of good wills that are joined together is a sort of road on which there are, as it were, certain steps for those ascending to happiness; but the entanglement of the bad and perverse wills is a chain by which he will be bound, who thus acts, in order that he may be cast into the exterior darkness" (XI, vi, §10).[14] Augustine's treatment of the Platonic command "Know yourself" in *On the Trinity* also shapes

Deguileville's didactic purpose. In his prologue the French poet exhorts
everyone to learn from the protagonist's experience:

Now let everyone come close and join in and listen carefully . . . this vision is
relevant to humble and mighty alike, without exception.

> Or (i) viengnent pres et se arroutent
> toute gent et bien escoutent . . .
> grans et petis la vision
> touche sans point de excepcion. (*PVH*, 15–16, 21–22)[15]

I think that self-discovery is the more valued by Deguilevile because of
Augustine's teaching that one's self is a starting point, however inadequate, from which to know God, in whose image one was made. As well
as being exemplary in itself, the pilgrim's pathway also offers a route by
which all his readers can better know God.[16]

The centrality of self-knowledge in the *Pèlerinage* accords with the
consistently human dimension of space in this poem. The places it offers—
house, path, hedge, coastline, ship—are all identified with human habitation or use. Place in this poem, that is, is conceived (as I said in my
Introduction) as what circumscribes body and as a model for thinking
about its true nature. For Deguileville, this means thinking about the difficulty, for the soul, of being embodied, in a body that is then situated
among the temptations of the earth. Despite the poem's human scale,
however, and despite the abundant illustrations in many of its manuscripts,
the places in which the pilgrim finds himself are often more *unheimlich*
than homely, and more a challenge to the visual than a manifestation of
it. Indeed, he is warned that his eyes are less to be trusted than his ears:

You must rely on your hearing, believe in it implicitly and trust it, through it you
will know the truth and be instructed.

> A l'ouir te faut apuier,
> croire du tout et toi fier,
> par li la verité[17] saras
> et par li t'en enfourmeras. (*PVH*, 2783–86)

In the revised version of the *Pèlerinage*, this warning is surreally amplified
when the pilgrim is persuaded to have his eyes transplanted into his ears
so as to be able to appreciate the teaching inscribed on his staff and stole.[18]
The notion of place that develops in the *Vie humaine* is thus intellectual

rather than physical. It is molded by the sheer difficulty of understanding what kind of "one" a man is and how it relates to the oneness of God.

In the next section I shall consider how the spatial paradoxes early in the poem make place at once visible and unimaginable, whole and divided; this in turn illumines the places associated with Penitence, patron of the Hedge. The motif of the divided path can then be seen as developing these paradoxes in order to analyze how the self is constituted. A concluding section will return to the wider history of the *cogito* as the context of Deguileville's allegory.

Paradoxes of Place

In Book 1 of both versions of the *Vie humaine* is a sequence of three discussions that suggest the complex character of certain places and of the boundaries that define them. The paradoxical places concerned are the tonsure/cloister, the relative domains of Nature and Grace, and those of human understanding (Science) and divine wisdom (Sapience). The last two are explored in response to the spatial enigma of the Eucharist, and so all of these places have in common the opening of the human onto the divine that is effected by the sacraments. This makes them apt precursors to the questions posed by the divided path of Penitence, itself related to the sacrament of confession, about how, in the human individual, an immortal spirit can somehow be located in a mortal body. This paradoxical presentation of place throughout the poem coincides with my observation, in the Introduction, that while place is an apt way of circumscribing thought, thought nevertheless does not belong in place and strains our attempts to imagine the *loci* in which it is placed.

The passage about the tonsure comes in an address by Raison to a crowd seeking holy orders. She tells them (*PVH*, 84off.) that the tonsure, the shaven head associated with fools, will be for them a sign of wisdom. With a rhyme that puns on (*de*)*partir* (depart/share in), she brings out the tonsure's double and contradictory function of both closing off (from the world) those who wear it and opening them up (to God):

Its round circle marks enclosure so that you have no care for the world, for you must cut yourself off from it if you wish to share in your God.

> Le cercle ront fait (la) closture
> que *du* monde n'aiez cure,

> quar de li vous faut departir
> s'a vostre Dieu voulez partir. (*PVH*, 899–902)

The key term here, *closture* (*PVH*, 899), brings out the symbolic parallel between the body and the place it inhabits by underlining that the tonsure is an enclosure which echoes, or replicates, the cloister. Its round shape recalls a defensive structure, such as a castle or tower. Thus at the same time as the ordained wear the *closture* on their bodies, they are also placed securely inside it:

Welcome this enclosure that encloses and immures you, severing you from the world.

> Biau vous soit donc (de) la closture
> qui vous enclot et (vous) enmure
> en vous du monde dessevrant. (*PVH*, 917–19)

While the pursuit of Raison is what cuts off the ordained from the beasts (*PVH*, 855–56), by means of the tonsure they are sheared for Christ as the beasts of his flock (*PVH*, 924–26). The line of the tonsure is thus multiply paradoxical. It designates both wisdom and folly, it both closes and opens, it is larger and smaller than the man who wears it, and it demarcates him from animals while marking him out as one.

A keen sense of paradox also comes through in the altercation between Nature and Grace Dieu that follows the transformation of bread and wine into body and blood in the Eucharist. Raison confesses that she cannot understand how this transformation has been effected, and Nature is indignant that her laws have been flouted. In Nature's view, she and Grace Dieu divide the cosmos between them. The sublunar world is hers; above the orbit of the moon, Grace rules. Bad-temperedly Nature complains at Grace's repeated interference in her domain. Grace's riposte is that Nature has misunderstood the nature of the boundary that separates them:

And for this reason if you were wise you would not speak of the limit that is placed between yourself and me, for it limits you, but not me; it prohibits you from passing beyond it because that it how I wish to draw the limit, but do not imagine that I am limited from entering there!

> (Et) pour ce, se fussiez bien saige,
> ne parlissiez (pas) du bonnage

qui est mis entre vous et moy,
quar il vous bonne, non pas moy;
il vous forsclot d'outre passer
pour ce qu'ainsi le vuel bonner;
mes a fin que n'i entrasse,
ne cuidiez (pas) que je bonnasse! (*PVH*, 1719–26)

The limit in question is surreptitiously affirmed as right by the homonymy between *bonne* "boundary" and *bonne* "good." Although it delimits the activities of Nature, it does not confine those of Grace. One way Grace illustrates the difference is by saying that Nature occupies the role of servant and Grace that of mistress. If Grace did not provide the world in which Nature operates, Nature would have nothing. Another explanation offered by Grace, implying a rather different relationship between them, is that Nature is merely a tool in her hand. Like the case of the tonsure, this example shows how the notion of place is bound up with that of hierarchy. Place, that is, is construed relative to value; it closes or opens, contracts or expands, depending on whether one takes the position of the lower or the higher term.[19]

In this argument, Grace cites Aristotle as an authority on place. But shortly after this, when the Eucharist is distributed to the faithful, Aristotelian physics too is shown to have its limits.[20] The seed of Christ's body, says Grace, has been baked by divine wisdom (Sapience) into a bread; for wisdom is capable of containing the whole world in a tiny box, or an ox in an eggshell (*PVH*, 2865–68). Charity required the bread to look small but yet be capable of satisfying everyone. In order for the bread to do so, even when it is shared out each part of it remains as big as the original whole:

For she made every part, however big or small, that was broken from the bread as large as the whole.

Quar de chascune partie
qui du pain estoit brisïe,
combien que fust petite ou grant,
fist elle chascune aussi grant
comme ensemble trestoute[21] estoit. (*PVH*, 2903–7)

Nature takes this as a further onslaught on her laws, and she summons Aristotle to argue with Sapience over it. The first part of the ensuing debate recapitulates the structure of that between Nature and Grace, in that

Aristotle is conceded to have some of the knowledge that pertains to Sapience but is nevertheless greatly her inferior, confined by inherent limitations that have no effect on Sapience. Their relationship is explained as being like that between a master champion (Sapience) and his ignorant apprentice, a remarkable image to which I shall return.

The argument then goes on to Aristotle's objection that the container cannot be bigger than that which it contains:

You know very well it's not reasonable for the vessel or house to be smaller than what is inside it.

> Bien savez que n'est pas raison
> que le vaissel ou la maison
> mendre soit de ce qui est ens. (*PVH*, 2933–35)

Sapience counters this assertion with the example of the heart. How big is a human heart? Aristotle has to admit that it could satisfy a bird's appetite but cannot itself be satisfied even by the whole world. Sapience then asks him to confirm that the heart must be capable of being full, since nature abhors a vacuum. Aristotle's answer, switching from the *Physics* to the *Ethics*, is that the heart may be filled by the sovereign good. Then, says Sapience, this good must be bigger than the whole world. Aristotle cannot contradict her (*PVH*, 3166). Sapience concludes: thus the heart, which is so small, can contain such a huge thing. Likewise a single person's memory can retain the population of two cities. Or again: a reflection of the whole face can be seen in the pupil of the eye; and a mirror, when broken into shards, reproduces many times over the same reflection it formerly presented in single form when it was whole.

The shift in reference in this passage from physics to ethics confirms that the concept of place is now topological and moral, rather than plotted with reference to physical location. And this is made explicit in what follows. Aristotle asks if these things are contained locally (*locaument*), virtually (*vertuaument*), or in some other way (*autrement, PVH*, 3221–22). Grace replies that they are not contained *locaument* but *autrement*. Some say the containment operates through imagination (*imaginaument*) and others that it depends on representation (*representativement, PVH*, 3228–31), but this is not adequate. What is essential, Grace insists, is to recognize that great *pasture* (nourishment) can be really contained within a small *figure*. That is, the sovereign good is *really* to be found inside the bread:

In exactly the same way the sovereign good is to be found within this bread, not imaginatively, nor representatively, nor moreover virtually, but placed and contained there bodily and really, presently and truly, without any pretense or deception.

> tout aussi dedens ce pain
> est vraiement (mis) le bien souvrain,
> non pas voir imaginaument,
> non representativement,
> non vertuablement sans plus,
> ains y est mis et contenus
> corporelment et reaument,
> presentement et vraiement,
> sans nule simulation
> et sans autre deception. (*PVH*, 3243–52)

Christ's body is contained in the Eucharist in a way that is paradoxical, ethical, and above all real.

These analyses of the place of tonsure/enclosure, Nature/Grace, and Aristotle/Sapience all rely on the notion of an inherent limit. Within the infinite space of openness to God there is an inherent limit, that of human enclosure and bodily restriction. Within the unlimited reach of God's Grace there is likewise an inherent limit defined by the limitations of the created world. And within the immeasurable profundity of divine wisdom the domain of strictly philosophical understanding is demarcated. This internal boundary is a source of paradox because its reality is ethical rather than geographical. Its shifting and troublesome character is conveyed through the images used to represent it.

As we have seen, Grace depicts Nature both as a subordinate, her handmaiden to whom she delegates tasks, and as a mere tool with which she presumably performs tasks herself. The image used to portray the relationship between Aristotle's science and God's sapience is more disturbing. Human science, says Sapience, is like a poor ignorant young man apprenticed to a master swordsman who generously instructs him and takes nothing from him. The two of them are then engaged as champions by two warring dukes. The master champion calls out to his student to ask why it is that two people have come to oppose him. The apprentice foolishly looks round to see who is being referred to, and as soon as his back is turned the master kills him. The combat has ended before it has even begun. This image, disturbing in its attribution to Sapience of such low cunning,[22] represents the hierarchical relationship between herself and human wisdom in terms of violent antagonism quite unlike the passive relation of tool to craftsman, or the domestic subordination of maidservant to mistress, evoked to explain the relationship of Nature to Grace. The reference to warfare links forward to scenes where the pilgrim receives a suit of armor to defend against his inner impulses, and where he is told by Raison that his spirit and his body are hostile forces. And the reference to Sapience facing two antagonists, although it is not spelled out in the poem, may suggest that the reason why human Science is disabled and instantly defeated is that it *may* indeed have two parties for whom to fight: the spirit and the body.

These images, then, show how defining a place of containment as a site of real hierarchy produces paradoxical results. The boundary between container and contained varies between being neutral, passive, or benign and being conflictual or even positively aggressive. We shall find this hesitation again when we come to examine the representation between body and spirit. Is the spirit contained within the body as if in a passive shell, or are they two active forces that are pitted against each other? The spatial paradoxes created by the notion of an internal limit also have implications for the relation between body and spirit. For while the body may be the place into which the spirit has been stuffed—as the pilgrim puts it— perhaps at the same time the spirit is greater than the body, encompassing it at the same time as it is enclosed within it? Or to state it another way, by analogy with these other examples of spatial paradox, perhaps the body should be seen as the "internal limit" of the spirit: not its diametrical opposite but a zone within the spirit in which the spirit's lucid rule is at best imperfectly acknowledged?

In *On the Trinity* Augustine invites his readers to reflect on the problematic character of the boundary between what he terms the "inner" and the "outer" man: "Well now! Let us see where the boundary line, as it were, between the outer and inner man is to be placed. . . . Since by the outer man we mean not the body only, but also its own peculiar kind of life, whence the structure of the body and all the senses derive their vigor, and by which he is equipped to perceive external things" (XII, i, §1).[23] Books X–XIV of his treatise are devoted to trying to work out the nature of this boundary, given that, as it were, something of the "soul" inheres in the body (as its "peculiar kind of life") and, conversely, that the body overshadows so many of the movements of the soul. Deguileville's approach to this question is first broached through the figure of Penitence, who occupies a liminal role somewhere between the inner and the outer man. The places with which she is associated reflect the complex nature of this division.

The Places of Penitence

Although not explicitly linked to the series of paradoxes I have just examined, the spatial representation of Penitence in the *Vie humaine* exhibits the same contradictions. Penitence is first introduced together with Charité at the point in the Eucharist where the bread is about to be distributed to the people (that is, repentance and charity are prerequisites for receiving the sacrament). She describes herself as a cleaning lady supremo, "guardian of the hidden island. I get rid of all the dirt before anyone comes in" ("gardienne (de) l'ille celee. / Toute ordure fai metre jus, / avant que dedans entre nus," *PVH*, 2050–52). She hammers, beats, and sweeps the human heart in order to induce in it true contrition, confront it with every single particle of wrongdoing, and cleanse it of its accumulated filth. The heart, as well as being an island, is a house with six doorways. Through five of them (the senses) enters dirt that then has to be swept out through the sixth (the mouth) by means of confession:

For so long as I am my mistress Grace Dieu's maid I mean to keep her house clean and not let any of the dirt remain.

> Quar tant com soie baiesse
> a Grace Dieu, ma mestresse,
> sa maison veul nete tenir
> sans nulle ordure retenir. (*PVH*, 2251–54)

Here, then, Penitence is seen as actively protecting an inner space for Grace against the polluting effects of the senses.

Subsequently, however, Penitence's spatial configuration is transformed. From actively policing the hygiene of an enclosed space, Penitence becomes an inert dividing line, identified with the Hedge that splits the path of life down the middle. On one side is the way of Occupation (Labor), represented by a man repairing old matting. But on the other side, Huiseuse (Leisure) is so much more alluring that the pilgrim chooses that path instead. Now separated from him by the Hedge, Grace Dieu calls out reproachfully. The Hedge, she warns, gets thicker as the path goes on. It belongs to Penitence, who culls her switches from its wood

(*PVH*, 6970–86). Raison's head pops up, likewise on the far side of the Hedge, to reiterate Grace Dieu's advice: the pilgrim had better come back through as quickly as he can. But in fact the pilgrim never manages to do so. The solution to this impasse comes only with the different place assigned to Penitence later on.

As with other paradoxical places, Penitence shifts in these two scenes from something contained to something containing, as the *locus* she is associated with mutates from an internal space to an external barrier. In the process she ceases to be an agent of reform and becomes an inert obstacle that the pilgrim himself must find a way through, and this too recalls the equivocations we encountered earlier between agency and passivity: for example, between whether Nature was Grace's tool or her maid. Whereas Penitence was earlier represented as enforcing a *cordon sanitaire* around a space for Grace Dieu to occupy, now she divides the pilgrim from Grace Dieu and Raison. By choosing the wrong path, the pilgrim has cut himself off from these figures, yet they continue to address his needs. As with the other paradoxical places, therefore, Penitence defines a hierarchy whose terms are differently situated. The Hedge divides the pilgrim from higher authorities, but not vice versa. The pilgrim is wrong to see the Hedge as permeable, given that he can't get through it himself; however, it *is* permeable in the sense that it can't prevent Raison and Grace Dieu from assisting *him*. In humorous confirmation of this, manuscript illuminations depict the heads of Grace Dieu and Raison bobbing up from time to time on the farther side of the thorn bushes.

The paradoxical topology of Penitence echoes, therefore, the poem's explicit spatial paradoxes, which is not surprising given that it, too, is a sacrament. There is one respect, however, in which Penitence differs from the others, namely, its reflexivity: the fact that it not only demarcates different domains but also mediates between them. While it condemns the pollution of the sensual body it also makes it clean for Grace Dieu; while it cuts the pilgrim off from Grace Dieu and Raison it also maintains communication between them. Reflexivity is central to the representation of Penitence in the last scene in which she figures. After meeting with all of the sins, the pilgrim recognizes his inability to get back through the Hedge and calls out to her (*PVH*, 10715ff.). Grace Dieu volunteers to lead him to Penitence provided he prays to the Virgin, whose intercession alone can enable him to regain God's favor (*PVH*, 10834ff.). When he complies and prays the famous ABC prayer, imitated by Chaucer, the result is a startling change of scene. The Hedge vanishes, and Penitence assumes a

humor

completely different guise—one worthy of a surrealist painting. Now she is a Fountain of tears issuing from a single eye in a heart formerly hardened into stone by wrongdoing, but softened sufficiently by Grace so as to see the state it has fallen into, and to weep with remorse (*PVH*, 11240ff). This mind's eye turned inward on itself, yet visible to the world so other sinners can wash in its tears, illustrates Penitence's complex reflexivity and the impossible topology that she occupies.[24] After washing in her Fountain the pilgrim is back on track. Although he must still undergo Tribulation and flounder for a while in the Sea of the World, the worst of his journey is behind him.

The different places identified with Penitence thus figure, successively, self-enclosure, division, and self-consciousness. I shall now look more closely at how this consciousness of self is arrived at.

Knowing One's Self: Memory

The protagonist's dream begins with a prebirth vision of the heavenly Jerusalem, to which he will try to return throughout his dream. The poem's epistemology is thus broadly Platonist in that it is premised on the soul's recollection of a truth that has become obscured by its entry into a body. As in the Augustinian tradition, the pilgrim is traveling not forward but *back* to his rightful home, from which he is exiled so long as he is embodied.[25] The pilgrim's "progress" is thus retrospective, his goal modeled on his past. This is clear in the scene where, following the Eucharist, Grace Dieu equips him as a pilgrim and gives him a staff named Esperance (Hope, *PVH*, 3679) surmounted by a pommel in which, along with Christ, an image of the heavenly city is reflected:

And there I saw that city that I was fired up to go to; just as I had seen and perceived it formerly in the mirror, so I saw it, to my delight, in the pommel.

> Et la vi je celle cité
> ou d'aler estoie excité
> aussi com l'avoie veue
> autre foiz et aperceue
> ou mirour, aussi u pommel
> je la vi, dont mont me fu bel. (*PVH*, 3445–50)

After all his misadventures with the sins, the pilgrim takes heart from the pommel's image of Jerusalem (*PVH*, 10748) before praying to the Virgin and progressing to the Fountain of Penitence. Recollection thus forms a significant strand in the attainment of self-knowledge.

Recollection of this primal illumination is accompanied by actively memorizing one's experiences in this world, a theme represented in the poem by the figure of Memoire. After giving the pilgrim his stole and staff, Grace Dieu provides him with armor consisting of the four cardinal virtues. Strength will protect the main part of his body and Temperance his head and hands, where the senses are primarily located, Prudence will be his shield, and Justice his sword. He puts the armor on but then immediately takes it off again, finding he cannot move in it. The exercise of these virtues would prove too restrictive. So instead it is carried for him by Memoire, who thus preserves on his behalf, even though he is unaware of her presence, the armor's injunctions. Memoire is described as being blind to the future; instead of her eyes being in her forehead, they project out behind her (*PVH*, 4891–92).

When the armor is first given to the pilgrim, it is made clear that its purpose is to assist him not against external threats but against what lies inside him. For example, the sword of justice is needed to parry the most intimate of threats:

for you cannot have a more redoubtable, a worse or more dangerous enemy, than what is closest to you, and what originates in you.

> quar anemis plus dangereus,
> plus mauvais ne plus perilleus
> ne pues avoir que tes privez
> et qui de toi sont dirivez. (*PVH*, 4298–300)

The armor is there to subdue the pilgrim's own assaults upon himself, which is why wearing it proves unbearable. When he asks Raison why Memoire, a frail young girl, can carry it when he can't, Raison throws this back at him in the form of another question, one I have already referred to: Is he a single being or a twofold one?

Do you know, she asked, who you are, whether you are a single or a double being, if you have anyone beside yourself to feed, manage, and care for?

> Ses tu, dist elle, qui tu es,
> Se tu es seul ou doubles es,
> Se nul fors toi as a nourrir
> N'a gouverner n'a mainbournir. (*PVH*, 5733–36)

Thus Raison's discussion of dualism is provoked by an inquiry into the nature of memory. I think this is because Memoire is liminal between mind and body. This is not what Raison says, however, and it will be best to look first at her account. (In the second redaction this dialogue is retained, but Raison is replaced by Grace Dieu.)

Knowing One's Self: Raison's Dualism

The pilgrim's response to Raison's asking whether he is *seul* or *doubles* is that he is so obviously a single being that he can't see the point of her question ("Je sui tout seul, bien le vëes, / Ne sai pour quoi le demandés," *PVH*, 5741–42). But he is wrong, says Raison. He is composed of warring elements:

You need to know that you are rearing your own great enemy. You yourself feed, water, shoe, and clothe him daily.

> Tu doiz savoir que tu nourris
> cil qui est tes grans anemis.
> De toi touz les jours est pëus,
> abevrés, chauciés et vestus. (*PVH*, 5747–50)

His spirit and his body, teaches Raison, are distinct. He must not identify with his body, which has enslaved his spirit, forcing it to pander to the body's urges when it is the spirit that should discipline the body through Penitence. His true being is his spirit, which was made by God and in his image. This spirit is immortal, the child of God; he is mistaken in styling himself son of Thomas de Deguileville, since only his natural body is inherited from his father.[26] This body, far from being where his self lies, is the enemy of the spirit. The internal war for which the armor was designed is spelled out here. Raison doesn't explicitly answer the question why Memoire can bear its weight while the pilgrim can't; but the implication is that it is because memory is spirit, not body.

To illustrate the pilgrim's dual nature, Raison allows him the experience of escaping temporarily from his body. The pilgrim is entranced by the weightlessness he experiences as he flies freely over its remains that lie beneath him crumpled on the ground. The scene is delightfully illustrated, MS fr. 12465, fol. 40, for example, depicting the abandoned body as a thin twist of cloth. Finding himself so liberated, the pilgrim is reluctant to resume his body, which is now in the position of the cumbersome armor he previously felt unequal to wearing. As soon as he dons it again, he feels himself grow heavy and darkened. That the body is merely the receptacle of the soul is made clear both by Raison and the pilgrim:

God made you, for you are spirit. He put you in the body where you are. He put you there to dwell there for a while and to test you.

> Il te fist, quar esperit es,
> et te mist ou cors que tu ez.
> Il t'i mist pour ens habiter
> une piece et pour esprouver. (Raison, *PVH*, 5993–96)

You call me a spirit thrust into my body here.

> Un esperit vous m'appelés
> qui en mon cors sui ci boutez. (Pilgrim, *PVH*, 6025–26)

It would, Raison contends, be as absurd to contend that the body bears the soul as to claim, she says, that clothes carry the body (*PVH*, 6125–30). The spirit acknowledges eternal truths, while his body does nothing more than darken its perception of the spiritual realm from which it came.

This dialogue with Raison about the vicissitudes of embodiment is yet another echo of the spatial paradoxes of Book I. On the one hand, the pilgrim's body is merely the receptacle for his spirit and has no essential relationship to him at all; on the other, his body is not an inert container but an active force. The first account is developed through images of the body as a cloud or a garment—a mere screen that blocks off spiritual light, or an inert burden to be shouldered. The second, however, comes to the fore when it is also said to be a sink of iniquity, endowed with its own will, a warring force within the containing armor of morality. (This last image in particular recalls the account of Sapience and Science as rival champions.) The body, then, is both a neutral, if obnubilating, container and a fearsome, overwhelming opponent. This contradiction, as with other spatial paradoxes, results from hierarchy. A comparison between the self and a ship effectively captures this spatial paradox (*PVH*, 6139–46). The steersman (the soul) is carried within the boat and may find himself at the mercy of wind and waves, yet his job is to control it, and in this sense it is he who carries the ship.

Raison's dualism is consequently equivocal. She is in no doubt that the soul has "being," but she is not clear whether the body does or does not. Sometimes she is adamant that the body is not being at all: "Mes tel[e] chose ne es tu pas" (*PVH*, 5981). The only reality would then be the spirit, with the body no more than an inanimate container for it. But at other times, in order to endow the body with agency, she discerns duality within the very properties of thought and will that she elsewhere presents as contents rather than container, and thus as spirit rather than body. The pilgrim, she says, has conflicting thoughts and desires, the negative parts of which are in fact "body" after all:

Thus, said she, your will is twofold and so is your thought. One wants to go and the other stay, one wants to rest and the other to work. . . . Therefore, you are not alone, rather you and your body are two, for two wills are not one but two, as anyone knows.

> Donques, dist elle, volenté
> tu as double et double pensé.
> L'un veut aler, l'autre arrester,
> l'un [le] repos, l'autrë ouvrer. . . .
> Donques, dist elle, n'es pas seulz,
> ains toi et ton cors estes .ii.,
> quar .ii.vouloirs ne sunt pas d'un,
> ainz sont de .ii., ce set chascun. (*PVH*, 5917–20, 5925–28)

Raison's distinction here between two wills parallels a passage in the *Confessions* where Augustine finds the "new will" of his converted self pitted against his old one: "So these two wills within me, one old, one new, one carnal, the other spiritual, were in conflict with one another" (VIII, v, §10).[27] Their conflict manifests the problematic boundary that Augustine speaks of in *On the Trinity*, in a passage I have already quoted: "Let us see where the boundary line, as it were, between the outer and inner man is to be placed. . . . Since by the outer man we mean not the body only, but also its own peculiar kind of life" (XII, i, §1). The effect of this problematic boundary is to redraw the initial dualism of container/body and contents/soul and to divide the soul in such a way as to endow the otherwise inert body with "carnal will," its own "peculiar kind of life."

When the pilgrim arrives at the Hedge of Penitence the reader is thus prepared to see this problematic dualism develop. To the outline I gave above of how the Hedge features in the topology of Penitence we can now add an investigation of how it contributes to this mapping of the "inner" and "outer" man.

Knowing One's Self: The Pilgrim at the Hedge

The narrative describes how the pilgrim's body persuades his soul to walk along the path of Huiseuse on one side of the Hedge, while Raison and Grace Dieu are on the farther side. The events that then unfold indicate that the soul, which has thus taken the "wrong" path, is dominated by those negative impulses that, in part of Raison's account (see the quotation immediately above), are ascribed to the body. This soul, if soul it is, has found it impossible to disentangle itself from its corporeality.[28] Thus it has fallen away from what it ought to be, the likeness of God, to which it could return through repentance, that is, by passing over to the farther side of the hedge.

It is helpful to remember, when reading this passage, that Augustine ascribes three aspects to the soul: memory, reasoning, and will, identified as the most evident imprint within man of the Holy Trinity because they are eternal and mutually interdependent (*On the Trinity*, X, xi). Understanding depends on memory and studious intent; but memory relies on understanding and the will to retain it; while the will depends on understanding and on having furnished good contents for one's memory. "Therefore, these three are one in that they are one life, one mind, and one essence" (*On the Trinity*, X, xi, §18; "Quocirca tria haec eo sunt unum quo una uita, una mens, una essentia"). Degenerating from this ideal, the memory, will, and reasoning powers that accompany the pilgrim on the wrong side of the Hedge interact mutually to keep him there, and to divorce him from what he has lost and ought to be.

I shall start with memory as represented by the figure of Memoire, who, despite Raison's alignment of her with the spirit, bears a strong imprint of corporeality.[29] The scene where the pilgrim is presented with the suit of armor presages an active pilgrimage, a *militia Christi*. But once the pilgrim has taken the armor off, he displays almost uncanny passivity in the face of attack by the sins and is repeatedly floored by them. Although the poem allegorizes life as a journey, much of its course is apparently effected lying down. Descriptions of the pilgrim in this supine position occur when his soul is separated from his body, when he has been defeated by one or other of the sins, and again at the end when he is ill in bed and about to die. The illuminations reinforce this by multiplying representations of the pilgrim lying on his back. Such images recall the miniature opening many of the manuscripts of the author lying on his bed and dreaming. Thus Memoire seems to operate at the level of the body, functioning not as a storehouse of abstract injunctions but as the reenactment of past posture. Although charged with carrying the virtues, there is no indication that she actively calls them to mind. Rather, the amount of time the pilgrim spends lying on his back implies kinship between the pilgrim's memory, his chosen path of leisure, and the first sin he meets there, Paresse (Sloth), the source of all the other sins. This is memory in corporeal rather than intellectual form.

Before the pilgrim ventured down this path, Raison had confronted him with his *double volenté*, of which the negative part loves only inertia and repose ("One wants to go and the other stay, one rest and the other work"; "L'un veut aler, l'autre arrester, / L'un [le] repos, l'autrë ouvrer," *PVH*, 5919–20). This is the part of his will that, in Raison's terms, is not spirit but the body, and it would appear to be this that accompanies the pilgrim down the wrong side of the Hedge. Once his will has degenerated from choosing Huiseuse to being overcome by Paresse, the first of the deadly sins to assail him, it loses the impetus to reform.[30] Deguileville represents this by having Paresse agree to release the pilgrim only on condition that he doesn't attempt to go back through the Hedge; as soon as he makes a move toward it she threatens him again. The farther the will lapses into sin, the denser the Hedge appears. Awareness that these sins are mortal, that is, cause the death of the soul, is expressed after the encounter with Ire (Wrath, *PVH*, 9025–26), when the pilgrim laments that he will die if Grace Dieu does not help him. With his will so misdirected it is not surprising that his memory for virtue is dimmed.

The split Raison has identified within the will she also ascribes to his thought (his *double pensé*), and it is clear from the way the pilgrim argues within himself at the Hedge that his capacity for thought is as much implicated in the body as are his indolent memory and slothful will. Although the text at this point distinguishes between the pilgrim's spirit as "I" (*je*) and his body as "it" (*il*), the two are hard to disentangle. The pilgrim's "I" wants to take the path of Occupation (Labor), but his body, finding Occupation repellent, refuses. The Hedge, "it" points out, although composed of thorny trees, is far from impassable and can be crossed at any time (*PVH*, 6719–24). The attractions of Huiseuse are such that "I" gives in immediately, feebly reiterating the body's conviction that he can get back any time (*PVH*, 6875–86). Grace Dieu and Raison exhort him to get back as soon as possible. But when "I" looks at even the thinnest parts of the Hedge he is overwhelmed with sympathy for how much the body would suffer if it had to struggle through the thorns. His reasoning has been quickly outargued by his body because that, in a sense, is what it already is. The distinction between "I" and "it" does not separate two entities; rather, it defines an internal limit whereby "I" is confined within "it"—it is the body that chooses which branch of the path to follow—even though "it" is supposedly inferior to "I." Although his "I" and his "it" are opposed, the two in fact act in concert to place the pilgrim on the opposite side of the Hedge from Raison and Grace Dieu. By the very act of reasoning, he has alienated himself from Raison and the divine power that sanctions her (*PVH*, 5189, 5219ff.).

In conclusion, the split of the Hedge makes the poem's dualism harder, not easier, to define. Although Deguileville speaks of the pilgrim's *esperit* as accompanying its body down the side of Huiseuse, his capacity for being in the likeness of God is located on the farther side, in Raison and the potential for Grace. Conversely, the soul that finds itself on the wrong side of the Hedge is a soul that is already internally split by its kinship with corporeality. Until the moment of remorse, when the pilgrim bathes in the Fountain of Penitence, the Hedge of Penitence keeps "him" internally divided in such a way as to separate him from what is most truly "himself." This stage in his self-knowledge is, at the same time, a state of loss and ignorance of self, an awareness of the self as fractured by divisions that are impossible to locate.

This insistence on failure and division is, however, precisely why Deguileville's investigation of self-knowledge and the nature of the self belongs in the Western history of the *cogito*.

Conclusion: Deguileville's Allegory and the Enigma of Cogito

An enormous amount has been written about the various manifestations of the *cogito*, from Augustine via Descartes to Lacan and beyond. This conclusion has the more modest aim of drawing attention to some of the similarities linking the *Vie humaine*, Augustine, and modern thinking where these throw light on the relationship in the poem between spatial dislocation and the complexity of the self as a "one."

In his treatise *On the Trinity*, Augustine asks, "Why, therefore, is it enjoined upon [the mind] that it know itself?" and at once answers: "It was, I believe, in order that it might consider itself and live according to its nature, that is, that it might desire to be ruled according to its nature, namely, under Him to whom it must be brought into subjection, and above those to whom it must be preferred" (X, v, §7).[31] In order to achieve such knowledge, the mind has to negotiate the various forms of uncertainty that afflict it in its embodied state. It is constantly a prey to doubt and, worse, to delusion and corruption. Yet this does not mean that it cannot at least be certain of its own operations. On the contrary, the certainty of existence can be inferred from the very process of casting doubt upon it, an argument later adapted from Augustine by Descartes: "Who would doubt that he lives, remembers, understands, wills, thinks, knows, and judges? For even if he doubts, he lives; if he doubts, he remembers why he doubts; if he doubts, he understands that he doubts; if he doubts, he wishes to be certain; if he doubts, he thinks; if he doubts, he knows that he does not know; if he doubts, he judges that he ought not to consent rashly" (*On the Trinity*, X, x, §14).[32] Some of Augustine's formulations in the *City of God* and in his treatise *Free Will*, likewise exploited by Descartes, are even more radical. I may be wrong about everything, says Augustine, but the fact of my being wrong demonstrates the existence of an "I" that is capable of error: "If [the skeptics] say, 'What if you are mistaken?'—well, if I am mistaken, I am. For if one does not exist, he can by no means be mistaken."[33] Augustine's next following phrase, "per hoc sum, si fallor" ("If I am mistaken, then I exist"), encapsulates the problematic of self-knowledge as it is developed along the divided path in the *Pèlerinage de vie humaine*. Although Deguileville's dreamer may aspire to know the self as a content—as a nature present and available to itself—he has to settle for awareness of the self as an agency defined precisely by its inability to possess that knowledge. When Foucault writes of a radical break between the Cartesian and modern forms of the *cogito*, then, he is neglecting this common ground between Augustine and modernity. The questions Foucault sees as characterizing the contemporary subject have been articulated from late antiquity: "How can man think what he does not think, dwell mutely in a domain that escapes him, animate, as with some kind of frozen movement, this figure of himself that presents itself to him as a stubborn external reality?"[34] Bewilderment at the dislocation between being and knowledge, at the troublesome disjunction (gap or overlap?) between the self as "I" and as "it," is precisely what Augustine and Foucault have in common.

Of course, Foucault may be right about the break between Descartes and modernity. According to some historians of philosophy, Descartes identifies his "I" with the agency that thinks so radically as to divorce that

"I" from the body. For Miles Burnyeat, "no ancient or medieval skeptic divides things up so that one's own body counts as part of something we have come to call the external world"; Descartes is the first to do this.[35] Augustine, on the other hand, does not identify himself exclusively with the "I" of thought. Aware of his corporeality, his "I" questions can always be recast as "it" questions; that is, he can ask both "Can I be certain that I exist?" and "What can the mind be certain that it is?"[36] A similarly incomplete identification of the "I" with the *esperit* is what brings about the spatial paradoxes associated with the Hedge in the *Vie humaine* where, as we have seen, *je* and *il* oppose one another and yet end up on the same path, separated from the path of Raison and Grace Dieu and yet in communication with them.

These fluctuating divisions in the self between an "I" and an "it" lie at the core of psychoanalytic thought, which theorizes them with reference to competing psychical agencies, some of them unconscious. Their most famous formulation is probably Freud's enigmatic "wo Es war, soll Ich werden" (literally, "where it was, I shall be").[37] Lacan, who returns repeatedly to the relation between psychoanalysis and Cartesian thought, sees Freud's main contribution to the *cogito* as having been to assert the coexistence, within the subject, of an "I" and an "it" that are located in paradoxically interrelated places.[38] Here, for example, Lacan brings out the parallel between Descartes' and Freud's reasoning that the fact of my doubting is evidence that I exist. Freud's position differs from Descartes', however, in insisting that the agency that thinks is unconscious and thus belongs in a place different from that of our conscious being; and that the thinking "I" has been displaced by a third person, an it or he, the "someone [who] thinks in his place": "In a precisely similar way, Freud, when he doubts . . . is assured that a thought is there, which is unconscious, which means that it reveals itself as absent. . . . It is to this place that he summons the *I think* through which the subject will reveal himself. In short, he is sure that this thought is there alone with all his *I am*, if I may put it like this, provided, and this is the leap, someone thinks in his place."[39] Following on from Lacan there has been a great deal of discussion of the various ways in which a psychoanalytical *cogito* might be construed, and how the categories of "I" and "it," and of "thought" and "being," would be combined in it.[40]

One way of reading Deguileville's personification allegory is as exploring this split within the pilgrim as *je* and as *il*. Various of the personifications, that is, can be read as "identifications," as ways of representing the self as a distinct, externalized, alien entity, what Foucault calls "this figure of himself that presents itself to him in the form of a stubborn, external reality" ("cette figure de lui-même qui se présente à lui sous la forme d'une extériorité têtue," *Les Mots et les choses*, 334). To this extent they all represent his *je* as an *il* (or rather, since the personifications are feminine, as a series of *elles*). In the episode of the Hedge the "one" of the pilgrim is realized in a multitude of such figures that fall into two distinct groups. There is the youthful trio of Memoire, Raison, and Grace Dieu, who between them represent in idealized form the trinity of mental faculties (memory, understanding, will) described by Augustine; and there is the nightmarish succession of horrible old women who represent his sinful bodily urges. These groupings could be read as identifying in the pilgrim a disjunction between the capacity for thought and the capacity for being: between his "I" as an "it thinks" or as an "it is." His thinking self is most obviously associated with the mental and spiritual faculties Memoire, Raison, and Grace Dieu; the self's existence as a weak, all too fleshly body would then be expressed through the personified sins, many of them (like Covoitise [Cupidity] with her six hands) explicitly associated with monstrous bodily excess. But equally, it could be argued, the poem affirms the being ("I am") of spiritual realities, whereas the capacity of the body to conceive and follow its own gruesome urges is all too graphically portrayed in the abominable *ça pense* ("it thinks") of the sins.

While the dream vision offers various possibilities of interpretation, what is most important about them from my point of view is that these two groups of personifications do *not* correspond with the division marked by the Hedge; Memoire and the sins fall on the *same* side. Thus dislocation does not rationalize division, it compounds it. The power of the poem's personifications is less that they externalize what is "inside" than that they render palpable the problem of an internal split whose nature is uncertain and shifting. The process of walking along the Hedge calls attention to this split but does not fix it. In this way, the decentering of the dreamer's self forms part of the broader, and systematic, concern with paradoxes of place in the poem, which, as we have seen, conceives place as real in a moral rather than a physical sense, and as riven by contradictory internal boundaries.

Describing the self in the *Pèlerinage de vie humaine* as split and decentered underlines the affinities between modern psychoanalysis and the medieval poem. But although it is psychoanalysis that has gone farthest in exploring the self as split, the rationale for this split in Deguilevile is the same is it is for Augustine, namely, the alienation of man from God. In the final book of *On the Trinity*, Augustine emphasizes the yawning gulf between such self-knowledge as we can attain and the knowledge of God to which we aspire. Even if the trinity within the mind is an image of the Holy Trinity, it leaves us looking, in the words of Paul, in a glass darkly (*per speculum in aenigmata*). Augustine recalls that some of Paul's translators, mindful of the rhetorical meaning of the term *aenigma*, have translated it as "allegory"—"those which signify one thing by another" (*On the Trinity*, XV, ix, §15, "quae sunt aliud ex alio significantia"). But, he goes on, not all allegories are truly enigmatic; *aenigma* is an especially demanding form of allegory. The *Pèlerinage de vie humaine* is, indeed, an enigmatic allegory in this sense, since it presents the pilgrim's struggle for self-knowledge as a means by which readers might attain some knowledge of themselves and of their salvation. The process of looking at an allegory of the self would be, as for Augustine, an allegory of the process of looking for God.

The *Pèlerinage de vie humaine* is about the one of the self as it journeys down its divided path, separated and united both in itself and in its relation to God, wresting knowledge even from delusion and self-deception. The poem's literary form—its use of place, personification, and allegoresis—is the means whereby this enigmatic progress is enacted. Place is vital to envisioning this pilgrimage, but on condition that we renounce trying to visualize it: the division of the physical from the spiritual, and their potential for union, are too real for us to see.

4

Universality on Trial in Machaut's *Jugement* Poems

IT IS EVIDENT THAT Machaut's *dits* are not didactic in the same way as the texts examined in the preceding three chapters. The major scholars who in recent decades have established Machaut's importance as an author and poet have all demonstrated how playful and equivocal he is, and how pre-occupied with the intricacies of form and literary discourse.[1] His elaborate rewriting and combining of past texts does mean, however, that his poetry is always in dialogue with didactic models, most consistently with Boethi-us's *Consolation of Philosophy*,[2] as well as with texts whose own engage-ment with didacticism is already complex, like the *Roman de la rose*.[3] Indeed, it could be said that Machaut is the first major French poet to extend the remit of didacticism so that it includes directions as to how to write poetry. Among his works, compositions as diverse as the *Prologue*, the *Remède de Fortune*, and the *Voir dit* can be seen as venturing farthest into this new didactic terrain, and even the *Jugement dou roy de Navarre* has been seen as studying "the conditions of possibility of lyrical writing."[4]

But Machaut is also and perhaps even primarily a poet who admonis-hes his readers on substantive matters. His *dits* promote his views on both love and courtly society—in particular, on the conduct of its leaders. The way Machaut pursues these twin themes is complex, however, and can perhaps best be grasped as a development of the dilemma of emotion and language that characterizes earlier courtly poetry. Lyric poets face a dilemma, in which they ask both, How can personal feeling be expressed or recognized otherwise than through language? and, How can anything personal in that feeling survive the alienation that it undergoes in the mill of its telling? Where earlier trouvères play ironically with the paradox or court sublime unutterability, Machaut creates pathos and comedy through first-person figures who find themselves unable to measure up to the ideals and traditions of institutions. The public courtly world and the intimate world of personal experience are always more or less at odds. Thus, while he is constantly offering advice on courtly conduct and advice to lovers, often indeed superimposing one on the other, there tends to be a divergence between the public and the personal poles of his teaching, and a comic-pathetic shortfall between principles and their realization. The exemplary mode, that staple of didactic writing throughout this period and one on which Machaut himself relies heavily, is thus always under a shadow of derision in his works.[5]

The result so far as the theme of this book is concerned is that, for Machaut, the "one" of individuality seems to be at odds with the "one" of generality, or the universal "one." In each of the works analyzed thus far, the various forms of oneness have been seen to be reciprocally interconnected. In the *Breviari* the individual lover-poet is integrated into a universal structure of divine love; in the *Ovide moralisé* the individual sinner is involved in potential community through the divine form; in the *Pèlerinage de vie humaine* the individual pilgrim, in his inner division, offers a means of apprehending the threefold unity of his Creator. My contention, then, is that the notion of "one" is decisively different in Machaut's *dits*. By suggesting that the individual subsists not through inclusion within the group but through its status as exceptional or excluded, Machaut implies that the universal, while it may be abstracted from individuals, does not include them. I shall explore this implication later in this chapter by comparing the respective influences of Boethius and Aristotle on the *Navarre*, in which Machaut's position is closer to Aristotle's. Machaut's views of oneness also lead to radical reflections on gender and sexual difference, which likewise have analogues in late medieval thinking, this time in the critique of Aristotle, as well as in modern gender theory. In his concentration on the excluded one, I shall argue, the concept of the universal is held up to scrutiny; it, rather than Machaut himself, is put on trial.

Spatially, Machaut's two strands of oneness, the social-universal and the singular-excluded, correspond with more public or more intimate settings. Some of the *loci* presented in his poems involve communities gathered together, generally indoors, in a recognizable dwelling or castle, where they give themselves over to social rituals, such dining and holding court. Others stress isolation or separation. But just as Machaut's themes tend to be superimposed, so these *loci* sometimes seem to morph into one another, and movements from inside to outside, or from collective to individual, are hard to trace. Often, moreover, the seemingly populous gatherings are composed of personified abstractions that could all be representing the internal makeup of a single individual, so that the public dimension is threatened with collapse back into the private.

This chapter will focus primarily on Machaut's *Jugement dou roy de Navarre*, a *dit* composed in 1349 or 1350, or possibly later,[6] as a companion and corrective to his earlier *Jugement du roi de Behaigne* that predates 1342, texts whose interconnecting structure Jacqueline Cerquiglini has described as "didactic."[7] In the *Behaigne*, a court is asked to adjudicate between testimonies of personal suffering brought before it by a knight and a lady. Who suffered more, the lady whose lover was killed or the knight whose lady left him? The court rules in the knight's favor, but its judgment is overturned in the *Navarre*, where Machaut himself is sought out by a personification eventually identified as Dame Bonneürté (Lady Happiness), tried, and condemned for having perpetrated what is now said to be the erroneous verdict of the earlier poem. As a punishment for deciding against the cause of women in the *Behaigne*, he is sentenced in the *Navarre* to compose a series of works defending them. In the last lines of the *dit* he undertakes to compose one of these commissioned pieces as soon as he has completed and presented to Dame Bonneürté the *dit* itself, which he trusts will propitiate her. In four manuscripts the *Navarre* is immediately followed by a *lai* called the *Lai de Plour*, composed in a female first-person voice, to show that Machaut carried out this promise; there is no evidence that he completed the other commissions.[8]

The "One of Exclusion" in the *Jugement* Poems as Negative *Exemplum*

One way of situating what I have identified as the "one of exclusion" in Machaut's writing is to see it as a development of the tendency in first-person didactic poetry for the persona of the self to serve as a negative *exemplum*, a model from whom to learn what *not* to do. The self-deprecating moralist is a familiar figure in medieval culture, from Marcabru to the lover in the *Roman de la rose* and beyond, and although Machaut certainly did not invent this device, he brought it to a high art.[9] Posing as the butt of one's own instruction leavens didacticism with humor and reduces the risk of causing offense to its actual targets. The *Pèlerinage de vie humaine* is a good instance of this strategy. Deguileville exaggerates the fallibility of his first-person protagonist by making him exhibit *all* of the sins and weaknesses that his readers might succumb to. From this perspective, the *Jugement dou roy de Navarre* can be viewed as a secular rewriting of the *Pèlerinage de vie humaine*. Deguileville's exemplary pilgrim, Guillaume, ventures out of his house after being enclosed there for nine months, then sets out on a journey, in the course of which he seeks to understand where the supreme good may be located (*souverain bien*, PVH, 3157, 3244, cf. Chapter 3 above); he is instructed in the virtues but neglects them and falls prey instead to the vices. Machaut's exemplary poet, also a Guillaume, shuts himself away in his house for several months before finally venturing out. Although hailed by a figure we later learn to identify as "supreme goodness" (*souvereinne bonté*, JRN, 1327), his demeanor at his trial suggests that he falls well below the standards embodied by the virtues. In both poems, Raison combines with an even more eminent Lady (Grace Dieu in the *Vie humaine*, Bonneürté in the *Navarre*) to criticize the protagonist roundly and exhort him to repent.

While broadly similar in theme up to this point, the endings of the two texts show how Machaut reverses the first-person exemplary figure from a position of inclusion to one of exclusion. Deguileville's Guillaume-pilgrim experiences contrition and is received into a monastic community; Machaut's Guillaume-poet fluctuates between being a learned authority and an inadequate fool and, whether on the grounds of superior intellect or moral blindness, persists in his disrespect toward his accusers. The negative aspect of his self-portrayal may be Machaut's way of assuming his public's (perceived or actual) disregard for him; that is, it may reflect the poet's social marginality.[10] Although Machaut's Guillaume-poet obeys the court's ruling, it can be doubted whether he ever really assents to it.[11] The end of the text, where he goes through the motions of submission, is tinged with bad faith, since his main gesture of atonement is to write up the very work in which his lack of repentance is flaunted—and to which he ostentatiously affixes his own name:

I the above-named Guillaume, surnamed of Machaut, have composed and rhymed this little book the better to acknowledge my wrongdoing.

> Je, Guillaumes dessus nommez,
> qui de Machau sui seurnommez
> pour miex congnoistre mon meffait
> ay ce livret rimé et fait. (*JNR*, 4199–202)

Moreover, for a professional author to receive three commissions is scarcely a punishment, while completing only one of them hardly suggests

overwhelming compunction. Resisting integration to the higher authority
in his text, he is presented in quite a different light from the individuals in
the works previously studied. The protagonist's singularity is symptomatic, for Machaut, of the situation of any one individual vis-à-vis the social
order.

"Advice to Rulers" and the "Court of Love" in the *Jugement* Poems

This failure of integration of the individual with a higher unity is also
played out in the tension between the didactic models that are called into
play in the two *Jugement* poems. Each of these *dits* features as its presiding
judge Machaut's patron of the time: John of Luxemburg, king of Bohe-
mia, in the first, and the young Charles, king of Navarre, in the second.
Each poem is in part a panegyric of the patron as a courtly ruler and dis-
penser of justice; at the same time, since the *dits* have an exhortative edge
to them, each commends to the patron his princely obligations. Both *Juge-
ments* therefore have one foot in the tradition of works offering "advice
to rulers," most explicitly in the *Navarre*, the prologue to which contains
social satire against unworthy conduct in the powerful.[12] Both poems are
also, however, slewed versions of another tradition: that of works presenting the "court of Love," where rival claims are disputed regarding some
aspect of love, and the judge has to adjudicate "d'amors, d'amant, et
d'amie," as the *Navarre* puts it (*JRN*, 1517: "regarding love, lover, and
beloved"). The form taken by the trial in both the *Behaigne* and the *Navarre* is a contest of love stories. In the first *Jugement* poem, it is the rival
tales of the lady and the knight that are repeated. In the second, a series
of *exempla* about the sorrows of male or female lovers are also told, so as
to bolster the respective positions of the disputing parties. The importance
of the court of Love tradition in these poems is brought out by their
manuscript context, since all of the copies containing the *Navarre* place it
last in a group after the *Behaigne* and the *Dit dou vergier*, a dream-vision
poem in which the God of Love lectures aspiring lovers from his seat in
the top of a tree.[13] Positioned with respect to these two didactic models,
both *Jugement* poems deal simultaneously with public matters of government and intimate matters of the heart; and the patron occupies the roles
both of real-world ruler and of the god Amor, the traditional judge in

the court of Love.[14] Both poems thus combine, and equivocate between, political and amorous themes in a way typical of Machaut's *dits*.

The reversible structure, whereby principles of government are turned inside out to probe the workings of the heart and vice versa, might be thought to be facilitated by the use of personification. In the *Jugement* poems, as in the *Dit dou vergier*, personified abstractions feature both as members of the court, counseling its rulers, and as attributes of the human lovers seeking advice or judgment. However, in none of the poems does the cast of abstractions work out quite as we expect it will. What initially seemed to be a single set of abstractions begins to pull apart, according to whether the talk is of love or of court procedures. Instead of cementing convergence, these figures highlight the strain between the general and the intimate.[15]

This incompatibility between the public and the private good is brought out in the *Navarre*'s treatment of personified abstractions. We are told that the Lady of the court, subsequently revealed to be Dame Bonneürté, is attended by twelve damsels representing twelve virtues that together instruct, wait upon, and embellish her. However, it transpires that this set is somewhat elastic and, moreover, that the manuscripts do not agree among themselves how it is made up.[16] For the sake of clarity, I have summarized some key aspects of the situation in the table given as Figure 8, which shows how "twelve" varies between eleven and fourteen or even more. One reason for the fluctuation is that many of the apparently "single" virtues comprise more than one personification. The very first to be cited, for example, combines Cognoissance (Knowledge) and Avis (Right Judgment).[17] Attemprance (Temperance) seems to divide into two when the personification of Mesure (Moderation) is chosen as juror; if Mesure is not an aspect of Attemprance, then she emerges out of nowhere as a further addition to the list. Foy (Faith) and Constance (Constancy) are introduced as if they were a single virtue, and they behave as one, since they have only one voice between them. However, for the numbering initially indicated to work, either they need to be counted separately or, alternatively, Pais and Concorde (Peace and Concord), likewise presented as one and with only one speaking part between them, need to be reckoned as two. And finally, in the course of the *dit* Prudence appears to be displaced by, or else renamed, Franchise (Candor, the generosity of spirit associated with aristocracy,[18] *JRN*, 2693ff.), given that the speaker referred to in the text as Prudence in line 2925 is addressed by Guillaume as Franchise in line 3009, and he is later rebuked by the jurors for his discourtesy to Franchise, not Prudence.

Of course, medieval authors were not always scrupulous over their lists.[19] But these discrepancies can also be seen as motivated according to whether the focus is on love or government. Attemprance figures high on the original list of virtues and speaks to moderate a lover's selfish desires, but Mesure takes up a role as juror. Foy and Constance, or Pais and Concorde, may be one virtue in matters of the heart, whereas in the public life of a court they may entail different qualities. Prudence is called for in the initial roll call of virtues but finds her place taken by Franchise when assessing personal emotion is at stake, as though social and moral feeling was more relevant here than an intellectual virtue. Or are we rather to understand that the Guillaume persona is too intellectually challenged to recognize Prudence, even when she looks him in the face? However we explain the fluctuations, the text betrays a lack of fit between the two didactic models on which it is based, "advice to rulers" calling for virtues rather different from those required by the "court of Love."[20] This discrepancy generates contradiction at the heart of the role of Dame Bonneürté, as I shall show.

Place

The status of the court(s) concerned is problematized by the use of place in these *dits*. The setting for the courtroom scenes is a castle (*Behaigne*) or manor house (*Navarre*), a *locus* most obviously appropriate for the "advice to rulers" tradition, since sessions of the court of Love usually take place in a garden or grove. Both poems, then, are primarily set in an enclosed, aristocratic space. In order to fill this space with the decorum appropriate to it, careful attention is paid to etiquette—who sits, who kneels, who stands, who talks to whom. The set-piece enumeration of the virtues in the *Navarre* is articulated as a tableau, defining the interior of the manor house with this circle of ladies-in-waiting who minister to and beautify their mistress. The way they are grouped, certain of them touching or speaking to one of their fellows, recalls the techniques recommended by arts of memory for remembering a series of interconnected ideas.[21] The function of the first of the virtues, Cognoissance, is to show Dame Bonneürté the difference between virtue and vice (*JRN*, 1155–59), which she does by having Avis lead the Lady to look in a mirror held by

Personification	Number ascribed in list v. 1155 ff.	Aristotelian equivalent	Role in legal proceedings	Also worn by Dame Bonneürté?	Narrative position and contribution
Dame Bonneürté		*felicitas* (trans. of Aristotle's *eudaemonia*)	plaintiff against Guillaume		1. narrates bestiary stories of turtle dove and swan
Cognoissance and Avis	*la premiere*	*cognicio scientifica et rationalis*	jurors	*Cognoissance* is associated with *Sobreté* in her *chemise*	11. sums up evidence, directs verdict
Raison		*ratio*, comprising *cognicio scientifica* and *rationalis*	spokesperson	mantle is *Bons Appensemens, courtois Parlemens, Scienteuse Introduction* and *Amiable Entention*	13. communicates decisions
Attemprance, wearing a garland of Souffrance	*la tierce*	*temperancia/conti nencia*	supports plaintiff	*Sobreté* is an effect of the *chemise*	2. tells story of girl who dies of love
Mesure (unless she is the same as Attemprance)	not mentioned in this list, only appears later	? *mediatas* (the mean, opposed to excess either side)	juror		12. sums up, and directs verdict
Pais (and Concorde)	*la quarte*	*concordia* (subsection of *amicitia*)	supports plaintiff	*Beniveillance* is source of her *pelice*	3. tells story of Dido
Concorde (unless she is part of Pais)			doesn't speak		
Foy (and Constance)	*la cincisme*	? *amator veri* (mean between boastfulness and mock-modesty)	supports plaintiff	*Loial Convenance* and *Ferme Fiance* form her belt	4. contests credibility of clerk story
Constance (unless she is part of Foy)			doesn't speak		

	la settisme (.vi.e in BNF fr. 1587)		supports plaintiff	one of her gloves (see Largesse)	5. rebuts clerk story with fable of the little graft
Charité	*la settisme* (.vi.ᵉ in BNF fr. 1587)	?*amicicia*	supports plaintiff	one of her gloves (see *Largesse*)	5. rebuts clerk story with fable of the little graft
Honnestez	*après*	*honestas* (decorum in conversation)	supports plaintiff	her robe is *Honneste Conversation*	6. contests clerk story
Prudence (the same as Franchise?), with Sapience in her heart	*la .ix.*³	?*prudencia* (Aristotle places her within *cognitio*)	supports plaintiff		7. bis. contests *Chastelaine de Vergy* and ring story (unless this is *Franchise*)
Franchise (unless she is the same as Prudence)	not mentioned in this list, only appears later	?*magnanimitas*	supports plaintiff	Franchise is the name of her *chemise*	7. tells *exempla* of Ariadne and Medea; contests *Chastelaine de Vergy* and ring story (unless this is *Prudence*)
Largesse taught by Noblesse and rebuking Advarice	*apres*	*liberalitas*	supports plaintiff	her second glove (see *Charité*) with *Noblesse* as the dye	8. contests ring story
Doubtance de meffaire watched over by Honte and Paor	*l'autre*	*timor ingloriacionis*; *verecundia*	supports plaintiff		9. tells story of Pyramus and Thisbe
Souffisance adorned with Pacience and safe from Fortune	*la dousieme*	*sufficiencia* (part of *justicia*; but also found in contemplative life)	supports plaintiff	provides gold ornamentation on her *pelice*	10. tells story of Hero and Leander

The order of the moral virtues (virtues of character) in Aristotle (Grosseteste's terminology): *fortitudo, temperancia, liberalitas, magnificencia, magnanimitas, honoris appetitus, mansuetudo,* [mean between ingratiation and churlishness, akin to *amicicia*], *amor veri* [= mean between boastfulness and false modesty], *decencia/dicere decora/honestas, verecundia/timor ingloriacionis* (not a virtue strictly speaking but a passion), *iusticia*. Intellectual virtues: *ratio* and its subdivisions—*cognicio scientifica* and *rationalis*, redefined as *ars, sciencia, prudencia, sapiencia, intellectus*. Conditions of the ethical life: *continencia; amicicia*. Further overall framework: *vita activa* (*honor, civilitas*) and *vita contemplativa* (*delectatio*).

Figure 8. Machaut's scheme of virtues in the *Jugement dou roy de Navarre*

the second virtue, Raison. Raison holds the mirror in her right hand, while her left holds a pair of scales. Pais holds Concorde by one finger, and Foy is accompanied on her right hand by Constance—as I have said, these virtues form pairs whose members between them constitute either one virtue or two. Blind Largesse gives away everything except honor, as instructed by Noblesse (Nobility), and reproaches Advarice (Avarice). Thus the internal architecture of the manor house is defined and furnished by its occupants, their postures, and their interactions. Yet while, as human figures, the virtues realize a public space, as rhetorical personifications they derealize it. The personifications have been crafted in order to render abstract ideas visible and memorable. They are clearly not *themselves* people but the actions or qualities *within* people and they belong not in a public space but an internal one, as the virtues practiced (or not) by the ruler, by Guillaume, and so on.

This equivocation between internal and external space is reflected in the way the poems are illustrated.[22] In both BNF fr. 1584 and 22545 the *Behaigne* attracts more illustration than the *Navarre*. After an initial depiction of the poet meeting with the lamenting knight and lady, we have pictures of them presenting their cases to the king and of his deliberating. The *Navarre* in these two manuscripts, by contrast, contains only one illumination, which represents the poet withdrawn in his house at the beginning of the text. The visual difference between the two *dits* implies that the action of the *Behaigne* should be read as taking place in the external world, and that of the *Navarre* in the mind of the poet. In BNF fr. 9221, however, the *Navarre* moves into the external world with the addition of a hunting scene; now it is the *Behaigne* that receives only a single, initial picture and otherwise leaves the reader to focus on the individuals' inner conflicts. The fullest range of illustration is that found in BNF fr. 1587. Here the *Behaigne* and the *Navarre* are run together as a single work in which the illustrations follow a rhythm from outdoor scenes to the indoor place of judgment, and from intimate settings to larger groups of people.[23] These visual treatments, by their equivocation between outer public debate and inner mental conflict, confront their readers graphically with the problem of how the "one" of the individual relates to the "one" of the public, discursive order.

BNF fr. 1587 is the only manuscript to include a courtroom scene in the *Navarre* (Figure 9) and thus assign the debate a space in what looks like social reality. The rubric reads "comme le roy de navarre se siet et la royne et les .xii demoiselles en estant devant le roy disputantes a l'encontre

Figure 9. Guillaume de Machaut at the court with the King of Navarre, Dame Bonneürté, and damsels; Machaut's head has been erased. *Jugement dou roy de Navarre*, BNF fr. 1587, fol. 86. Reproduced by permission.

de guillaume de loris" ("how the king of Navarre is seated with the queen and the twelve damsels standing before the king arguing against Guillaume de Lorris"). What is particularly fascinating about this image is that the poet's head has been rubbed out, as though his presence within the court were being negated. The disjunction between the singular individual and the social institution is eloquently realized in this act of censorship or vandalism. Machaut's effacement from the illumination of his own text nicely captures the development I have described from a negative persona to a figure of exclusion.

There is another aspect to the use of space in the *Navarre* that is worth mentioning. The social architecture delineated by the personifications is abruptly and surprisingly reconfigured at the end of the poem. The detailed portrait of Dame Bonneürté toward the end is an echo of Boethius's portrayal of Philosophy at the beginning of his *Consolation of Philosophy* and, like its model, includes lengthy description of clothes that represent the Lady's qualities. Her outfit (described for us by Avis) comprises a *chemise* called Franchise, gloves of Charité and Largesse, a robe of Honneste Conversation (Decorous Living), and various other meaningful items whose merits overlap substantially with the virtues embodied in her ladies-in-waiting (see the table in Figure 8 for details). Her attendants, it seems, have taken their duty to adorn their Lady (*JRN*, 1314–17) so literally as to transform themselves into her garments, underwear included.

The setting of the *Jugement dou roy de Navarre* in a manor house that is at the same time an individual's internal, moral space *and* a multi-tiered suit of clothing distances the notion of "place" from anything that can readily be visualized. The capacity of this setting to morph from one shape to another is characteristic of dream-vision poetry, to which this *dit* belongs even if the motif of the dream itself is missing.

Boethius on the Nature of the Good

The *Jugement dou roy de Navarre* attests Machaut's abiding fascination with the model followed by so many medieval dream poems, the *Consolation of Philosophy*. As I have said, it culminates in the portrayal of an ideal female figure reminiscent of Lady Philosophy as she appears to the imprisoned Boethius. Machaut's *dit* even preserves in reversed form the penal context of the *Consolation*. Boethius's Philosophy consoles a convicted prisoner, but the Lady in the *dit* is determined that Machaut *should* be convicted; it was she who went in search of him, charged him with his offense, and organized the trial. Her consolatory role, if she has one, emerges only obliquely, when the jurors have finished their deliberations. By contrast with her forceful manifestation to Boethius at the beginning of his dream, she is identified to Machaut only at the end of his poem. Machaut is exhorted to note her qualities and draw strength from them so as to be able to endure the verdict that is about to be passed on him. This consolation has a hollow ring, however, given that the verdict is one that she has been seeking all along—she is his accuser, not his helpmeet (*JRN*, 4060–68).

The Lady is only named as Bonneürté in line 3851. But although her identity has been withheld until this point, clues are offered from the time of her first appearance. With Raison's help she sees

Whatever God and Nature can bestow on a happy (fortunate) person. That is, avoiding evil and doing good, and not seeking harm to anyone.

> Quanque Diex et Nature donne
> a *bonne eüreuse* personne.
> C'est le mal laissier et bien faire,
> e non voloir autrui contraire. (*JRN*, 1169–72, my emphasis)

With Souffisance (self-sufficiency) she rises above Fortune so that "she is extremely happy and perfectly virtuous" (*JRN*, 1299–300, "tant par estoit *bonne eüreuse* / et parfaitement vertueuse," my emphasis). She has every grace and merit crowned with "souvereinne bonté" (*JRN*, 1327, "sovereign goodness"). These hints point to Dame Bonneürté being a personification of the "supreme good," which is what Philosophy seeks, in Book III of the *Consolation*, to teach Boethius to recognize. Some of Philosophy's argument is echoed in the *Navarre*: for example, that self-sufficiency (Souffisance) not Fortune is the means to happiness; perhaps also that worldly power or pleasure are not in themselves sources of happiness but "sidetracks" from the road to it (*Consolation of Philosophy*, III, prose 8). However, just as the consoling role of Dame Bonneürté is an ironic reversal of Philosophy's, so in general Boethius's teaching on happiness and the supreme good seems to me to be undermined in the *Jugement dou roy de Navarre*.

Philosophy contends that there is but one supreme good, which is God, and that consequently when we identify happiness as a supreme good we must see that "God is the essence of happiness" (*Consolation of Philosophy*, III, prose 10: "Deum esse ipsam beatitudinem necesse est confiteri"). Human beings aspire to participate in the divine, and it is through union in this One that goodness, happiness, and our very existence are secured (*Consolation of Philosophy*, III, prose 11). The tone of the *Navarre* is far removed from this exalted religiosity. Far from promoting the integration of the individual with a higher One, Machaut exploits his comic disjunction, and in this sense his poetic practice is non- or even anti-Boethian. There is no epiphanic union, no elevation of the spirit to the divine, at the conclusion of the *dit*. As William Calin puts it, "Machaut does not renounce love poetry in favor of a higher truth, the only Truth and Love for a canon at Reims."[24] On the contrary, if Machaut's own supreme good is in any way furthered by the poem, it is in being instructed to go on writing. In the *Navarre*'s elaboration of Bonneürté as supreme good, the Boethian framework is undercut by other intellectual models.

In inquiring what these may be, I am not expecting to pin down a single, uncontestable source for Machaut's thinking. He is a poet and not a philosopher or theologian; moreover, the poetry of the *Navarre* is comic, frivolous—even, at times, scurrilous. But as Margaret Ehrhardt has suggested, Machaut's portrayal of the virtues was probably influenced in some degree by Aristotle's *Nicomachean Ethics*, which Machaut is very likely to have studied.[25] Ehrhardt herself doesn't pursue the Aristotelian angle, looking instead to traditional medieval schemes (the cardinal and theological virtues and those associated with the gifts of the Holy Spirit) to explain Machaut's choice of personifications. Given Machaut's divergence from Boethius, however, the comparison with Aristotle merits further investigation.

Machaut's Virtues and Aristotle's *Nicomachean Ethics*

Ehrhardt's main ground for suggesting the influence of the *Ethics* is that Aristotle discusses twelve moral virtues that assist human beings in their striving after the supreme good in the active life, just as Machaut, in the *Navarre*, depicts Dame Bonneürté as *souvereinne bonté* waited on and supported by twelve personified virtues. This formal similarity aside, Ehrhardt sees little relation between the virtues Aristotle enumerates and the personifications Machaut creates. Her conclusion is not without justification so long as one doesn't look beyond the moral virtues in Aristotle. Of course, if the intellectual virtues are included, then the Aristotelian scheme no longer numbers twelve; however, there is, as I have said, a good deal of doubt whether Machaut's does either. Taking account of *all* of the Aristotelian virtues produces a significant number of equivalences between Machaut's nomenclature and that of the standard Latin translation of the *Ethics*, by Robert Grosseteste (see Figure 8). Worth noting are the term *felicitas*, which Grosseteste uses to translate the Greek *eudaemonia* and which corresponds well with Machaut's *bonneürté*, and the term *sufficiencia*, cognate with Machaut's *souffisance*. The fact that these words are also used by Boethius enables Machaut to draw both sources into dialogue with each other in his *dit*. Another point to note is that Aristotle's moral virtues are enumerated primarily with reference to the political life (*vita civilis*, 95b17). Aristotle's positive attitude to *civilitas* contrasts with the negative evaluation of worldly power in Boethius but is reflected in that aspect of the *Navarre* which functions as an "advice to rulers" poem. Thus both the *Navarre* and the *Ethics* endorse as "virtuous" the social practices of decorum, generosity, and the avoidance of dishonor (Honnestez/*honestas*, Largesse/*liberalitas*, and Doubtance de meffaire/*timor ingloriacionis*). This political and courtly orientation is consonant with the decidedly secular presentation of Foy and Charité in Machaut's poem. They may, in other contexts, be theological virtues, but there is nothing theological about them in the *Navarre*.

At this level of broader, intellectual sympathy between the *Ethics* and the *Navarre* (as opposed to equivalences between the terms they use) is the rationalism that dominates their approach to ethics. Aristotle's argumentation proceeds from the moral to the intellectual virtues. While the moral ones are important for the active life of a public figure, Aristotle accords a higher value to the contemplative life that is entirely given over to thought: "That which is proper to each thing is by nature best and most pleasant for each thing; for man, therefore, the life according to intellect is best and pleasantest, since intellect more than anything else *is* man. This life therefore is also the happiest" (*Nicomachean Ethics*, 1178a5–8).[26] Machaut, although less rigorous and more playful, broadly observes the same priorities. He appoints as jurors and spokesmen of the judge the intellectual virtues Cognoissance, Avis, Raison, and Mesure,[27] leaving to the active or moral virtues the role of witnesses and debaters in the trial—a role they do not always acquit with distinction.[28] As a result, the trial in the *Navarre* progresses, like the *Ethics*, from the active to the intellectual level. And near the poem's end, the active and contemplative ways of life are explicitly distinguished by Raison. Some people, she says, lead a contemplative life that is so far removed from the world that it cannot inspire emulation; and so Dame Bonneürté is obliged to promote the cause of contemplation among the active:

And so [Bonneürté] returns by the active path to incite those who enjoy discussion to speak about the benefits of the contemplative life. And as a result, many are filled with good intent and bow to her teaching and instruct themselves to be conscientious and eager in becoming contemplatives.

> Or revient par la voie active
> pour esmouvoir ceuls de parler
> qui tiennent volentiers parler
> des biens de contemplation;
> dont maint, par bonne entention,
> s'enclinent si a sa doctrine
> que chascuns par soy se doctrine
> d'estre diligens et hastis
> de devenir contemplatis. (*JRN*, 3948–56)

Finally, Machaut's poem reflects the metaphysical, as well as the ethical, aspects of Aristotle's text. Although less elaborately, Machaut too is interested in the relation between ethics, action, chance, and human nature, as, for instance, in the passage where Lady Bonneürté's identity is dramatically revealed by Raison:

The lady's name is Happiness, and she holds the hand of Assurance from among Fortune's followers. For there is no one Fortune could strike low if the lady wishes to oppose it. And when she wants, for some particular concern, to intervene in Nature, you can see her do so without the need for any intermediary. . . . It is true that Nature is responsible for the bringing a child up to live and smile, but Happiness it is that leads him to the domain of well-being until such time comes as it is apparent in him that Happiness adorns him.

> La dame a nom Bonneürté,
> qui tient en sa main Seürté
> en la partie de Fortune;
> car il n'est personne nesune
> cui Fortune peüst abatre,
> se la dame le vuet debatre.
> Et quant elle vuet en Nature
> ouvrer par especial cure,
> la la voit on sans nul moien. . . .
> Voirs est que Nature norrit
> par quoy li enfes vit et rit;
> et Bonneürtez le demeinne
> tout parmi l'eüreus demainne
> tant qu'il est temps qu'en lui appere
> que de Bonneürté se pere. (*JRN*, 3850–59, 3871–76)

The deliberations at the end of the trial are punctuated by gales of laughter (*JRN*, 3513, 4032, 4057), so we are clearly not in a wholly serious philosophical text. Nevertheless, the broad sympathies of the *Navarre* seem to me to be Aristotelian, and this is true of the central question that preoccupies me, the question of the universal.

Aristotle's *Ethics* and the Question of the Universal

The status of the universal is, as I have indicated, the point at which Machaut's divergence from the Boethian model is most apparent; and it is significant for this book because it marks a way of approaching the theme of "one" different from that in my earlier chapters.

Aristotle engages from the outset in dialogue with Plato, asking whether the *summum bonum* is a "one" and of what kind. As Grosseteste's translation puts it, Does the supreme good exist *quod universale*

(96a10, "as a universal")? The answer is that that there is no single universal good, because "good" is realized across the categories. Thus "it is manifest, then, that it will not be something universally common and one" ("manifestum quod non utique erit commune quid universaliter et unum," 96a25). "The good" does not correspond with a single idea (96b25, "non est igitur bonum commune quid, secundum unam ideam"). Rather, it is locked into the particular; for example, a good doctor heals a particular sick man (97a10). Good is not a thing in itself but the completion or perfection of an aim, which differs according to different circumstances.

As we see these ideas echoed in the *Navarre*, we take the measure of Machaut's ironic disengagement from the Boethian One. When Raison identifies Dame Bonneürté to Guillaume, she stresses the plurality of her manifestations.

Now I wish to inform you openly how she manifests herself in some but not in all.

> Or vous vueil je dire en appert
> en quelles manieres elle appert,
> en aucunes, nom pas en toutes. (*JRN*, 3881–83)

Bonneürté appears in prosperity, friendship, victory, good dealings of all kinds, and success in love:

She is prompt in furnishing all kinds of good things, and doing so makes her more merry and cheerful; she is a friend to all good people. She appears in all forms of entertainment, in jousts as well as tourneys, to raise up knighthood and bring the deeds of brave men to the knowledge of ladies; there honor increases and disgrace vanishes. . . . If Happiness manifests itself by nature, good luck, or justice among knights, it also appears among the clergy.

> Elle est a tous biens mettre a point;
> s'en est moult plus gaie et plus cointe;
> elle est de tous les bons acointe.
> Elle appert en mains esbanois,
> tant en joustes comme en tournois,
> pour chevalerie essaucier
> et les fais des bons avancier
> a la cognoissance des dames.
> La croist honneur; la chiet diffames.
> . . .
> Se Bonneürtez par nature
> par fortune ou selonc droiture

appert en la chevalerie
elle appert aussi en clergie. (*JRN*, 3906–14, 3925–28)

This passage continues with the praise of the contemplative life that I've already cited. The diversity of forms adopted by Bonneürté accounts, perhaps, for the strange morphing of settings in the *Navarre* and also the fact that Guillaume is initially unable to recognize her.

The fact that Aristotle sees ethics as a set of activities that take place at the level of the individual does not mean that his discussion of it is not pitched at a universal level. For instance, his outline of the active virtues is subordinate to the universal principle of observing the mean between excesses, while his account of the intellectual virtues is, as we have seen, in no doubt as to their absolute superiority. And the practice of virtues, too, is enhanced by universal knowledge, even if it is always targeted at individual circumstances. Doing good does not require universal knowledge, but universal knowledge makes it likelier that one will do good: "It would seem, then, that the detail is worked out with more precision if the care is particular to individuals; for each person is more likely to get what suits his case. But individuals can be best cared for by a doctor or gymnastic instructor or anyone else who has the universal knowledge of what is good for every one or for people of a certain kind" (*Nicomachean Ethics*, 1180b10–15).[29] An obvious way in which this relation between universals and particulars is rendered in Machaut's poem is by the use of personified abstractions. The personifications are rhetorical representations of universal concepts, and the nature of such individual human beings as are found alongside them might be thought to be determined with reference to these concepts. The fact that the universals involved here are human virtues makes this insight especially palpable: the poem dramatizes for us what individual people are like in terms of universal "states" (*habitus*, 1106a10).[30] Even if different universal concepts (personifications) are needed for the "advice to rulers" as compared with the "court of Love" dimensions of the poem, they remain the means whereby our ethical understanding may be advanced (or not, as the case may be).

So how do the various groups or individuals fare in this poetic court? The king of Navarre, while his portrait is tinged with humor, is flatteringly represented as attended by all the virtues and counseled by the intellectual ones. According to the poem's allegorical logic, these establish a framework for good government and the good ruler will attain *bonneürté* provided he practices them. The distinction between the active and the contemplative life might be thought to favor Machaut, who, as a clerkly author, would be in a position to lay claim to the latter. The Guillaume persona, on the other hand, is hounded and condemned by Bonneürté as someone fundamentally unworthy. Capable as the supreme good is of taking on many different forms, his particularity remains one of obstinate exclusion from it. And where the court of Love is concerned, the relation to *bonneürté* is also a negative one. Aristotle dismisses pleasure (which Grosseteste translates as *delectacio*), except for that of the mind (*speculacio, contemplacio*), as not conducive to happiness. And the debate at the heart of both *Jugement* poems—who suffered more, the knight whose lady left him or the lady whose knight died?—involves lovers competing over how *little* happiness they get. The character who embodies happiness, Dame Bonneürté, is in the bizarre position of condemning Machaut for failing to record how *un*happy women can be.

I said at the outset of this chapter that the roll call of the virtues in the *Navarre* is elastic and seems to fluctuate according to whether government or love is uppermost. This divergence is at its most striking, then, with relation to the supreme good, *bonneürté* itself. Good lovers and the narrator stand in a negative relation to happiness, and as such are the opposite of good clerks and rulers, whose relation to it is positive. In the remainder of this chapter I shall look more closely at this negative dimension of Machaut's didacticism, the "one of exclusion," as it is realized in the figures of the narrator and of lovers.

The Excluded One of the Narrator

As in other *dits* by Machaut, there is a distinction in the *Navarre* between an authoritative author-function and his comic fall guy and alter ego. This is a feature of his writing that has attracted extensive critical attention, and so as not to labor the obvious I shall focus here only on how it relates to the problem of happiness.

Happiness, *bonneürté*, the poem (like Aristotle) tells us, is achieved by practicing the virtues, and the best happiness comes from pursuing the intellectual virtues. But if the *Navarre*'s author, who is after all responsible for conceiving the poem as a kind of *Ethics*, might reasonably lay claim to the intellectual virtues, the conduct of his persona falls short even of the moral ones. At these extremes, author and narrator are poles apart. The problem arises, though, that this division is not consistently maintained.

The author's claim to set forth a universal scheme of virtues wavers in and out of credibility as his persona's shortcomings constantly intrude onto the intellectual pretensions of his poem and push it toward burlesque.

The incident that sets the tone for the whole poem is the sequence near its beginning where the author-protagonist first meets Dame Bonne-ürté. The poet has unheroically shut himself indoors while France suffers the ravages of plague, war, and other calamities. But now calm prevails, and he goes hare-coursing. He is summoned to the company of a grand lady, whom he at first fails to see. Such indifference toward happiness is significant, and will be a subject of lasting reproach. When he is brought before her, he acknowledges her only as a courtly lady to whom he owes gallant service; there is a hint of courtship to the relationship on both sides. She also recognizes him, however, as a scholar and somewhat incongruously declares that she is going to make a game of him. Legal language is humorously bandied about. Is the trial really only a joke? When she accuses him of having written disobligingly of women, Machaut asks her to specify the passage she means. His *oeuvre*, he says, is too vast for him to reread; and even if he were to, he couldn't be expected to read it with her eyes. Their relationship now looks like that between the intellectual and the censor—the authorities did, after all, burn books convicted of error, and this looks like the fate awaiting Machaut himself. In response the lady summarizes the earlier *Jugement* and insists he retract it. Machaut, however, prefers to proceed to trial, where he will vigorously undertake his own defense. During this four-hundred-line passage the relationship between the two characters has been constantly shifting. The persona of the narrator is both an unworthy figure ignorant of the supreme good and a scholar who punctures the pretensions of a bogus and oppressive authority. He both is drawn to utmost felicity and flirts with a self-important courtly lady who is determined to bully him. Neither perspective triumphs over the other. The resistant particularity of the narrator excludes the possibility of his achieving happiness while at the same time lowering reflection on happiness to an unseemly confrontation between a particular man and woman.

The protagonist's subsequent behavior throughout the proceedings amplifies this burlesque tone. He proves unreceptive to all the arguments of the virtues. Indeed, he becomes more and more obnoxious as the trial proceeds, alternately fawning on the personifications with hypocritical praise for their fine speeches and deriding them for failing to address the issue, or for playing straight into his hands. His manners degenerate completely in the altercation with Prudence/Franchise, where he launches into an attack on women as inconstant, superficial, and incapable of commitment, and then refuses to listen to the storm of protest that his onslaught provokes. What these altercations effect, then, is that (from the narrator's perspective at least) the personifications are no longer universal abstract qualities but individual, flawed women. His refusal to accept them as authoritative means that, indeed, they do not *seem* authoritative to the reader. As in the initial encounter with Dame Bonneürté, the point of resistance to thinking in universal terms becomes identified with whatever constitutes sexual difference.

The author has been put on trial for defaming women, and the narrator's behavior during it shows that he is incapable of respecting them. As a misogynist, he can (apparently) be neither virtuous nor happy. Although Dame Bonneürté pursues him, it is not with the view to imparting any of her nature to him. She is the embodiment of happiness, but her sole intent, as he sees it, is to rejoice in her own merriment "and plunge me into melancholy" ("et moy mettre en merencolie," *JRN*, 591). It seems that Machaut agrees with Aristotle that there is no single, universal model of happiness. What the courtly tradition contributes to Aristotelian *Ethics* is the recognition that its universality is blocked not just by the differences in particular experiences of happiness but also by the partiality that results from sexual difference.

The Excluded One of the Grieving Lover

Dame Bonneürté dislikes and wants to confound the narrator's misogyny. However, this does not mean that she rewards lovers. Although Happiness is the plaintiff in the case and her attendants are all witnesses in her favor, the sole purpose of the trial is to establish just *how* unhappy a grief-stricken woman can be. In taking up his own defense, the narrator must lodge the converse claim that men are unhappier still. Both parties compete in the court of Happiness in order, paradoxically, to have their exclusion from her realm recognized. At the core of the text, then, is this impasse, where the demand to have one's pain acknowledged is constantly brought up short against the other's inability, or refusal, adequately to concede it. Love, though it might seem to be the opposite of misogyny, is equally snagged on the thorn of sexual difference and positively exults in its misery.

In the *Jugement du roi de Behaigne* the tales of woe that prompt the proceedings in the *Navarre*—the narrative of the lady whose lover was killed in combat and the knight whose lady left him—are repeated again and again. Immediately striking about these stories is their lack of reciprocity: one is neither the same as nor the converse of the other. The lady had a perfect knight, but he died. The knight thought his lady was lovely, but he was deceived, and she left him. In a sense the grieving woman retains her object even in its loss: her attachment to the value of her lover is unshaken. But from another point of view, she has lost it more definitively, to death. Since her knight was everything to her, she has lost her reason for living. This is why, in her view, she suffered more. The knight's case is different. He was entranced by his lady's beauty and thought she loved him, so when she leaves him he suffers what Žižek calls "the loss of loss": he has lost not just the object but also his desire for it.[31] If the bereaved lady has been deprived of her future happiness, the knight has been robbed of his past, for he feels stripped of the joy he thought he had. There seems, to cite the Lacanian tag,[32] to be "no sexual relation" in the *Jugement* poems because there is no common obstacle for men and women to overcome; instead, the impossibility of union is figured differently, via a different impediment, for the two sexes.

The effect of misogyny is to reify sexual difference, instituting "women" as categorically different from (and inferior to) men; and in the *Behaigne* it seems that the pain of love has the same net effect. Despite the lopsidedness of the knight's and the lady's narratives, the knight is the subject of both: they are both mainly about what a fine, noble, loving, and so on, man he was. In both stories, too, the woman turns out to be lacking; she is left deprived of her reason for living in the first story; and she turns out never to have had any substance in the second. In the *Behaigne*, then, gendered identities are enforced through repetition of the same basic narratives, which are then reiterated with variations in the *Navarre*. The association between gender, citation, performance, and melancholy, which Judith Butler has enabled us to see as defining of heterosexuality, is also legible in the *Navarre* where both parties constitute their identity as "male" or as "female" by repeatedly reenacting their loss of their loved one before the judge.[33]

In between writing the *Behaigne* and the *Navarre*, Machaut composed two *dits,* in each of which the central metaphor escalates the difference between men and women into one between species. In the *Dit du lyon,* a lion understandably finds it difficult to make headway with a lady;

in the *Dit de l'alerion*, a human narrator complains at his inability to retain the love of a series of birds of prey. Do the different relations to discourse of male and female characters in the *Navarre* continue to solidify gender difference as categorical? The female personifications and the male narrator cite different kinds of stories in defense of their positions, the personifications drawing on classical or other clerical narratives and the narrator citing recent vernacular literature and anecdote. Sylvia Huot has suggested, too, that male and female characters evince different forms of melancholy in the *Navarre*, the men dramatizing it, the women succumbing to it.[34]

It seems to me nevertheless that Machaut's treatment of gender and sexual difference in the *Navarre* operates differently from the way it does in the earlier *dits* and that, in his careful negotiation of particularity and universality, he is wary of abstracting from individual identity to a category such as gender. Although gender differences are humorously acknowledged, the individual suffering lover is ultimately defined not in function of a universal but by exclusion from it. By way of preface to developing this position, I shall take a detour through the critique of Judith Butler made by Elizabeth Wright in the course of her typically illuminating exposition of Lacan's views on sexual difference. Lacan's well-known if still baffling formulas represent masculinity and femininity as internally inconsistent and mutually incompatible ways in which speaking beings locate themselves in relation to the universal symbolic order.[35] A result of this, as Wright points out, is that the shards of discourse repeated in what Butler calls "citation" are not clean-edged, self-contained units. On the contrary, as Wright puts it, " 'Citation' involves an incalculable private element and it is this which can make visible the 'deceit' of the symbolic. If the real is indeed that within which subjects carry out the performances that the symbolic has provided, then, as Lacan's formulae illustrate, the real will cross the binary of feminine and masculine unexpectedly within those constitutive repetitions."[36] Gender identity, Wright is arguing, is as much undone as done by citation because the element that returns is not a constitutive element of either identity (or a necessarily visible part of the citation) but the trace or remainder of the impossibility of the sexual relation that each individual bears as his or her own private scar. If the *Behaigne*, the *Alerion*, and the *Dit du lyon* set out to recast this impossibility in the consoling form of gender opposition, the form that misogyny likewise embraces, the *Navarre* as a whole is more subtle. Unlike the *Behaigne*, it opposes not a man and a woman but Guillaume and a series of personified abstractions

who, while feminine, are also at least potentially the qualities internal to
Guillaume (and the judge). Sexual difference, that is, lies as much within
as between individuals; it is, as Wright puts it, "the real [that] will cross
the binary of feminine and masculine unexpectedly."

The story-telling competition that unfolds in the *Navarre* tracks this
private scar of sexual difference borne by all human beings, male and female. The grief that the other cannot or will not hear is the "incalculable
private element" in any one speaker, his or her resistant singularity that
exposes the "deceit of the symbolic," the pretension of language to universalize and explain. In Dame Bonneürté's court, that is, the supreme
good to which lovers aspire is to be acknowledged as suffering the greatest
incommunicable pain. Each speaker lodges a bid to be recognized in his
or her profound unhappiness. Submission to Happiness consists in exclusion from it, at least as it is publicly understood. In addition to taking the
Ethics into the domain of sexual difference, Machaut moves it beyond the
pleasure principle.

The Wandering Remainder and the Worm in the Tongue

The movement of the "incalculable private element" that undoes symbolic cohesion or intelligibility, and thus challenges universal categories
(like gender), can be traced through the various stories that Guillaume
and the personifications cite in support of their respective positions. In-
eluctably, as the tales are told, these positions shift. The initial opposition,
inherited from the *Jugement du roi de Behaigne*, is between grief at death
and grief at infidelity. But as the stories accumulate they acquire surplus
features that cause the whole debate to drift from its starting point. Thematically, the surplus elements are the death of the woman (instead of, or
as well as, that of the man); the infidelity of the man (instead of, or as well
as, that of the woman); and madness. The *exemplum* of Dido, for instance,
is told by Pais to illustrate the "woman's" point of view and is therefore
supposed to confirm the greater intensity of grief of a woman whose lover
has died. However, it does nothing of the kind. Instead, we have a man
who is unfaithful (Aeneas leaves Dido), and a woman, Dido, who goes
mad and kills herself. By the end of the trial, the stories—those of Pyramus
and Thisbe, Hero and Leander—involve the deaths of *both* the man *and*
the woman. This constant redrawing of the boundary lines enables the
defendant to claim, with some justice, that his opponents' stories don't

support their case, even the reverse. With equal force, they repudiate his stories as implausible, tasteless, and open to question. These exchanges raise interesting questions that are in turn debated. Is Love subject to Nature or the other way round? Is death the ultimate affliction or a merciful release? Is madness a form of suffering or a means of escape from it? As the citation of models continues from one side to the other, the boundary between the genders keeps shifting. By the end, all are emphatically seeking to demonstrate the capacity for love and suffering—for love *as* suffering—in which death, loss, and madness can afflict us all.

One sequence of tales strikes me as especially revealing. Machaut's story of the clerk of Orléans is initially adduced as an example of a man grieving at female betrayal, but it veers around to focus on a man driven mad by suffering.[37] The blow of losing his beloved is so terrible that he loses his mind, tears off his clothes, appears deaf, never speaks except to rave unintelligibly, sleeps only on dunghills, refuses food and drink, and rampages over the countryside unless forcibly restrained, living in this way for twenty years. This story provokes an onslaught of criticism from the virtues, which comes to a head with Honnesté (Decorum) demanding to know how the clerk can be accounted unhappy. Once he has gone mad, isn't he just following his own desires?

He has lost his memory, judgment, social sense, and understanding; from which one can clearly infer that there was nothing that he wanted except having his heart set on the great follies that he was committing. When he used to sleep on a dunghill, this was his relaxation, this his bed, this in every respect his delight, where he slept most refreshingly.

> Il avoit perdu sa memoire,
> sens, maniere, et entendement;
> dont on puet vëoir clerement
> qu'il n'avoit point de volonté,
> fors que le cuer entalenté
> des grans soties qu'il faisoit.
> Quant en .i. fumier se gisoit,
> c'estoit sa pais; c'estoit ses lis;
> c'estoit de tous poins ses delis
> ou il dormoit a grant repos. (*JRN*, 2579–99)

Guillaume's reply is that madness is not a relief from pain but an expression of it, and to justify this claim he tells what I find the most interesting of all this poem's *exempla*. Pointing out that the first cause underlies all subsequent causes and their effects, he stresses the importance of locating it. Remove the first cause, and the subsequent causes will then disappear too. Take the case of a mad dog. What causes the madness is a worm that has pierced the dog's tongue. This prevents the dog from eating and drinking; as a result, the dog goes mad; when it is so mad that it can no longer bark is the time to worry that it will bite. If the worm were to be taken out, the dog would recover. The same is true of the clerk.

And thus I say that this clerk was struck through with just such an obscure sickness; and so I say to you that the blow of this great ill that his body felt was what reduced him to the state he was in.

> Aussi di je que cils clers poins
> fu d'une maladie obscure;
> dont je vous di que la pointure
> dou grant mal que ses corps sentoit
> le tenoit en point qu'il estoit. (*JRN*, 2685–90)

This "worm in the tongue" is a graphic image of the invisible lesion that, as Machaut insists, leads to visible signs being misinterpreted.[38] The clerk's worm in the tongue is a pain so intense as to be incommunicable even to himself, since it disguises itself from him as derangement. All of the characters have a worm in the tongue that impedes their communication and binds each of them to his or her own inadmissible, unique partiality.

Conclusion

The *Jugement dou roy de Navarre* proposes a public world where the supreme good of *bonneürté* is revered. The political and contemplative lives are alike positively subject to it. However, the narrator is an instance of a particular subject who defines the rule of Happiness by defying it. Likewise, the lovers in the exemplary stories are subject to Happiness only in the sense that they measure themselves by the extent of their exception from it. Like the worm in the tongue, private passion is a cause legible only in secondary causes and their effects. It is the point of singularity that marks a gap or failure in the universal concept and means that, for lovers, supreme good is the same as unspeakable woe.

In pursuing this singular "one of exclusion" the *Jugement dou roy de Navarre* may be responding to contemporary thinking. From Aquinas onward, and gaining ground in the works of Duns Scotus and Ockham, there is anxiety (as we saw in the Introduction) about the way, following Aristotle, uniqueness is lost to knowledge because things are known to us only via the generalizing grid of language. The particularity of an individual thing, that is, is known to us by virtue of the universal categories abstracted from it, while its singularity remains unknown. As Pierre-Christophe Cathelineau puts it: "The core of Aristotelian ontology remains essentially that of the individual uncognizable in itself and known only through the language of knowledge as expressed through genera and species."[39] In reaction to this, philosophers speculated whether we might, despite Aristotle's assertions, be able to know a singular thing—the "this-ness" (*haecceitas*) of a thing, as Duns Scotus was the first to call it. Singularity might shadow the domain of human intellectual understanding while remaining excluded from it, but it might be available to us to intuit. Machaut's poems suggest awareness of contemporary preoccupation with *cognitio singularis*, even though he traces singularity in relation to bodily drives—sexuality, madness, and death—which is *not* what Scholastic philosophers are after when they talk about "this-ness."[40]

What are the implications for the *Jugement dou roy de Navarre* as a didactic poem? The personal is found to be discrepant with the general and the public good at variance with private (dis)satisfactions; but the inadmissible, embarrassing, and comic incapacity of the intimate to find its place within the institutional points to it as the basis of truth. Didacticism, as a result, is founded on the exemplary value of the unsaid, of what cannot be told. When Raison speaks of "those who are secretly wise" (*JRN*, 3941) in the contemplative life, and the consequent need to advertise it to others, maybe her remarks speak to the secrecy of all of our mental processes. Similarly, Bonneürté's shirt, called Franchise, respects the incommunicability of love's secrets in such a way as to found knowledge on silence:

[Her shirt] is called Franchise in order to make secret lovers free and to enrich them with Seriousness on behalf of Silence with the agreement of Knowledge.

> [Sa chemise] est appellée Franchise
> pour secrés amans afranchir
> et de Sobreté enrichir
> en la partie de Silence
> parmi l'acort de Congnoissance. (*JRN*, 4081–84)

If knowledge is based on silence, it is not going to be found in language. By the same token, "realism" becomes the domain of the unexpressed but intuited singular, which alone is "real," while the reality of the universal "one," whether Boethian or Aristotelian, is found to be merely a constructed, verbal fiction that has more in common with the nominalism of a thinker such as Ockham.[41] What one man calls "unhappiness" another may call "happiness," and one person's view of "woman" may be rejected by another.

Although the argument I have put forward in this chapter sounds abstract, it is in fact exactly the contrary. My point is rather that Machaut, in common with other fourteenth-century thinkers, sees shortcomings in an abstractive concept of the universal. He sets out to anchor knowledge and reality in the particular and the singular, while at the same time conceding that these are what subvert or limit thought. When the universal is put on trial in the *Navarre*, it is the singular one that wins.

Understanding, Remembering, and Forgetting in Froissart's
Le Joli Buisson de Jonece

FROISSART MAY NOT BE the greatest poet of the fourteenth century—that title probably goes to Machaut—but his *dits* are uniquely powerful as a result of the way they combine, or collide, intellectual schemes, narrative invention, visual images, and intricate patterns of sound. The impact of his works relies not on his exquisite command of any of these elements individually but rather on the exhilaration of the complex play between them. This chapter is about the most ambitious of his *dits amoureux*, the *Joli buisson de Jonece*, which, seemingly composed in late 1373, was probably also his last. I concentrate on the place referred to in its title, the curiously named "merry bush" in which the major part of the poem takes place.

A dream-vision poem in which a shrub provides a seriocomic setting for a farrago of erotic, epistemological, and theological concerns, the *Joli buisson de Jonece* clearly acknowledges the tradition of the *Roman de la rose*. In the branches of this bush Froissart sets out both to relive youthful passion and to fathom his own nature as part of the cosmos. Eventually he renounces sexual love and redirects his devotion to the Virgin, under whose influence the bush is reconfigured as, among other things, the Tree of Jesse from which she sprang. This chapter, then, has points of contact with the *Breviari d'amor* (see Chapter 1), in which thought is likewise mapped onto the structure of a tree. The way the *buisson* changes as it passes from secular to religious registers also shares common ground with the *Ovide moralisé* (see Chapter 2), on which Froissart arguably draws (see below). In his probing of universality and singularity Froissart probably has most in common with Machaut. While in Machaut the singular "I" defines universality in terms of its exclusion from it, in Froissart, it does so

└ through its own voluntary eclipse. In the "merry bush of Youth" Froissart discovers both how difficult it can be to remember and—at least where certain experiences are concerned—how some things are best forgotten. He concludes, not without humor, that some aspects of his self have to be consigned to oblivion for the sake of his soul.

The treatment of memory in the *Joli buisson de Jonece* is made more complex by the fact that Froissart is both reviving allegedly intimate memories and rewriting an earlier poem.[1] Just as the *Jugement dou roy de Navarre* recapitulates and reverses Machaut's earlier *Jugement du roi de Behaigne*, so the *Joli buisson* reworks and ultimately rejects Froissart's *Espinette amoureuse* of 1369. In the *Espinette* the first-person narrator reaches the age of fourteen and experiences the confusions of his first love affair: a tangle of joys and pains, flowers and thorns, emblematized by the little hawthorn of the title. In the *Buisson* he has matured to a sober thirty-five. Despondent at his inability to write, he is advised by Philosophy to look at a portrait of his lady that he put away ten years ago; poetic creativity is rekindled, and he produces the first of a flurry of *forme fixe* lyrics. Froissart then has a dream in which the goddess Venus, who had assumed guardianship of him by the little hawthorn tree in the *Espinette*, escorts him to the *buisson* and leaves him with his double or mirror image, Jonece, custodian of the bush. Here Froissart revisits his earlier courtship, starting again in adolescence, only to find his desire more acute but just as inconclusive as in the earlier work. As Froissart wittily reviews questions of love and desire under the tutelage of Jonece, and later of one the bush's principal denizens, Desir, it is unsettling to discover that none of the "memories" he is apparently revisiting quite matches the earlier poem. Desir wishes him to use his experiences in the bush as the basis for a didactic poem about love (*JBJ*, 3093–97). But Froissart has found the intensity of his feelings overwhelmingly painful. On waking he recognizes their folly and recasts some of the lyric poetry he had composed in the bush as a *lai* to the Virgin. His reward for putting behind him his past love and its poetry is that now he can truly become a didactic poet. The rubrics, indexes, and explicits of both the manuscripts that transmit the *Joli buisson de Jonece* attest his success, since they remind their readers that Froissart is a priest and alert them to the *moralité* as well as the amorous sentiment to be found in the texts.[2]

Froissart's fascination with memory and forgetting shows him to be in tune with fourteenth-century thought. We have already seen memory used to question the relationship between mind and body in the *Pèlerinage de vie humaine*. But Froissart's treatment of the theme is not Augustinian, like Deguileville's. It is closer to Scholastic debates that used Aristotle's *On Memory* to explore questions of oneness, both universal and singular.[3] For Aristotle, memory is a bodily phenomenon, since it is a product of time and the passage of time is perceived by the senses.[4] It is the imprint (or "sensible species") of a particular experience that is only brought into the sphere of the intellect by the mental act of reminiscence. All animate species have memories, but man alone has the rational powers that enable him to reminisce, that is, to engage in the intellectual activity of calling memories to mind. Medieval discussions of memory continue the distinction between memory and reminiscence.[5] However, Christian commentators found unacceptable Aristotle's view that memory, as a bodily deposit, would die with the body. For example, they believed in the afterlife as a time for retribution; for this, the soul would need to recall its sins after death. If memories were to survive the body, wouldn't they need to be intelligible, mental, and universal? But if so, how could we remember singular things, given that, as Aristotle asserted, only universals are intelligible, while the singular is strictly outside the field of what can directly be known? Should one argue, against Aristotle, that memory can somehow both be intelligible and nevertheless retain knowledge of the particular? In this way, the nature of memory provided a testing ground for debates about the relationship between universality and singularity in the field of knowledge. The solutions philosophers devised to these questions were, as we shall see, extremely relevant to the kind of poetry Froissart was writing, since they focus on the act of remembering as an experience that can itself be remembered. Short-circuiting the opposition between memory and reminiscence, philosophers focus on subjectivity as constructed through a particular subject's memorial acts, while allowing that the particular *objects* of memory sink into oblivion.

These ideas will be developed below. I shall show how the implications for the subject of memory and forgetting are especially acute when encountered in the context of a dream, and I shall compare Froissart's nightmarish experiences with the famous "dream of the burning child" discussed by Freud. But first I shall consider the *joli buisson* of the *dit*'s title, since not only is it the setting of Froissart's dream, it is also presented as the place where thought is mapped.

The *Joli Buisson* as a Place of Thought:
The "Maistre en Philozophie"

The description of the *joli buisson* confirms that while, as Aristotle said, "without an image thinking is impossible,"[6] some thoughts are decidedly harder to visualize than others. In becoming the "merry bush" of the *dit*'s title, the little hawthorn tree of the *Espinette amoureuse* has inflated alarmingly into a huge spherical growth that has no stem or trunk (*JBJ*, 1380) and floats above the ground in a shimmering blue-white haze (*JBJ*, 1409–13), a model of elusiveness and mutability (*JBJ*, 1417–18). Wherever Froissart stands he seems to be at its midpoint (*JBJ*, 1395–402); the more he looks at it, the less he can take it in (*JBJ*, 1374–75). Disappointingly, but perhaps not surprisingly, there is no attempt to depict the bush in the text's manuscripts.[7]

Drawing on the instruction he received, Jonece tells us, from his "maistre en philozophie" (*JBJ*, 1559), Jonece informs the dreamer of the bush's nature. The bush, according to this teacher, has universal significance. It is a figure of the firmament, and in its shade lies the world of nature with all the various species of creature it contains. Comprising seven branches that correspond to the seven planets and to the seven ages of man, it also systematizes all of the possible qualities that humankind can pass through in the course of time:

I often heard him [= my philosophy master] compare the dome of the firmament, as we habitually see it, to a bush that is perennially green. And I have it well in mind that, in order more completely to explain his thinking, he figured the little leaves of this bush as proportional to the stars that are beyond number. In addition, he included in his teaching the shade under the bush, which he generalized as, and converted into, the world of Nature, which . . . gives to every individual, male or female, the distinguishing characteristics that are common to them, so that each has its own quality. Proceeding to a moral reading of the above figure, in order for it to be the more complete, he located as many as seven branches in this bush—as my memory of the astronomer serves me—which he made out to be so resourceful and so masterly that everything that could be born or be included under their sway depended on them. And he represented these clear, distinct branches as the seven planets. . . .

> Pluisieurs fois li [le maistre en philozophie] o comprendre
> le firmament, qui est reons
> 1565   que coustumierement veons,
> a .i. buisson vert en tous tamps.
> Et encores sui bien sentans

que, pour plus plainnement parfaire
l'entension de son afaire,
1570   il figurait tout par raison
les foellettes de ce buisson
as estoilles qui sont sans nombre.
Avoec ce, il comprendoit l'ombre
dou buisson, qu'il universoit
1575   a Nature et l'i conversoit,
la quele . . .
1582   . . . donne a cascun et cascune
sa proprieté si commune
que cascuns a se qualité.
1585   Revenans a moralité
de la figure dessus fette,
a fin qu'elle soit plus parfette,
en ce buisson jusqu'a .vii. branches
mettoit, selonc les ramembranches
1590   que j'ai del astrologiien,
et celles de ci grant engien
et si magistraus faisoit estre
que trestout ce qui pooit nestre
ne desous leurs eles comprendre,
1595   a e lles estoit a reprendre.
Et ces branches cleres et nettes
figuroit il as .vii. planetes. . . . (*JBJ*, 1563–97)

Jonece's exposition here is an amalgam of metaphysical and rhetorical terms. The first half (to line 1584) presents the bush as pedagogical device devised by his teacher to explain the makeup of the cosmos. The second proceeds to "moralize" it as the seven planets and the variations in their influence on which all the ages of mortal life depend. The rhyme *branches : ramembranches* (*JBJ*, 1589–90) evokes the rhetorical use of places as mnemonic aids, suggesting that the "merry bush" is also a device for "placing" groups of attributes in a numbered sequence.[8] So the *buisson* is a way of representing both the eternal structure of the universe and the time-bound experience of man, both abstract metaphysics and embodied perception. The framing of the account with references to Jonece delving into his memories shows to what extent a person's capacity to understand universal being is conditioned by the vagaries of his subjective situation. While this reflects the turn toward psychology taken by the "universals debate" in the fourteenth century, it also leavens the passage's didacticism with irony as the reader is led to doubt the credentials of either Jonece or Froissart as reliable guides to the higher understanding purportedly disclosed in the bush. Indeed, on the face of things, Youth's merry bush is an incongruous place to find universal enlightenment!

The presence of irony is confirmed by the uncertain use (or misuse) of Scholastic vocabulary. First we are told that the bush represents the heavens. The expression "l'entension de son afaire" could simply mean the teacher's "intent," his "meaning," but *intentio* designates the way (such as universal concepts) the intellect directs itself to a thing, and *son afaire* would then designate the conceptual content of the bush/cosmos.[9] Next we learn how Jonece's teacher commented on the shade under the bush ("l'ombre dou buisson"), which he "comprehended," "universaliz-ing" it as and "converting" it to the sublunar order of Nature. The verb *comprendre* (*JBJ*, 1573) might correspond in philosophical usage to *compre-hendere* (as opposed to *apprehendere*) where it can mean to understand something exhaustively, rather than to perceive it confusedly or partially, or by analogy with something else. Given that the human intellect cannot fully directly cognize either singulars or matter, such comprehension is beyond its scope—human knowledge is inevitably based primarily in our conceptual apparatus, our reception of form.[10] Comprehension in this to-talizing sense is precisely what is placed out of reach by our reliance on universals (invoked in the following line). So to claim, as Jonece seems to do, that his teacher "could fully comprehend the shade under the bush and universalized it under the concept of Nature" may be a contradiction in terms—that is, if *universer* does indeed mean "understand in universal terms."

A difficulty here is that *universer* seems not to be attested anywhere but in this passage and may simply be a made-up word; certainly the pre-tentious rhyme *universoit* : *conversoit* (*JBJ*, 1574–75) suggests a tongue-in-cheek attitude to Scholastic terminology.[11] Is Froissart poking fun at Jonece for his shaky memory of his schooldays, at his dream persona for mistaking what Jonece told him, or at his own capacity as a poet to record what he learned in his dream? Whichever of these possibilities is the case, the irony continues with the word *conversoit*. A technical term in a number of Scholastic disciplines, *convertere/conversio* can refer (among other things) to the rhetorical transformation of one structure into another, or a logical operation involving the derivation of one proposition from another (e.g., "no man is a stone" can be converted to "no stone is a man"). Aquinas also speaks of knowledge as necessarily resulting from the "con-version" of mental images into intelligible species.[12] The expression "tout par raison" a few lines earlier (*JBJ*, 1570) might simply mean "quite reasonably" (which is how Fourrier glosses it), but could it also mean "in strict proportion (as part of an argument by analogy)" and thus suggest understanding by recourse to conversion. The point of Jonece's master's teaching would appear to be that he can only "fully comprehend" his object of knowledge if he compares it with or transforms it into something else, which would again be a *contre sens*.

The playful tone becomes more overt with the introduction of Nature, who has the semicomic role assigned to her by Jean de Meun in the *Roman de la rose*. She never gets a day off (*JBJ*, 1579–80) but is constantly busy assigning to all individuals their *propriété commune* (*JBJ*, 1582–83). Here the use of Scholastic language gets if anything more vexed. *Proprietas* is one of the Aristotelian concepts that Porphyry sets out to define in the *Isagoge* (§56); he distinguishes four senses of the term, of which the most significant is that which defines a species by the fact that it belongs necessarily to all the members of that species and to no other beings. Jonece appears to use the word *propriété* in this sense, since it is said to be common to *cascun* and *cascune*, that is, to be what unites individuals, male and female, in a particular species.[13] But when we are then told that *cascun* has its own *qualité* (*JBJ*, 1584), emphasis seems to pass instead to the individual. For Aristotle (*Categories*, 8b25ff.), *qualitas* is one of the nine categories of accident, the one which encapsulates the "what-kind-ness" of a substance; it comprises such characteristics as states, conditions, abilities, affections, color, shape, and so on. That *qualité* in line 1584 refers to what distinguishes one individual from another is confirmed when Jonece glosses the seven branches of the bush as the seven ages of man. Governed by the seven planetary influences, these ages group all the various qualities that can be associated with an individual man in the course of his life, and that characterize him *as* an individual within the species "man." As his exposition advances, then, Jonece's attention shifts away from the world of substance under the bush (all the identifiable species of creature that live in its shade, in the domain of Nature), and turns instead to their varying accidents. This switch concords with the bush's floating structure and shimmering indeterminacy of color, which can be seen as inviting—or challenging—the reader to visualize the fluctuations of accidental qualities.

It seems, then, that the merry bush is being proposed as a version of Porphyrian tree: one that maps not the category of substance (Porphyry's own example, see Chapter 1) but rather that of *qualitas*. Unlike the resplendent "albre d'amor" of divine Love in the *Breviari*, Porphyry's tree has here been diminished, trivialized, and rendered comic as the jolly shrub of human mutability. A Porphyrian tree of quality is, of course, highly apposite to personification allegory, since most of the personified abstractions that people this and other *dits* are qualities in this sense. Venus, one of the planets and hence equated with one of the bush's branches, has already made her appearance in the poem. Jonece, guardian of the bush, is likewise an "age of man," and the other figures Froissart meets in the bush are further expressions of human conditions, states, capacities, or affects, such as the "damsels" serving his Lady: Maniere, Atemprance, and so on (*JBJ*, 2406ff.). When the poet receives instruction on the meaning and structure of the *buisson*, therefore, this is also a semi-comic, self-reflexive move to represent to him the genre in which he is composing. The whole passage illustrates that medieval allegory is, as Matthew Bardell puts it, "a privileged way both of expressing thought and of thinking about expression."[14]

This account of the bush is ascribed to a philosophy master and recorded by a poet, and so it is not surprising that it veers between metaphysics, epistemology, rhetoric, and poetics. Its initial offer of comprehension surpassing the human intellect is retrenched to one of universal intellection that proceeds by proportion and conversion. This in turn is framed by comic reminders of how difficult it is to remember things, so that the primary condition of universal understanding becomes the quality of the individual mind attempting that understanding. As the passage develops, the world of substance under the tree is metaphorically overshadowed by the ramifications of mutable attributes that are its branches. These at least, it is implied, might be able to be memorized, or else be translated into the poetic conventions of a *dit amoureux*. This passage, then, both epitomizes and ironizes the principal themes of this book; Froissart's *joli buisson* resonates not just with other *dits* involving garden settings but also with other didactic trees, philosophical and memorial. The merry bush as a place of thought shifts unsteadily between notions of oneness as cosmic, universal, and singular, relying as it does so on appeal to a scarcely envisionable visual image in which to "place" a skein of poetico-philosophical ideas.

The Joli Buisson as Conceptual "Philosophical Tree"

The Porphyrian tree recast as "albre d'amor" in the *Breviari d'amor* is hard to visualize because it is simultaneously right way up and upside down, singular and plural, sprouting from roots top and bottom and from its center. Froissart's dream of a rootless, floating system of branches with no trunk and constantly changing colors makes his version of Porphyry's tree just as difficult to picture, but very different as a place of thought. Froissart probably didn't know the *Breviari*, which was not diffused in Northern France. I think, however, that the mutability of his "philosophical tree" owes much to the *Ovide moralisé*, in particular the episode in Book IV where Perseus wins the golden tree from Atlas. The moralist's historical gloss suggests that Atlas is a precursor of Jonece's "maistre en philozophie":

He was a master of philosophy. He knew so much of the art of astronomy that he knew how the whole firmament was ordered and how it moved.

> Mestres fu de philozophie.
> Tant sot de l'art d'astronomie,
> qu'il sot de tout le firmament
> l'ordenance et le mouvement. (*OM*, IV, 6304–6)

The way the gloss subsequently develops confirms that Froissart knew this episode and offers more pointers on how to read the *buisson* as an "arbre de philozophie."

First, the moralist explains that the reason Atlas was said to carry the world on his head is that the tree of all philosophy was a conceptual structure:

He had a rich and worthy orchard, which is to say his heart or his books, where the whole art of philosophy was freely planted, which is signified by the golden tree.

> Un vergier ot riche et honeste,
> c'est son cuer ou ce sont si livre,
> ou plantee estoit a delivre
> toute l'art de philozophie,
> qui l'arbre doré signifie. (*OM*, IV, 6313–17)

Winning the tree means coming to resemble Atlas in wisdom (*OM*, IV, 6327); to do so, one must concentrate "on learning philosophy" ("en aprendre philozophie," *OM*, IV, 6330). The "arbre de philozophie" in the *Ovide moralisé* is thus mental and internal. It maps a person's inner conceptual grasp of the world (unlike the tree in the *Breviari*, which is presented as a guide to the world's actual structure). Read in this light, the outline of Froissart's *buisson* would correspond not so much with the universe as with a person's mental apparatus laboring to understand the universe. The formlessness of the bush might then reflect not just the shaky reliability of Jonece's recall, or Froissart's recording, or both, but the purely mental or verbal character of the *philozophie* purveyed by Jonece's *maistre*. And the slippage between ontology and rhetoric in Jonece's presentation would be justified (if still somewhat comic), since, if the tree represents the mental and verbal character of epistemology, by the same token it concedes the kinship between philosophy and poetry.[15]

Second, the *Ovide moralisé* tree, like the *buisson*, acts as a pivot between secular and religious perspectives. After the historical gloss, the moralist interprets the Atlas episode in Christian terms. His garden is now seen as figuring Gethsemane (*OM*, IV, 6342ff.) or the Virgin (*OM*, IV, 6499–517), and the golden tree as the Cross, the tree of life, assumed by Jesus-Perseus from Atlas, now interpreted as representing God the Father, source of all knowledge and wisdom. The tree is further read as an ethical and spiritual allegory; for example, it is said to have four main branches, which are the four cardinal virtues, and which then produce smaller branches (*OM*, IV, 6559–65). In Froissart's *dit* a similar program, although ordered differently, "moralizes" (*JBJ*, 1585) the *buisson*'s branches as the ages of man before interpreting it typologically as the burning bush or the Tree of Jesse. Read from the standpoint of this gloss, the instability of Froissart's floating bush would indicate that it is inevitably caught up in the process of mutation whereby the Christian subject reformulates pagan thought in line with the Christian revelation. When Froissart first sees it, he is unable to visualize the "form" of the bush of which he "informs" us ("Pour ymaginer de quel fourme / Li Buissons, dont je vous enfourme, / Estoit," *JBJ*, 1372–74). Its shimmering mutability would be a sign that it was already inviting him radically to recast it in something more like its true (i.e., eternal, Christological) form.[16]

The Porphyrian tree in the *Breviari* is rooted top and bottom in God's love for humanity and the human capacity to love God. It is a realist tree in the sense that it traces the flow of the divine essence through the universe. Froissart's version of Porphyry's tree has no anchorage in external reality but instead moves with every wind that blows (*JBJ*, 1419–20) until it becomes equated with "Jesse's root" ("la rachine Jessé," *JBJ*, 5396). If what it maps is "real," it is so only in the sense of being an inner, conceptual reality that is constantly shifting according to the subjective position of the one who thinks, and the language he or she uses to think with. To transcend the accidents of human perception the bush needs to articulate a language of revelation, for which Froissart reaches in the concluding *lai*:

It is the resplendent Bush that does not diminish but grows and raises up all good things according to the divine plan. And its Son, as Saint John tells us, is the pleasant fire that does not consume but illumines all hearts that put their trust in him who came down once upon a time among his children, inspiring them and breathing upon them, giving them full power to convert all errant hearts, and made them so great as to be able to speak and understand well all languages, without distortion.

> C'est li Buissons resplendissans,
> non amenrissans,
> mais croissans
> et edifians
> tous biens par divine ordenance.
> Et ses Fils, ce dist sains Jehans,
> est li feus plaisans
> non ardans,
> mais enluminans
> tous coers qui en Lui ont fiance,
> qui descendi, ja fu li tamps,
> entre ses enfans
> inspirans
> et yauls alenans,
> et leur donna plainne possance
> de convertir tous coers errans
> et les fist si grans
> que parlans
> et bien entendans
> toutes langhes sans variance. (*JBJ*, 5402–21)

The newly pious bush promises an inspired and irresistible language that will put an end to worldly error—and the anxieties of philosophy.[17]

Philozophie and the Consolation of Memory

Froissart's rapid embrace of eternity at the end of the *dit* reacts against the fascination with time and remembrance that dominate the rest of the poem. I have examined Jonece's reminiscences of his schooldays; I want to look now at the opening section where Boethius's *Consolation of Philos-ophy* is recast so as to commend memory as the crucial and consoling good.

The *dit* begins with the melancholic Froissart in dialogue with his thoughts (*JBJ*, 102) gradually personified as Philozophie (*JBJ*, 191), a name that both recalls Boethius's Philosophy and anticipates Jonece's "maistre en philozophie." Froissart is dejected because, although he feels Nature intended him to be a poet, he has lost his inspiration. Philozophie urges him to emulate the Romans, who taught their children studiously to "fathom their true nature" (*JBJ*, 118, "leur nature encerquier"): the disci-plined inquiry into (one's own) nature forms another link between this sequence and the one by the bush. Froissart really must pull himself to-gether, Philozophie chides, lest he disappoint his audience. When Froissart seizes on this as a pretext to count up the money his many patrons have given him, she sharply reminds him that reputation is worth more than financial reward. He can recover his natural talent by reflecting on the past and calling his previous creativity to mind (*JBJ*, 462–68). Elaborating via an allegory the Aristotelian distinction between reminiscence as a mental act and memory as a material trace, Philozophie directs him to seek out a portrait long since stored away in a strongbox:

"Set your thoughts on that [i.e., on remembering what you have stored]!" "Yes, lady, I am doing. What is it meant to be? By my soul, I don't know. Remind me." "Gladly I will. You must have somewhere close to you a strongbox in which long ago—more than ten years since—you placed, and I recall this well (since it's my job to talk to you about it) a beautiful and propitious image made in the likeness and the imprint of your true lady as she was then. Even if you have not since taken it out, you should still have it there. I beg you, go and find out: you know the way there well enough and you will find the image that I am describing to you on parchment, portraying her figure and her face. . . ."

          475   Or y penses.—Si fai je, dame.
                 Que voelt estre? Ne sçai, par m'ame!
                 Recordés m'ent.—Volentiers, voir.
                 Tu dois par deviers toi avoir
                 un coffret ens ou quel jadis—
          480   il y a des ans plus de dis,—
                 tu mesis, et bien m'en souvient,
                 (puis que dire le me couvient),
                 un ymage bel et propisce,
                 fait au semblant et en l'espisce
          485   que ta droite dame estoit lors.
                 Se depuis tu ne l'as trait hors,

encores le dois tu avoir.
Je t'empri, or y va savoir:
tu y sces moult bien le chemin,
490 et tu veras en parchemin
L'ymage que je te devis,
pourtraite de corps et de vis. . . . (*JBJ*, 475–92)

The *coffret* (*JBJ*, 479, "strongbox") containing the portrait echoes the *coffres* (*JBJ*, 398) where Froissart stashed his patrons' largesse, but it is also a standard image of a "treasure house" as the place where memories are stored.[18] The analogy between memory and a picture is a commonplace of medieval thought. It goes back to Aristotle, who analyzes its implications in his treatise *On Memory*: "It is clear that we must conceive that which is generated through sense-perception in the soul and that part of the body that is its seat,—viz that affection the state of which we call memory—to be some such thing as a picture" (450a 27–30).[19] Like a portrait, a memory is valued "as a likeness, and not in its own right" (*On Memory*, 451a14, "sicut imaginem et non secundum se"; cf. Froissart's term *semblant*, *JBJ*, 484).[20] Memory is produced when sense perception imprints on the mind a "sensible species" (*espisce*, *JBJ*, 484), which is then stored as a phantasm or *imago* (*ymage*, *JBJ*, 483). For Aristotle, the way we access these phantasms intellectually is by means of a chain of thought that moves backward in time, experiencing similar antecedent moments until we reach the one we are seeking (*On Memory*, 451a17–18). Similarly in the *dit* (*JBJ*, 477) the act of *recorder* or reminiscence will take Froissart to the *ymage* that is the trace in fantasy of memory's imprint; the rhyme *chemin* : *parchemin* (*JBJ*, 489–90) metaphorically casts the access of reminiscence to memory as the "path" to the "parchment" where this imprint was made. The fact that the painting is preserved on a parchment page also brings to mind the common medieval image of memory as a book (books in the Middle Ages often being stored in strongboxes).[21]

The process whereby a memory is laid down is teasingly elaborated in the next following lines when Philozophie praises the craftsman's skill in painting and recalls Froissart's role in commissioning what, it is now clear, is a portrait of his lady. When Froissart sees it, Philozophie claims, he won't fail to recognize in it his youthful inspiration. Froissart then recalls having the portrait made "by a wise and worthy painter" (*JBJ*, 533, "Par .i. pointre sage et vaillant"), wrapping it and putting it away some seven years ago. I think that these teasing allusions are a disguised form of boasting about his own creative powers, and that in retracing his steps to his memory-portrait of his lady, Froissart is also revisiting his own previous writing in her praise. The act of reconnecting with his earlier inspiration, signaled by his opening the coffer and finding in it the parchment, causes him at once to burst into a *virelay*. The *ymage* of his lady is "highly consoling" (*JBJ*, 733, "de grande consolation"), just as Achilles consoled himself with looking at Polyxena's portrait (*JBJ*, 698, "en regardant s'i console"). In this rewriting of the *Consolation of Philosophy*, what Froissart finds consoling is not his own thoughts (personified as Philozophie), still less a scheme of thought, but rather the acts of thought that are associated with the production and retrieval of memory.

This view of memory as performative is characteristic of the later Middle Ages, when Scholastic thinkers developed and radicalized the Aristotelian account. At the heart of their concern, as I have said, lay the distinction in *On Memory* between memory as a sensory trace and reminiscence as an intellectual activity; this fed directly into the medieval thinkers' difficulty in conceding that there can be no intellectual cognition of the particular experiences that are remembered. Their response was to postulate that memory *could* involve intellectual knowledge of singular events if by "memory" was meant the intellectual recall of the subject's own prior states of mind. If I remember a thing, I have to recall experiencing it, and thus its existence as a singular thing, even if I don't have intellectual knowledge of it as such. The object of memory is lost to cognition, but the experience of remembering has been preserved. By revisiting its prior acts, the subject is able to call to mind a previous encounter with a singular thing, even if the form in which it is recalled is a universal one, and thus the thing itself eclipsed.

Aquinas's own concession to the memory of singulars, when he grants that the mind may be aware of it own production of *phantasmata*, involves such a process of reflection on one's own thought processes.[22] When in the *Joli buisson de Jonece* first Philozophie and then Froissart recall having the portrait painted and put away, this double reflection on prior mental acts may be alluding to this influential account. Duns Scotus's position, described in these terms by Janet Coleman, is analogous: "When a man reminisces, he actively seeks to recall a mental image that corresponds with his continuously present universal understanding of something. He does not remember past *things* in themselves; he remembers past acts of knowing the formal aspects of things through sensible and intelligible species which represent those things in modes peculiar to active mind. He remembers only that which had and still has intelligible being for him."[23]

Memory, then, becomes the rehearsal of the mind's earlier acts. Duns Scotus's formula "I call to mind myself having seen, or having known, that you were seated" ("recordor me vidisse vel nosse te sedisse")[24] is recapitulated by Ockham: "I do not recall any such thing [as speaking, writing, disputing] except insofar as I recall myself hearing or seeing someone do them" ("De talibus [speaking, writing, disputing] non recordor nisi quatenus me recordor audivisse vel vidisse eum talia facere").[25] The use by both thinkers of the verb equivalent to Froissart's *recorder* (*JBJ*, 477) confirms that it is right to see this as meaning "remember" and not (as in Fourrier's glossary) "dire, déclarer, exposer."[26]

There are grounds, then, for seeing the Philozophie-portrait sequence in the *Joli buisson de Jonece* as reflecting not just Aristotle's *On Memory* but also later medieval developments on the same theme.[27] Throughout the episode we discover less about the portrait than about the subjective events associated with it: memory is identified as the act of remembering the act of committing something to memory. In this way, memory becomes a history of consciousness; it becomes constitutive of identity; and this explains its appeal to Froissart as a topic of first-person poetry. As Zink has put it, "[Froissart's] poems construct a representation of the self structured by the process of reminiscence, by the making present of memory to consciousness, where consciousness is nothing other than the reflection of memory."[28] Not only does Froissart remember remembering his lady, but the means whereby he does so is by remembering his own past writings. The identity recalled or reconstituted in the *dit* is that of himself as a poet.

"Bush" Versus "Portrait"

Connections between the episode of the portrait and the exposition of the bush are clearly signaled. At stake in both is access through thought ("philozophie") and memory to "nature" and thence to poetry. Yet the two scenes are also diametrically at odds. Philozophie's exhortation to look for the portrait is about intellectual understanding leading (or not leading) to memory; Jonece's reminiscences of his "maistre en philozophie" are about memory preserving (or failing to preserve) intellectual understanding. The "bush-portrait" dialectic, in other words, lies at the heart of the problematic of oneness in *Le Joli buisson de Jonece*, since it questions our capacity to know singulars and/or remember universals. To what extent can we claim universal knowledge in the present of singular events that happened in the past? Does our understanding of universals depend on contingent states that diminish our ability to remember the reasoning that would lead to them? Both aspects of this dialectic are treated with a degree of humor. As we saw, there is ineptitude, contradiction, or slippage within the teaching ascribed to the "maistre en philozophie." Likewise, Philozophie's words to Froissart about the value of memory depend on Froissart's questionable recall of Boethius; they don't deliver the promised "consolation" or the renewal of past experience. I shall here consider the dream world within the *dit* to see how it further explores, via this failed encounter of "bush" and "portrait," the one of universal understanding and that of the remembered singular.

While his dream is born of nostalgia for his boyhood, Froissart is aware that it may mislead as much as reveal:

It is everywhere said that the mental images caused by things, of which—whether they come from on high or from the depths of the abyss—one is intensely mindful, exist in their own right and are also so powerful that they often manifest themselves as apparitions in the way one mentally imagines them.

> On dist en pluiseurs nations
> que les ymaginations
> qu'on a as coses sourvenans,
> dont on est plenté souvenans,
> tant sus terre com en abismes,
> sont si propres d'elles meïsmes
> et si vertueuses ossi
> que souvent apperent ensi
> qu'on les ymagine et devise. (*JBJ*, 838–46)

Froissart's memory is not entirely under the control of reminiscence; it plays tricks on him.[29] Although he can retrace his steps to the portrait, his dream brings him face to face with his lady, not as she was when it was painted but as when he first met her many years before, at the beginning of the *Espinette*. And this purportedly remembered love affair also diverges sharply in the *Joli buisson* from the way the *Espinette* described it. True, it is inconclusive in both *dits*. But in the earlier poem a series of external and apparently fortuitous obstacles bars the poet's access to the lady, whereas in the *Joli buisson* courtship is impeded by the lady's own Refus, Dangier, and Escondit (Refusal, Resistance, and Denial), and is relegated to the status of a dream that the lover himself will repudiate. While the *Espinette* holds out hope of love in the future, the *Joli buisson* consigns it to impossibility.[30] Concomitantly, the *Joli buisson* doesn't recapitulate any of the external events of the previous poem but (in imitation of the *Rose*) unfurls an entirely internal, psychological world of personified abstractions and their interaction.

Does memory rear up involuntarily and impose itself on the dreamer's mind, as the last quotation implies? In the *Joli buisson de Jonece* it seems rather that Froissart has distorted the events of the *Espinette* in line with his present melancholic, introspective, and frankly middle-aged mindset; in other words, it seems that reminiscence has distorted memory rather than that memory has outplayed reminiscence. Thus, for example, although in the dream he fondly believes that he is reentering the world of Jonece, in fact he hasn't changed his persona from the dit's opening. Venus presented him with Jonece as with his double from the past; but if we calculate Jonece's age from what he tells us about his memories of his university experiences "more than ten years ago" (*JBJ*, 1557), he is most likely the dreamer's double as he is *now*, at thirty-five.[31] The dream offers only the illusion of being young again. Froissart remains affected by the thoughts of his own mortality that were assailing him before the dream began (*JBJ*, 811–26), to which he returns as soon as it is over (*JBJ*, 5156ff.). Although (in Zink's phrase) "structured by the process of reminiscence," *Le Joli buisson* also attests the difficulty of remembering the past. By definition, what is past cannot be present: all we can call to mind is a generalized (universalized) version of it as it touches us now. Coleman puts it in a nutshell when she says that, processed by the intellect, the past can only be "of necessity, present and generally meaningful in an exemplary way."[32] The portrait may have been made in the past, but it remains outside the realm of the intelligible, associated not with understanding but with sensation, and Froissart's "memory" of it is not a memory at all but a confused reconstruction of a system that he wishes to be exemplary.

We first witness this traducing of the past by the present when Froissart compares himself to Achilles. In no known text, according to Philip Bennett, does Achilles console himself by looking at a portrait of Polyxena; the parallel has been forged on the basis of Froissart's own case.[33] The two series of *exempla* recounted in the dream by Jonece and Desir similarly subordinate historicity to present preoccupation. Jonece's theme is the mental preservation of youthful love, while Desir illustrates, by contrast, the lethal effects of sexual passion. Both sets of stories wryly inflate Froissart's current anxiety about his former love to the level of universal truth.

Jonece's stories reassure him that dreaming of his lady as if she had not aged since their first meeting is quite normal, while Desir's adduce analogues to his sufferings as a lover. But while capturing Froissart's particular concerns in general terms, the stories also bring the notion of exemplarity into disrepute. Jonece's tales are flagrantly fictional, pure works of imagination, while Desir misrepresents or misremembers well-known myths.[34] These stories are produced to order as expressions of the personified abstraction that tells them. Universal youth and universal doom seem equally fabricated and equally specious.

As a result, the dream world of the *Joli buisson de Jonece* represents the one of universality and the one of singularity as caught in a vicious circle. The particular cannot be called to mind except in a generalized form; but the form that it adopts is conditioned by the particular state one is in. What can be known to the intellect at any one time is inevitably conditioned by the imprint of particular past experiences that remain unknown. Our thought is overwhelmingly (or exclusively) abstract, but our capacity for it is qualified by particular concrete circumstances that lie outside it.

Remembering the Unknown: The "Buisson en Creux"

The unknown may, however, persist: namely, as the holes or gaps in the bush in which Froissart's "I" is insistently located and which, once past the teachings of the "maistre en philozophie," loom larger in his experience than do its branches.

When Froissart first sees the portrait, it opens up before him a gap alight with sparks:

When I hold it in my thoughts and look at it, it reminds me of time past and everything my heart used to feel when I gazed at my lady, for love of whom I was all ablaze. Now I have uncovered the fire and opened up the little gap through which the sparks fly that set fire to me, leaping up once more and bringing back to life that blazing fire.

> Quant je l'ymagine et regars
> le tamps passé me ramentoit
> et tout ce que mon coer sentoit
> lors que ma dame regardoie
> pour la quele amour tous ardoie.
> Or ai je le feu descouvert

et le petit pertruis ouvert
par ou les estincelles sallent
qui me renflament et rassallent
et ratisent cel ardent fu. (*JBJ*, 615–24)

This passage recapitulates one from the end of the *Espinette* that also represents the poet set ablaze by the sparks of love:

For you, my sovereign lady, I have received much pain and am cut out to receive much more. I speak truly in this, for the longer I live, the more the flame of love for you sets me on fire. The live, burning spark burns and glows in my heart, and will never cease at any hour of the day or night.

Pour vous, ma dame souverainne,
ai recheü tamainte painne
et sui encor dou rechevoir
bien tailliés. Je di de che voir,
car, come plus vif, et plus m'enflame
de vous li amoureuse flame.
En mon cuer s'art et estincelle
la vive et ardans estincelle
qui ja ne prendera ja sejour
heure ne de nuit ne de jour. (*Espinette amoureuse*, 3881–90)

The words *ardre* ("burn"), *estincelle* ("spark"), and *enflame* ("inflame") and their cognates from these lines in the *Espinette* are reiterated not only in the passage I have just quoted from the *Buisson* but from thereon forward too. What, however, the *Buisson* passage introduces that is not in the *Espinette* is the *pertruis* (*JBJ*, 621, "aperture, gap"). It makes no sense in this context, where Froissart is retrieving the picture from his coffer, but is, as it were, the gap around which the branches of the bush will later form. Once the dream is under way, and Froissart has fallen into the company of Desir, the sense becomes clearer that this gap, while formed by the *buisson*, is in a sense also prior to it.

Riding piggyback on Desir in the course of a game, Froissart is suddenly aware he has caught fire (*JBJ*, 3056–59). The only explanation he can think of, in an agony of flame, is that the fire has somehow reached him through a *pertuis*:

And I don't know where such a fire could have arisen or reached me except that I can see and make out a kind of window or opening in the bush, indeed, I made it earlier with my finger: it is certainly right I should pay for this naughty deed, for through it I often saw the sweet comportment of my sovereign lady as I look high and low at everything. This burning has come through there, I can't see any other way it could have got in. Is that right, Desire?

> Et si ne sçai mies par u
> telle ardeur puist venir ne nestre,
> fors seuelement q'une fenestre
> a le maniere d'un pertruis
> dedens che buisson voi et truis,
> se l'i fis je orain de mon doi:
> certes, moult bien comparer doi
> che meffait, car par la souvent
> ai je veü le douls couvent
> que ma tres souverainne garde
> quant bas et haut par tout regarde.
> Ceste ardeur est par la entree,
> car je n'i voi nulle autre entree.
> Dites, Desir, ai je dit voir? (*JBJ*, 3071–84)

For the dreamer, the bush is not a branching structure but rather a series of holes around which the branches form a frame, or an obstruction to be poked into a further hole by his eager finger. When he made this *pertuis* he himself was hiding in the *croes* ("hollow," *JBJ*, 2962) of a little *buisson*, a bush-within-the-bush; covered over with leaves, he was still able to keep a beady eye on his lady (*JBJ*, 2967, 3121–25). Later, when Desir approaches her on his behalf, he will once more retreat into this leafy hole (*JBJ*, 3785–86). His dodging and spying continue to the end of the dream (*JBJ*, 3895–96) so that in the end he seems to be almost a prisoner within the bush (*JBJ*, 4368–69).

The *buisson* is, as we saw, a place of thought; but in making it full of spy holes and hideaways Froissart seems to imply that there are places *outside* thought that are, at the same time, contained *within* it, places that (as bushes within the bush) replicate but also invert it into *croes* (hollows). While the *buisson* proper is a place of intellection, this "buisson en creux" is associated with sensations: those of being covered over, peering out, and catching fire. On Desir's back, Froissart burns, shouts with pain, and calls for help:

It seems to me that there is fire all around me, and that all of me is burning and in the midst of flame. And so I cry out, "I am all burning and in flames! Desire, Desire, put me down! . . . I can feel the fire catching me, burning and setting light to all of me. Go and call whatever men and women you can find and tell them to come and help me, for truly I am burning away to ash and can feel nothing but fire and flame."

> Il m'est advis de toutes pars
> que che soit feus et que tous ars
> et que je soie enmi le flame.
> J'escrie lors : "J'ars tous et flame!
> Desir, Desir, mettés moi jus! . . .
> Je sench le feu qui me sousprent,
> qui tout me bruïst et esprent.
> Issiés de chi et appellés
> cheuls et chelles que vous volés;
> dittes qu'on me viegne secourre,
> car vraiement j'ars tous en pourre,
> ne je ne sench que flame et fu." (*JBJ*, 3056–60, 3064–70)

As he burns in the flames that reach him in the gaps of the bush, Froissart "remembers" his passion from the *Espinette* as a return of sensations that exceed what can be grasped intellectually. His feeling of disintegration—of being reduced to ash (*JBJ*, 3069)—marks his eclipse as a subject in the face of this irresistible upsurge of intensity. Contrary to the reminiscence guided by Philozophie, this memory is emphatically *not* consoling, and his ultimate objective will be to forget it.

Memory, Forgetting, and the "Dream of the Burning Child"

Froissart's dream presents striking parallels with one discussed by Freud, parallels worth exploring because the disagreement between Freud and Lacan over the dream's meaning turns on precisely the issues with which I am concerned here: understanding, memory, and forgetting, and their implications for universality on the one hand and singularity on the other.

A father whose son has just died has a nightmare in which the child walks toward him in flames, asking reproachfully, "Vater, siehst du denn nicht, daß ich verbrenne?" "Father, can't you see I'm burning?" As though himself transfixed by the horror of the dream, Freud returns to it repeatedly in *The Interpretation of Dreams*, struggling to reconcile it with his thesis that dreams express the fulfillment of a wish.[35] Lacan scorns Freud's optimism, arguing instead that the dream stages the subject's encounter with something unbearably traumatic; to underline the potency of his own reading he likewise keeps repeating the child's words, "Père, ne vois-tu pas, je brûle?"[36] In the *Joli buisson de Jonece*, where the dreamer is himself the one in flames, the nightmare is even more horrific and the reiteration more insistent: "J'ars tous et flame. . . . Je sench le feu qui me sousprent, / Qui tout me bruïst et esprent. . . . Car vraiement j'ars tous en pourre, / Ne je ne sench que flame et fu" ("I am all burning and in flames! . . . I can feel myself catching fire, burning. . . . I am burning away to ash and can feel nothing but fire and flame").

Lacan's objections to Freud deploy terms taken from Aristotle's *Physics* that in their original context are, I think, particularly relevant to Froissart's dream. These terms are *automaton* and *tuché* ("fortune"). For Aristotle, they denote two potential causes of events that fit uncomfortably into his analysis of causation because they are indeterminate and don't command general assent. Lacan seizes on the concept of *automaton* as corresponding to his idea of the symbolic order, or the pleasure principle; it is arbitrary, impersonal, inhuman, and generates repetition ("the repetition compulsion") along the network of signifiers. By *tuché* Lacan understands what lies beyond the pleasure principle: the cause as an unarticulated trauma that reverberates through subsequent acts and reappears on the borders of thought without ever being captured in it, and that he calls the Real (*le réel*): "By real is meant that which always returns to its place—to that place where the subject insofar as it thinks, where the *res cogitans* [of the subject] does not encounter it."[37] When the real "returns" in this way, it constitutes a form of memory that is not consciously remembered—indeed, from the perspective of consciousness it is forgotten—but that *is* repeated in behavior.[38] According to Lacan the dream of the burning child is an instance of traumatic *tuché* or inadmissible memory, whereas Freud's interpretation assigns it only to *automaton* as something amenable to comprehension.

The way Lacan elaborates the distinction between *automaton* and *tuché* is directly relevant to Froissart's "merry bush" as a system of branches and holes. As propounded by the "maistre en philozophie," the bush resembles the vast impersonal structure of *automaton,* its branching pathways conveying thought in a mechanical way that makes it universally intelligible.[39] Froissart's position in the gaps in the bush exposes him to the shock of *tuché*, the unbearable intensity of that which, lying outside thought, nevertheless conditions its shape. In Lacanian terms, Froissart's dream of the burning child is an encounter with the real and, as such, a memory of something inadmissibly private that demands to be forgotten but that nevertheless repeats itself insistently.[40] Of course, Froissart could not have known the use that Lacan was going to make of Aristotle's *Physics*. However, it is interesting to observe how Aristotle's text illumines his own "dream of the burning child," and in a way that (as it does for Lacan) connects it to the question of what can or cannot be universalized.

In Latin, Aristotle's *tuché* is translated as *fortuna* and *automaton* as *casus*. The pseudonym taken by Desir in the course of the game where Froissart catches fire is "bonne aventure," or *fortuna* in its benign aspect (cf. *Physics*, 197a25), so Froissart's encounter with Desir is literally a brush with *tuché*. The key element in Aristotle's definition of *tuché* is that it is "unaccountable" (*Physics*, 197a19). The oldest Latin translation renders this as "outside reason" (*extra ratione*); Aquinas's commentary goes further, saying that it is "without reason" (*sine ratione*).[41] Crucially, however, whether outside or without reason, *tuché* is defined *with respect to* reason. What, for Aristotle, differentiates *tuché* from *automaton* is that whereas *automaton* refers to a random natural accident, *tuché* is related to human thought, choice, and action. Being hit by a randomly falling rock is *automaton* (197b29), whereas chancing to get money from someone when calling on him or her for a quite different purpose would be *tuché* (196b33–197a5). Aristotle concludes, "It is clear then that chance [*tuché*] is an accidental cause in the sphere of those actions for the sake of something which involves choice. Thought, then, and chance are in the same sphere, for choice implies thought" (197a6–8).[42] Or, more simply, "Chance [*tuché*] is in the sphere of action" (197b2).[43] "In the sphere of" here means "exists within" rather than "is integrated to," just as the gaps and holes exist within the sphere of Froissart's universal bush. *Tuché*, Aristotle is saying, is the unthought within thought, the unchosen within choice, the passive within agency (and by implication it is that which is unavailable to reminiscence and hence remains unremembered within memory). The motif of encountering fortune or *bonne aventure* in the *Joli buisson* would thus be related, by Aristotle, to the difficulty of locating the unthought within the "place of thought."

Tuché, says Aristotle, is "unaccountable" in that it is impossible to universalize or generalize about, "for an account [*ratio*] is what holds always or for the most part" (197a19–20).[44] Froissart likewise sees fortune as incapable of supporting any ethical conclusion or worthwhile generalization:

You [fortune] are so contrary [*or*: so full of contradictions?] that there is nothing good or exemplary to be said about you that could or should please.

En toi [fortune] a tant de contraire
qu'on n'en poet dire ne faire
nul bien ne nul exemplaire
qui puist ne qui doive plaire. (*JBJ*, 3732–35)

Tuché resists universality, according to Aristotle, because it is "accidental," a term that implies both "happening by accident (as opposed to by design)" and "resulting from an accidental (as opposed to defining) quality." Aristotle gives as an example the causes of house building. The ability to build houses is an inherent cause, a cause *per se*, of a house being built, but an accidental cause might be that the builder responsible was pale or musical. "That which is *per se* cause is determinate [*finita*], but the accidental cause is indeterminable [*infinita*]; for the possible attributes of an individual are innumerable [*infinite*]" (196b27–29).[45] Froissart's experience of *tuché* or fortune, following this line of argument, would result from the accidents that make him one person rather than another, that is, from his chancing to be the particular individual that he is.

Froissart's misadventures therefore pertain directly to his position within the merry bush. The bush, by virtue of mapping (as I have suggested it does) the Porphyrian tree of *qualitas*, articulates accidents as a universal category. But his brush with *tuché* or fortune takes place in the gaps, and it is "outside reason" and unaccountable within its reasoning structure. The accidental qualities that he has as a singular being make him burn with desire. The searing pain of this memory can't be rationalized in the bush, and therefore has to be forgotten.

The Consolation of Forgetting

The treatment of fortune in the *Physics* draws it into the same orbit as the *Consolation of Philosophy*, where Philosophy invokes Aristotle in the course of her exhortations to Boethius to withstand the vicissitudes of fortune. I have already noted the Boethian footprints on the opening of the *Joli buisson de Jonece*. Desir, a pale imitation in this of Philozophie, does his best to comfort Froissart over being reduced to ashes (*JBJ*, 3406, 3450); he exhorts the lady to be consolatory too (*JBJ*, 4419); but real solace comes only when Froissart wakes up and uses the wits God gave him to distance himself from his dream (*JBJ*, 5091–98). In the cold light of day he compares his nightmarish visions with the spiritual interests of his soul:

Picturing these things in my mind, I drew something of a comparison between [them and] my life and interests, and said that I had no business to think of such idle things, for they are tortures and harmful to the soul.

> En ceste ymagination
> fis un peu de collation
> contre ma vie et mon affaire
> et di que je n'euïsse que faire
> de penser a teles wiseuses,
> car ce sont painnes et nuiseuses
> pour l'ame. (*JBJ*, 5156–63)

This passage recalls and inverts one from the beginning of the *dit* where Froissart looked at the *ymage* for the first time:

And still I draw comparison with the portrait I had, and find great consolation in it. May God grant that good come to me from it, for it is right/rational that I should remember my beautiful lady. . . .

> Et encores en mon ymage
> preng nouvelle collation
> de grande consolation.
> Or doinst Diex que bien m'en couviegne,
> car c'est raisons qu'il me souviegne
> de la belle. . . . (*JBJ*, 731–36)

Both passages rely on medieval accounts of reminiscence as an intellectual act that enables people to effect rational comparison (*collatio*) between the *intentiones* (meanings) that are the products of remembering, resulting from the *imagines* in the *imaginatio*.[46] At the beginning of the *dit* Froissart's intellect decides in favor of memories of his lady; at the end it does a *volte-face*, instructs him to banish those memories as "idle," and directs his thoughts to objects more beneficial to his soul.

In the remaining lines of the *dit* Froissart makes short work of forgetting everything he had initially worked to remember. His singular experiences are swept aside by a tide of pious generalities. The experience of burning alive is reinterpreted as a reminder of the body's mortality (*JBJ*, 5166). Authorities endorsing spiritual nourishment are cited. Souls are asserted to be more important than bodies. Even the notion of sin is dissolved in an indefinite plural as "some unattractive vices" (*JBJ*, 5179, "aucun vilain visce"). Only the lexical weight of a few key words like *ardre* and the inarticulate imprint of rhyme survive from his earlier passionate *forme fixe* lyrics in the concluding *lai* to the Virgin. As the merry bush mutates into the burning bush and the Tree of Jesse, the *dit*'s complex and witty standoff between the universal and the singular, memory and understanding, dissolves in the embrace of a transcendental One, an out-pouring of personal devotion in line with the universal church.

Conclusion

In his *Confessions* Augustine claims to be able to picture his childhood: "Thus my boyhood, which is no longer, lies in past time which is no longer. But when I am recollecting and telling my story, I am looking on its image in present time, since it is still in my memory" (*Confessions*, XI, xviii, §23).[47] Such a claim is dispelled by Froissart as he dreams in the bush of Youth. At every turn the *dit* acknowledges the lack of fit between time-bound singular experiences and the timeless universal mode available to their expression. Froissart's dream is an attempt to enable him, via the metaphor of the tree and its gaps, to "see" the universal and the particular at the same time, but even in a dream they are hard to visualize, and when one awakes they retreat at once into invisibility:

Dreams often bring those great invisible wonders which seem visible while one sleeps.

> Amainnent li songe souvent
> les grans mervelles invisibles
> qui samblent en dormant visibles. (*JBJ*, 5107–9)

Memory as the making present of the past and irony at the expense of our limited exercise of reason are the first casualties of this misfit; but reminiscence, subjectivity, the play of imagination, humor, and the possi-bility of writing poetry are included in the payoff.

Froissart does not altogether deny the possibility that we might have some knowledge of singulars that would be rooted in the body. But the traces of memory and, worse, its repetition in behavior risk being disturb-ing. Philozophie fruitlessly tenders the hope he might once again write love poetry, and the "maistre en philozophie" offers a rationale for secular reflective poetry on human nature. But if Froissart wants to be a poet—and he is convinced that it is his nature to be one—then his best bet is for his accidental passions to be reduced to ash in the "place of thought," so that it can be reconfigured as a site of Christian truth. The route that Froissart traces from boyhood desire to mature didacticism is ironic, humorous, and self-deprecating, but in the end he decides that the one of his own individuality is best forgotten if he is to enhance his chances of being united with the eternal One.

Melancholia, Allegory, and the Metaphysical Fountain in Christine de Pizan's *Le Livre du Chemin de Long Estude*

I BEGAN THIS BOOK with the Sybil's summons to Christine de Pizan, in her *Livre du Chemin de long estude*, to follow her "to another and more perfect world" ("en autre monde plus parfaict," *CLE*, 649) where she will better understand this world's plight. My final chapter is devoted to analyzing the thought to which Christine directs us in this poem, and the principal place she uses in order to do so: the fountain of the Muses on Parnassus, a home to poetry and philosophy combined.

The *Chemin de long estude* recounts a dream that takes place after Christine has been sorrowing over her husband's death and the chaotic state of the world. In imitation of Dante's journey with Virgil in the *Divina commedia*, she finds herself escorted by the Cumaean Sybil to the fountain of the Muses, and from there through history, around the world, and into the heavens. The Sybil takes her up to the firmament, the fifth circle of heaven, to gaze on the majestic order of the stars and planets, then back down to the first circle of air, where she witnesses a debate between four "Destinies" or "Influences" that rule the world below: Noblece, Chevalerie, Richece, and Sagece (Nobility, Chivalry, Wealth, and Wisdom). They have been summoned by Raison (Reason) to explain their part in the world's problems, which they hear about via a messenger from the distraught figure of the Earth. The Destinies agree that what is needed is a single leader who will be respected by all and thus put an end to strife; each proposes an unnamed candidate, but they cannot agree among them which to appoint. Finding it impossible to reach a decision, Raison remits the matter to the court of France. Christine's fortuitous presence throughout the debate, which she has been transcribing as it goes on, makes her the ideal messenger. She and the Sybil are just returning to earth when, by mischance, her mother wakes her up from her dream. However, the prologue to the completed poem appears to have been written in fulfill-ment of her mandate from Raison, since it dedicates the *dit* to Charles VI in fulsome terms.

The *Chemin de long estude* is one of several works by Christine that explore how generality can be abstracted from the particular being to which she has the greatest access, namely herself. Divesting the *dit* of much of the whimsy that had characterized it in the hands of Machaut and Froissart (not necessarily a wise decision), Christine uses her first-person experiences as a widow with academic aspirations and dependent children as a springboard for didacticism. Composition of the *Chemin de long es-tude* was under way in 1402 at the same time as another of her verse *dits*, the *Mutacion de Fortune*, which likewise begins autobiographically before turning toward universal history. Then in 1404–5 Christine adopted prose as her medium. The resulting works, the *Avision* and the *Cité des dames*, perform the same shift from concrete personal experience to universal in-sight, where politics, philosophy, and theology are intertwined.[1]

This chapter will address the relation between autobiography and universality in the *Chemin de long estude*, concentrating on the fountain of the Muses as the place of thought from which the didactic poem is produced. I shall argue that Christine's awareness of the problematic rela-tion between embodied individuality and intellectual universality leads her to personify her ideas in a series of metaphysical female figures who are, as it were, born from this fountain: the Muse Calliope, the Earth, and Wis-dom itself in the figure of Sagece. Drawing on Julia Kristeva's account of allegory as the expression of and remedy for melancholy, I shall contend too that these dream-vision personifications offer a way of compensating not only for her personal bereavement but also for the impasse at the heart of Aristotelian epistemology as Christine understands and experiences it.

Christine and Universality

Any discussion of universality in Christine de Pizan must begin by ac-knowledging Earl Jeffrey Richards's contributions to this topic.[2] In his essay "French Cultural Nationalism and Christian Universalism in the Works of Christine de Pizan," Richards discerns a tension in Christine's thought between what he calls Christian universalism—an Augustinian conception of history as salvation for the whole of Christendom—and categories of difference, such as nationalism. Citing her *Livre du corps de policie* of 1406, he says: "The remarkable feature . . . is that Christine proposes French examples as universal ones. . . . Christine does not celebrate France for its particular indigenous traits but for its universality, which translates as France's ability to serve as a representative for Christendom" (84). This characteristic of her thought he traces back to the *Chemin de long estude*, "in which France is chosen as the land from which the new universal monarch will be selected" (85). At the end of the same essay he points out the parallel between national difference and gender difference: "Christine's predicament lies in the conflict between her universalism and her endorsement of the categories of identity and alterity themselves" (90). In Richards's view, Christine's "fragmentation of human culture according to national or religious lines" (90) falls short of the universalist ideal. On the other hand, he thinks she does succeed in transcending her gender, since, to quote a later article by him, she "proposes what amounts to a female theodicy, a new female-centered universal history of humanity where women's experiences afford the literal sense of the creation itself."[3]

While recognizing the importance of Richards's remarks, I have reservations about some of his assumptions. Richards writes as though the particular and the universal were alike available to Christine, and as though she had a choice between operating on one level or the other or else combining them. By articulating the problem as he does, I think Richards misrepresents its terms as Christine would have understood them. The universal is not related to the particular as a class is to its members in the way Richards seems to imply; Christine is not extrapolating on the basis of one representative (herself, France) to a group (humanity) of which it is a part. While the universals debate is many things, it is not an argument about taxonomy. Rather, it is about negotiating certain fundamental philosophical aporias, such as the lack of congruence between what exists (particulars) and what can be known (universals); or the incompatibility between experience (singular things are perceived via the senses) and reasoning (universal categories are manipulated by the intellect). Given that the only tools with which we can think are universal ones, how can we make sense of individual experience? But given that reality exists at the level of the individual alone, how can we grasp human nature and its needs? In choosing to combine autobiography and didacticism, Christine de Pizan pitches into the heart of this problematic. She repeatedly alludes to Aristotle's formulation of it in his *Metaphysics* and was evidently aware

too of Aquinas's *Metaphysics* commentary. More than any of the other
authors discussed in this book, Christine demonstrates first-hand knowledge of how Scholastic philosophers canonically approached what I have
been calling "the complexity of one."[4]

In the *Chemin de long estude* the citation from Aristotle admittedly
takes the form of a commonplace. Sagece claims that she, more than the
other Influences, holds the key to human nature:

And the created world by nature desires to know. And it is the rightful and ultimate goal to which humanity directs itself, in consequence of which my assertion
is true, that without knowledge it is imperfect.

> Et par nature
> desire savoir creature.
> Et est la droite fin derreine
> la ou tend creature humaine;
> dont est vraye m'entencion
> que sans lui n'a perfeccion. (*CLE*, 5179–84)

This is a paraphrase of the well-known opening of Aristotle's *Metaphysics*:
"All men by nature desire to know . . . the animals other than man live by
appearance and memories, and have but little of connected experience;
but the human race lives also by art and reasonings" (980a21, 980b26–27).[5]
Experience and how human beings make sense of it are Aristotle's theme
here; as Andrea Tarnowski has shown, they also lie at the heart of the
Chemin de long estude.[6]

The opening of the *Metaphysics* details how multiple sensory perceptions are processed into unitary experience through the agency of memory, and then how multiple experiences are processed into one judgment
by means of what Aristotle calls "art." The Latin text used by Aquinas
makes it clear that the key difference between experience and art is that the
former belongs on the level of particulars, the latter on that of universals:

Now in men experience comes from memory; for many memories of the same
thing produce the capacity of a single experience. And experience seems to be
somewhat like science and art.
   But in men science and art come from experience. . . . And art comes into being
when from many conceptions acquired by experience a single universal judgement
is formed about similar things.[7]

The progression in Christine's writings from the multiplicity of her various
experiences toward an affirmation of some general finding marks its

indebtedness to this understanding of Aristotle's epistemology. For example, in the *Cité des dames* Christine refers to this framework when she asks Raison to reassure her that women have the capacity to extract expertise from past events so as to acquire wisdom in the present and prudence as regards the future:

> That is to say that they have opinions as to what is best to do and what should be left, and that they have memory of past events whereby they develop expertise from instances that they have seen, and wisdom in the management of things present, so that they have foresight regarding those that are to come.

> C'est assavoir qu'elle ayent avis sur ce qui est le meilleur a faire et a ce qui doit estre laissié, souvenance des choses passees, par quoi soient expertes par l'exemple que ont veu, sages ou gouvernement des choses presentes, qu'elles ayent pourveance sur celles a avenir. (*Cité des dames*, 196)

A similar passage, explicitly referring to *Metaphysics* I, is found in Christine's praise of wisdom in her *Livre des Fais et bonnes meurs du sage roy Charles V* (II, 21); its three aspects are there said to be "memoire, intelligence et pourveance."

In the *Cité des dames* Christine also refers to Aristotle's disagreement with Plato over the concept of form. Plato taught that the multitude of things, even though they are always changing, derive their being from participation in one Idea or Form. The matter from which they are drawn, although also an underlying unity, is realized as the duality of great and small, the fundamental principle of diversity from which numbers derive. In *Metaphysics* I, 6, Aristotle attacks Plato's account, showing how it results in a plethora of contradictions and unnecessary or unhelpful distinctions. He counters that matter is inherently undifferentiated, and that duality and multiplicity inhere in form, since it is by virtue of their forms that individuals are constituted. As Aquinas in his commentary puts it: "For when something is generated it receives a form, and the same form numerically cannot become the form of another thing that is generated but ceases to be when that which was generated undergoes corruption. In this argument it is clearly apparent that one matter is related to many forms and not the reverse, i.e., one form to many matters. Thus it seems more reasonable to hold that unity pertains to matter but duality or contrariety to form. . . . This is the opposite of what Plato held."[8] Judging by Christine's summary of *Metaphysics* I in the *Avision*, this would appear to be the crux of her understanding of Aristotle's arguments, which she reduces to the observation that Plato invested matter with the duality of the great and the small (*Avision*, 125). She continues by agreeing with Aristotle that form is located at the level of the individual being:

For form is the first cause of being and thus it is that whereby every thing has its being, the first cause both of it and of our knowledge of it.

Car fourme est principe de l'estre et ce que cest doncques comme ce par qui toute chose a son estre soit le principe delle et de sa cognoiscence. (*Avision*, 128)

The abstraction of knowledge from an individual requires us to recognize its form, which is the "principle" or first cause of its being; apprehended by the senses, this form is then the origin and cause of intellectual knowledge by which we grasp its universal nature.

Some kinds of knowledge, however, are more accessible than others. Aquinas distinguishes between knowledge that proceeds directly from the definitions of physical things, which is available to everyone (e.g., that the whole is bigger than the part), and knowledge that requires reflection on abstractions (e.g., knowledge of a concept such as "quantity").[9] And clearly when it comes to judging and reasoning on the basis of one's knowledge, some individuals are better equipped than others. Thus Christine's quest for knowledge in the *Chemin de long estude* is located from the outset in places to which we are bidden to follow her, but which are also defined by their limits, and by her personal limitations. The delimiting of place in the *dit* circumscribes her own particular place as a historically situated individual, in addition to defining the place of thought.[10]

Place and Circumscription

The limits of place are enshrined in Christine's very title. The Sybil explains to her that there are two paths, the highflying way of the mystic and the literally pedestrian way of prolonged study, the *chemin de long estude*. The first is accessible to very few indeed; the second is possible only to the highly literate, as the fact that it is a quotation from Dante confirms.[11] The Sybil makes no bones about the mystics' way being simply beyond Christine; however, her scholarly proclivities fit her to attempt the second. Awareness that the poem excludes a whole other realm of knowledge is implied also by the figure of Sagece, who has two books in front of her, one open, the other closed (*CLE*, 2310–12). The open book I take to be the one of study; the closed book records a higher, and incommunicable, wisdom. Christine thus admits that there is a domain that her understanding cannot include. Its secrets are known to God and the mystics, but they remain secret from the author herself.

The Sybil, it is true, gives Christine a vision of the heavens. No one can make this ascent except on his or her own individual ladder. Christine's will take her to the firmament and no farther; this is the highest point she can aspire to reach. It is given to her by Ymagination (*CLE*, 1640) and is made of Speculation (*CLE*, 1647). It takes all her strength for her to see anything, so dazzling is the brilliance of the light (*CLE*, 1789–800). The Sybil explains to her the names and movement of the heavenly bodies; Christine is awestruck by their sublime order and sense of hierarchy, so different from the chaos and conflict she was lamenting on earth. She feels a moment of kinship with the poets, such as Ovid, who had described these realms before her. But (with a modesty that is perhaps more assumed than real) she acknowledges that their wonders exceed her understanding:

But I couldn't sufficiently understand their grandeur, despite my efforts, because my mind is too simple.

> Mais trop pou povoye comprendre
> leur grandeur pour tout mon estude,
> pour mon entendement trop rude. (*CLE*, 2024–26)

So the Sybil escorts her down to a lower circle, that of air (*CLE*, 2060–61). The view from here could not be more different: Christine sees unfurl before her the seething turmoil, murderous conflicts, and terrible disasters that are going to afflict the world—some of them too secret for her to reveal. The human experience of disorder to which such events give rise is the problem to which the four Destinies, themselves the occupants of this level of the heavens, are trying to find a solution in the form of an ideal prince. And it is here that Raison holds court, attended by the virtues. Thus, apart from the brief ascent to the fifth heaven, Christine's "route of long study" confines her to what can be known from the vicissitudes of historical experience and the knowledge that reason painstakingly abstracts from it by study.

Since much of the debate between the Influences relies on *exempla*, it too turns on the value of what can be learned from the experience of historical individuals. The progression in the *Chemin de long estude* from

Christine as exemplary figure to whole catalogues of other exemplars is similarly found in the *Mutacion*, the *Avision* and the *Cité des dames*. Sagece in particular uses *exempla* to bolster her argument, a fact which of itself implies that wisdom can be gleaned by reflecting on particular instances of behavior. In practice, however, arguments supported by examples prove inconclusive, given that Sagece fails to win over the other Destinies to her point of view, and Raison is powerless to reach a decision. This suggests that, while universals are known and particulars are not, it's not easy to obtain agreement about *what* exactly it is that is known. Indeed, although Christine identifies herself with Sagece (see below), all of the other Destinies advance some very cogent claims for their part in the eventual world order, reminding us that power, money, or force are all facets of human reality that need to be taken into account. The debate thus also reminds its readers that a truth which cannot be imposed by power, money, and force may remain a truth unheeded. Didacticism is not just about the propounding of a truth but also about its enforcement.

The sheer difficulty of processing experience intellectually is also emphasized at the end of the *dit,* whose wryness is the nearest Christine comes to humor in this work. When it proves unable to reach a decision, Raison's court can think of no better solution than to refer the world's problems back to the world itself to deal with. The route of long study ends up being, if not a cul-de-sac, at least a short round trip. This is borne out by the circular structure of the text: the dedication to the French court at the beginning fulfills the instruction given to Christine at the end to remit the debate to the French court. The quest for enlightenment, which begins in Christine's autobiographical experience, has to be concluded in the actions taken by another human individual.[12] The location of the faculty of reason in particular human bodies, although it limits knowledge, is also the condition of exercising it.

Christine's Places of Thought: From Study to Fountain

All through this book I have argued that the places with which thought is associated in medieval didactic poetry are defined with reference to the human body, and this is especially evident in the *Chemin de long estude*, where, despite their cosmic range, it is strongly implied that Christine's travels take place inside her own head. The dream that makes up most of the *dit* is first prompted by her sorrowful reflections in her study:

I had retired alone to a small study where I often take pleasure in looking at books.

> Je m'estoye a par moy mise
> en une estude petite,
> ou souvent je me delite
> a regarder escriptures. (*CLE*, 172–75)

Chancing upon Boethius's *Consolation of Philosophy* consoles her temporarily for the misfortunes of her own life, but when she goes to bed she suffers a further bout of melancholy about the chaos and conflict that assail the world in general. She then falls asleep, and the last text she had read, Boethius's, overdetermines the beginning of her dream as the Sybil appears to her in the role of Lady Philosophy. The Sybil, one of the most constant figures of female authority in Christine's texts, brings her own textual history in her train.[13] The plethora of literary allusions that ensues once the dream is under way, and that includes Virgil, Dante, Ovid, Alan of Lille, the *Roman de la rose*, and the *Ovide moralisé*, as well as innumerable historical *exempla* and moral reflections, takes the dreamer in fantasy back into the study she has just left.[14] If we interpret *estude* as referring to a place rather than an activity (as it does in the last quotation) the *dit*'s title could roughly be translated as "The long way round my bookshelves." Like the *Cité des dames*, the *Chemin de long estude* is a creative rereading of Christine's own library. Her study, that is, is a place of thought because it is the place where she herself sits, reads, and thinks. The ensuing text is a journey around the mind of a reader who is also a scholar and a woman, with the particular experiences that this conjunction brings.

The first major *locus* in Christine's dream, and the place to which the Sybil first escorts her, is also the place where much of this reading is condensed, namely, the fountain of the Muses on Mount Parnassus. This scene is dense with poetic allusiveness as the fountain compounds the *loci* of previous texts: most obviously Ovid's *Metamorphoses*, the *Ovide moralisé*, and the *Roman de la rose*. Also named the "fountain of wisdom" ("fontaine de sapience," *CLE*, 984–85) and the "fountain of learning" ("fontaine de clergie," *CLE*, 1091), its waters are said to have been drunk by all the famous philosophers, poets, and sages. The fountain marks the start of the two paths to enlightenment and is where Christine embarks with the Sybil on the path of *long estude*, itself actually described as an open book:

But this [path] we have entered, flatter than an open parchment, is reserved for the educated.

> Mais cestui plus que parchemin
> ouvert, ou nous sommes entrez,
> si est reservé aux lettrez. (*CLE*, 932–34)

As Christine contemplates this *chemin* together with the Sybil, the range of poetic allusion widens to include Dante and Virgil.[15] The fountain, then, is a kind of alfresco transformation of Christine's study, where the authors she has read congregate around her and the books themselves make up the landscape.

The Sybil advises Christine that even if she is not on a par with the glitterati frequenting the fountain (*CLE*, 1084, "de si haute escole"), she can nevertheless drink from and bathe in its streams. This sense that Christine is just one member of a vast company who all gather around the same waters is an aspect of what could be called the "metaphysics" of the fountain: its insistent invocation of the theme of "the one and the many." Reading the *Consolation of Philosophy* in her study has brought her to a place that materializes this key philosophical theme.[16] The single fountain is comprised of a multitude of ducts and rivulets:

And flowing onto the clear shingle through more than a thousand ducts there descended charming rivulets from that broad fountain.

> Et de celle fontaine lee
> par plus d'un miller d'uissellés
> dessendoient beaulx ruissellés
> sus clere gravelle courans. (*CLE*, 832–36)

Similarly, the path toward it on which Christine travels with the Sybil comprises many paths (e.g., *CLE*, 710, 714, 728, 733, 740, 777); and the wonderful place comprises many places (e.g., *CLE*, 738, 741, 785, 789). The heartland of poetry is clearly also being flagged as a philosophical *locus* where the multiplicity of paths, rivulets, and places between them make up a single aim, fountain, and place of thought. It is noteworthy that although the reference to Aristotle's *Metaphysics* comes much later in the text, Aristotle is the first named of the sages who drink from the fountain's streams. The fountain inscribes from the outset of the dream the idea that the unity of the universal arises from multiple physical exposure to the particular.

Christine's solitary book-lined study fills her with melancholy, but the gregarious fountain of the Muses proves an inspiration. To borrow David

Hult's description of the fountain in the *Roman de la rose*, it functions both as "an allegorical fountain and a fountain of allegory."[17] From its waters, I shall argue, the rest of the poem pours forth; its allegory, or practice of "other readings," conjures up an "other world," the *autre monde* of the Sybil's summons. Whereas in the *Rose*, as Hult demonstrates, allegory is generated by the capacity for internal difference within the crystals, Christine's dream fountain functions as a metaphysical spectacle, manifesting the "one" of the universal as if it were materially present in the same way as the many individuals (ducts, places, paths) through which we know it. At the same time, Christine and her readers are implicitly reminded that in order to conceive the unity of the universal we don't have to experience every single one of these particulars—indeed, it would be impossible for us to do so. The many ducts (paths, places, and so on) are, among other things, the different textual currents of *sapience* or *clergie*, and the route of long study, however prolonged, cannot include them all. Like the fountain in the *Rose*, only half of which can be seen at a time, this is a place that, however much it appeals to the sense of sight, cannot be seen in its entirety by any one person.

As Christine's vision unfolds, it offers a series of female figures through whom, I shall argue, she develops this metaphysical spectacle that cannot wholly be visualized. Christine's study had been a place of abject melancholy, but the fountain is (literally) a source from which emerge glorious female figures: the Muse Calliope, the Earth, and the figure of Sagece, all of whom, I shall argue, abstract in barely visible form successive universal forms of Christine herself. They are not, as she is, a corporeal figure; their being depends on reasoning and reflection. The union of poetry and philosophy that is implied in the fountain enables these ethereal transfigurations of her particular, melancholic female body. In their sublime but elusive reality, these figures stage the recognition that the universal alone can be cognized, and that it is so on the basis of a bodily particularity that remains shrouded from knowledge. Later I shall have recourse to Kristeva's writing on melancholy and allegory to explain the emergence of these allegorical figures but first I examine their presentation in the text of the *Chemin de long estude*.

The Muse Calliope

Although the episode of the fountain is dripping with verbal reminiscences of the *Roman de la rose* and (I am maintaining) plays a generative role in the allegory similar to Guillaume de Lorris's fountain, Christine's fountain is not that of Narcissus but the fountain of the Muses; its source is not *Metamorphoses* Book III but Book V, the aftermath of Perseus's adventures; its subject is not doomed love but epic quest, which, when glossed by the moralist of the *Ovide moralisé*, turns into a quest for divine enlightenment.[18]

In Ovid's *Metamorphoses* Book V, Pallas the goddess of wisdom, after helping Perseus defeat the Gorgon Medusa, goes to Mount Helicon to see the fountain that sprang up when the marvelous horse Pegasus, born from Medusa's blood, struck the ground with its hoof. The nine Muses have adopted the fountain as their home; nearby in the trees are nine magpies, formerly called the Pierides because they were the daughters of a certain Pierus. Wanting the fountain for themselves, the Pierides had foolishly challenged the Muses to a poetry competition, with occupancy of the fountain as its prize. Not surprisingly, the Muses won and the Pierides lost; as punishment they were turned into foolish, chattering magpies. Pallas, whose informant is the Muse Calliope, hears recited the two poems that competed for this prize. That of the Pierides is short and cursorily describes the transformations undergone by a series of gods in their wars with the giants. The winning entry, by Calliope, Muse of eloquence and epic poetry, is also set in the time of the giants but relates at length the story of Ceres and Proserpina, a story inset with a whole series of metamorphoses. Much like the Orpheus sequence in Book X (see Chapter 2), the episode of Pallas at the fountain assumes a self-reflexive function. The rival stories illustrate potentially right and wrong ways way of narrating the *Metamorphoses*, in which the voice of the Muse, with the goddess of wisdom as her audience, becomes ironically entangled with that of Ovid.

Christine's account of the fountain is shorter than Ovid's. She stresses how clear its water is, says that there are nine ladies bathing in it who seem very authoritative (but does not say they are the Muses), mentions the marvelous winged horse (but does not name Pegasus), and enthuses over the beauty of the whole place; the Sybil is needed to identify the mountain as Parnassus or Helicon (*CLE*, 978–79). Christine's show of ignorance is disingenuous; it is plain that she knew not only Ovid's treatment of the scene but also its adaptation in the *Ovide moralisé*. The terms in which she identifies the fountain ("fontaine de clergie" and "fontaine / dont sapience doit venir") are those used by the moralist (see *OM*, V, 1674, 2462, 2473–74). The fountain's link with study, and thus with *long estude*, is also present in his gloss, which calls it the place "where the nine Muses are studied" (*OM*, V, 2494, "ou les neuf Muses s'estudient"), and where Pallas is invited to join them in study (*OM*, V, 1707–8; compare *CLE*, 1093–95).

There is very little in the *Moralisé*'s allegoresis of the fountain that Christine does *not* in some way retain. Its stream is glossed as figuring the pursuit of wisdom, love, and knowledge. It leads to the worship of God, since God is wisdom. In this respect the fountain represents the unattainable, given that knowledge of God is beyond human capacities and no one can fathom its borders or its depths (*OM*, V, 2339–45). This gloss would seem to lie behind the Sybil's distinction between the mystics' way and the route of long study. The moralist's injunction to seek to know the world and oneself (*OM*, V, 2362–65) encapsulates, though without acknowledging its problems, the conjunction of autobiography and encyclopedism in the *Chemin de long estude*. For the *Ovide moralisé*, the world is a place of affliction and betrayal, a diagnosis that is commonplace enough but certainly chimes with Christine's own melancholic reflections. The way the moralist describes the quest for self-knowledge as an act of rereading a text (*OM*, V, 2394–401), in which errors must be scratched out and corrections written in (*OM*, V, 2403, 2411, 2418–24), has also been internalized in the *Chemin de long estude*, whose bookish landscape emends the literary bases on which it rests.

With their home thus "amended" to a "stream of philosophy" ("dois de philozophie," *OM*, V, 2463), the role of the Muses in the *Ovide moralisé* is transformed from what it was in Ovid. The word *philozophie* or its cognates ring every few lines, the moralist's other favorite words in this passage being *clergie*, *science*, and *estude*. Mount Helicon is now identified with the human brain (*OM*, V, 2488–89). The Muses hold the keys to philosophy (*OM*, V, 2505), which are the nine mental faculties that are the prerequisites for intellectual reflection (love of philosophy, love of study, judgment, selection, and so forth, *OM*, V, 2507–23) and that occupy the three "cells" or mental faculties of apprehension, reasoning, and remembering (*OM*, V, 2533–37). A man equipped with these can become a philosopher (*OM*, V, 2540). By the same token, the traditional role of the Muses as inspirers of literature is downgraded and relegated to the Pierides, whom the moralist explicitly identifies with the false Muses of poetry chased away by Philosophy in the opening book of Boethius's *Consolation of Philosophy*: "'Who,' she demanded, her piercing eyes alight with fire, 'has allowed these hysterical sluts to approach this sick man's bedside? . . . These are the very women who kill the rich and fruitful harvest of Reason with the barren thorns of Passion'" (I, prose 1).[19] In this way the competition between the true and false Muses assumes reflexive value for the *Ovide moralisé* too, but now the issue is not the right and wrong way of narrating the *Metamorphoses*, it is the rival claims of pagan poetry and Christian philosophy. The authority of the sapiential Muses is annexed by the Christian thinker as he chases away the "hysterical slut" of Ovidian verse.

As with Ovid and his moralist, the way Christine recasts the fountain reflects on her conception of herself as a poet. Like them, she benefits from implied identification with the Muse. R. L. Krueger has suggested that, because the philosopher and poets the Sybil names as benefiting from the Muses are all men, Christine's fountain is "a site of exclusively male privilege."[20] I think rather that, by situating herself as Calliope talking with Pallas, Christine identifies with the arts of thinking and expression on which both poetry and philosophy depend, and thereby feels empowered both to know and to write about the world. Poetry's philosophical ambition is conveyed stylistically in this part of the text by the emphatic use of rich rhymes that integrate landscape to intellect, such as *lettree : contree* (*CLE*, 863–64), *passage : faire sage* (*CLE*, 865–66). It is also brought out thematically in the next ensuing scenes, where Christine, with the Sybil, tours the universe and learns the name of everything she sees. Adam may have named the world's first creatures, but these two women assume intellectual mastery of it. Their female mastery is underlined in Figure 10, from BL Harley 4431 (the so-called "manuscrit de la reine," believed to have been copied by Christine herself). This image depicts the author (the larger of the two women) and the Sybil talking together and looking toward the Muses in a way that both privileges poetry (since Christine is the dominant figure) and stresses its philosophical remit.[21]

As Calliope, Christine's ambition is in some ways greater than that of either of her models. By refraining from naming the Muses or the competition with the Pierides, Christine enables her fountain to be at once poetic (as in Ovid) and philosophical-theological (as in the *Ovide moralisé*). She seamlessly encompasses the pagan and the Christian (the same breadth is also found in her Sybil, since the Sybils were recognized in the Middle Ages as Christian prophets). Thus, in her vision, Christine fulfills the philosopher's obligation to know the world, which forms part of gloss on the fountain in the *Ovide moralisé*, and then remakes that world in poetic language. Calliope is never present in the text, however, even as a personi-

Figure 10. Sybil summoning Christine to the fountain of the Muses in the *Chemin de long estude*, BL Harley 4431, fol. 183. Reproduced by permission.

fication. She is there by inference or, I would rather say, by abstraction. She remains utterly invisible and incorporeal, as befits a universal concept. Through her, Christine reinvents herself, from the unhappy widow that she was, as the transcendent art of Poetry. Does this perhaps represent a recognition that the singular embodied self remains excluded from knowledge? Does it perhaps offer an escape from the anguish of her own particular life experiences? I return to these questions later, after considering Christine's other abstract identifications.

Mother Earth

After Christine's tour of the cosmos with the Sybil, and her arrival in the part of the heavens where Raison rules, there arrives a deputation on behalf of La Terre, also called Rhea, Ceres, or Isis (*CLE*, 2603–6). La Terre's complaints are read by a figure called Loquence (*CLE*, 2589, Eloquence). Since Calliope is the Muse of Eloquence, Loquence's address to Raison can be seen as repeating the Ovidian encounter between Calliope and Pallas, recasting it in an allegorical, euhemerist form. In the *Metamorphoses*, Calliope's prize-winning poem is about Ceres's quest for her daughter Proserpina, who has been abducted by Pluto, king of the underworld, and Christine's Ceres figure briefly alludes to this tragedy (*CLE*, 2656–58). Thus, although La Terre's lament comes about fifteen hundred lines after Christine has left Parnassus, it directly continues the episode of the fountain and is a further outpouring from its allegorical waters. By recasting this episode from the *Metamorphoses*, Christine confirms her identification with Calliope— especially given that her Ceres (unlike Ovid's) is represented by a written text that, with its ABABCDCD rhyme scheme, is metrically distinct from the surrounding octosyllabic couplets. Christine-Calliope-Loquence is clearly making an effort to impress her audience of Pallas/Raison![22]

As with the fountain episode, Christine's presentation of Ceres/Earth is shaped not only by Ovid but also by the *Ovide moralisé*. Her method is essentially the same in both cases: she takes the allegoresis of Ovid offered by the *Moralisé* and turns it back into a narrative that, in its breadth of literary resonance, has an even greater universality than the moralist's. The moralist reads Ceres as the Church, "our mother and nurse" (*OM*, V, 3048, "nostre mere, nostre nourrice"), rescuing her daughter, humanity, from diabolical seduction. This interpretation elevates Ceres from a literal, individual mother to a metaphorical, universal one.[23] Christine's Ceres is likewise a universal mother afflicted at having lost all her children. But her laments, which pick up the vocabulary of the *Ovide moralisé*, are over the state of the whole world, not just her daughter:

this maker made me the nurse and sole mother of all of the transitory world and of all bodies possessing volume and tangible matter.

> cellui facteur
> me fist des choses corrompables
> nourrice et singuliere mere
> de tous corps compas et palpables. (*CLE*, 2622–25)

As Loquence reads on it becomes clear that La Terre's lament is also modeled on Nature's complaint in Alan of Lille's *De Planctu Naturae* and her "confession" in the *Roman de la rose* (though it lacks the burlesque elements of either). La Terre complains that her creatures are consumed by violence—what mother would not be distressed to see her children intent on destroying one another (*CLE*, 2639–42)?—and repents giving birth to them (*CLE*, 2653–54). The loss of Proserpina seems slight in comparison with what she is now suffering. With a nod to the *Consolation of Philosophy*, La Terre declares that the world's ills are caused by human desire for the "illusory goods of Wealth" (*CLE*, 2679–80, "les biens vains / . . . que Richece depart"), and she asks Raison to resume guidance of human conduct.[24] In only just more than a hundred lines, Christine has swept into her *dit* a series of major literary and philosophical works in addition to the *Moralisé*. As with the scene at the fountain, she has taken care to not to expose any rifts between pagan and Christian culture. Unlike the *Moralisé* poet, she does not distance herself from Ovid but subsumes him into her rich internal library.

As this last remark implies, I think we should read Christine's voice of La Terre as not just a personification but an identification of herself. Essentially, the Earth Mother's lament replicates Christine's own miserable reflections, at the start of the *dit,* about the universe seeming to be at war with itself. Here Christine condemns the world's all-engulfing violence (*CLE*, 323–414) and blames Nature. Nature/Earth repeats the charge (*CLE*, 2636–42) and blames Richece. In La Terre, who personifies everything bodily but is herself not physically present except as a written text, Christine universalizes her own melancholic laments, elevates them to a cosmic scale, and places them before the throne of Raison.[25]

The lamentations of both Christine and La Terre sketch the first outlines of the debate between the Destinies that Raison will convoke in response. This debate is not the most enjoyable part of the *Chemin de long estude*; it lends support to Christine's recognition that that there is something pedestrian about the route she has chosen. But the role played in it by Sagece comes closest to representing Christine's own thinking about the problems she and the Earth have raised.

Sagece

Asked by Raison to account for the state of things on Earth, Richece passes the buck to Noblece, who in turn blames Chevalerie, who directs responsibility back to the other two; the presence of any or all of these three Destinies might have caused this strife, whereas Sagece's fault, it transpires, lies only in her absence, in the fact that no one paid her enough attention. Although all four Influences are universal figures that make the experience of historical reality intelligible, Sagece's position is thus formally differentiated from the others; she is intended to stand apart. The Destinies are then invited to prescribe an ideal prince, which they inevitably do in light of the qualities they personify. Each of the first three does her best to supplant the others, claiming their achievements would be impossible without her own (no nobility without chivalry, no chivalry without the wealth to pay for it, and so on). The order in which they speak—Noblece, Chevalerie, Richece—revives the assumption from which Raison began and echoes Christine's gloomy diagnosis before her dream, that Richece dominates human behavior and is the main reason for war. In this second round of the debate Sagece speaks at far greater length than the others. A walking, talking library of *sententiae* drawn from classical and patristic sources, and of *exempla* from all historical periods, Sagece follows the humanist trajectory already set in the *dit* of combining pagan and Christian elements without drawing attention to potential incompatibilities between them.[26] Her encyclopedic reading enables her to rebut the accounts her fellow Destinies give of themselves and to redefine the moral and intellectual bases of all three; she is especially dismissive of Richece. The wisdom she embodies is, she maintains, a fusion of learning, sapience, and virtue that is valid throughout history:[27]

Wherever sapience is widespread one also finds virtue and constancy, strength, and an abundance of wisdom that, however circumstance may change, does not diminish or puff up men's minds. Its intent is never altered or deflected from its rightful purpose. Without doubt, learning is worth more than any wealth, as Alan [of Lille] says in his book.

> La ou sappïence est commune,
> la est vertu, la est constance,
> la est force et grand abondance
> de sagece, qui le corage
> n'appetice në en hauçage
> ne maine pour mutacion
> des choses. Son entencion
> ne sera ja nul temps muee
> de son droit point ne remuee.
> Que scïence trop mieulx, sans faille,

> que nule autre richece vaille
> en son livre le dit Alain. (*CLE*, 5196–206)

The solution to conflict lies in finding order and permanence, which Sagece alone can provide:

For as long as the world keeps turning on its course it will head for confusion if it is not governed by order; no thing can last without order, nothing endure. And where does order come from? Is it not from wisdom, its partner?

> Car tant qu'il [*sc*. le commun cours du monde] dure a la reonde,
> se par ordre n'yert gouverné,
> a confusion ert mené;
> ne sens ordre ne peut durer
> nulle chose et riens endurer.
> Et dont vient ordre? N'est-ce mie
> de Sagece, qui est s'amie? (*CLE*, 5062–68)

A prince who submits to this order—one who is wedded to Sagece herself—offers the best hope of resolving conflict.[28] Through these allegorical nuptials, the prince will be able to extend wisdom to others, increasing the virtue of all individuals and preparing for their glorious metamorphosis into creatures of eternity. Sagece thus proposes herself as the necessary supplement to any political structure that Noblece, Chevalerie, or Richece could give rise to; she alone can transcend earthly mutability and offer a lasting recourse against its inherent tendency to discord.

Clearly Sagece is presented as the *dit*'s most important spokesperson. In what sense, however, can she be said to be generated from the fountain? The answer, I suggest, is that she personifies its sapiential value; as a "fontaine de philozophie" it can flow but not speak; to be articulated, this philosophy requires at least metaphorical embodiment. Sagece is first described as being accompanied by two daughters, Sapience and Science, which is to say that she comprises both these qualities. Sapience and Science are both identified with the fountain; indeed, they are echoed in its twin names of "fontaine de sapience" and "fontaine de clergie." As a combination of *sapience* and *science/clergie* (terms she herself reiterates innumerable times), Sagece is the wisdom that issues from the fountain; indeed, she *is* the fountain. In this way she is the closest the *dit* comes to the goddess Pallas, who, in the Sybil's account (unlike in Ovid's), is said actually to live at the fountain, in its world of *clergie, science*, and *philozophie*:[29]

Now [says the Sybil] I have told you the whole truth about this beautiful place
and the surroundings of the fountain of learning, where one can learn astrology.
Philosophy lives there, and Pallas used to as well, and I think she still does for she
[*or:* the fountain?] is unchanging; and so does all learning that clerks go sowing
throughout the world.

> Or t'ay je tout le voir appris
> de ce beau lieu et du pourpris
> de la fontaine de clergie,
> ou l'en apprent astrologie,
> et Philosophie y repaire
> et jadis y ot son repaire
> Pallas, et croy qu'elle a encore,
> car telle qu'elle fu est ore;
> et toute scïence ensement
> que clers vont au monde semant. (*CLE*, 1089–98)

It is characteristic of Christine to suppress divinity from the pagan pantheon and reinterpret its gods as human qualities. As the voice of Pallas/
wisdom/philosophy, Sagece is not only the "lead" Destiny but also the
figure whose statements, articulating the thought "placed" in the fountain
and applying it to lived historical circumstance, are the closest to being
programmatic for the whole *dit*.

  For this reason Sagece can be seen as an identification of Christine.
In Sagece she finds an answer to the problems that she raised first in her
own voice and then in the voice of La Terre. Wisdom personified does not
just provide a framework in which these problems might be solved; in her
metaphorical body she also constitutes something approaching a physical
presence in which Christine's melancholic presence from the beginning of
the *dit* is raised to the universal and dignified as sublime. Armed with this
insight, we can now consider in more depth the transition from melancholy to allegory in the *Chemin de long estude*, and their joint relation to
metaphysics.

Allegory and Melancholy

Kristeva's account of allegory in *Soleil noir: Dépression et mélancolie* will
illumine the way in which Christine's fountain as "place of thought" generates an allegory that is not just a "reading otherwise" but also develops
the fountain's potential as a metaphysical spectacle. For Kristeva, allegory

is a way of transacting with the loss that is the root cause of melancholy. Melancholy orchestrates the psyche around a loss to which it clings, and allegory both marks the space of that loss and retrieves it as artifice, permanence, and beauty. While melancholy confronts the metaphysical implications of loss, allegory renders them beautiful. We see all these processes at work in the *Chemin de long estude*.

The most obvious loss is the death of Christine's husband, which plunges her into depression at the beginning of the *dit*:

And I was overwhelmed by the weight of grief, becoming like a recluse—listless, gloomy, lonely and weary, never taking a single step without a tear in my eye, a prey to mortal sorrow.

> Si fu de grief dueil confuse
> et devins comme recluse,
> matte, morne, seule, et lasse,
> ne pas un seul pas n'alasse
> que n'eusse la larme a l'ueil,
> demenant mon mortel dueil. (*CLE*, 119–24)

Before she falls asleep, Christine is in a state of near despair as her melancholia inflates this grief to encompass all the misery and strife that tear human life apart. In her dream, the figures of La Terre and Sagece universalize this loss of her husband as the engulfing loss of all order, security, and happiness.

This escalation suggests that, as Kristeva argues, melancholy is not just a reaction to the loss of a specific object that might be replaced; it translates a deeper, ontological deficit in which the subject suffers alienation from what Kristeva calls "la Chose" ("the Thing"): "The narcissistic depressive is in mourning not for an Object but for the Thing" (*Soleil noir*, 22, "Le dépressif narcissique est en deuil non pas d'un Objet mais de la Chose"). By the "Thing" that is lost, Kristeva designates "the real that resists signification, the pole of attraction and repulsion, the home of sexuality against which the object of desire will detach itself" (*Soleil noir*, 22, "le réel rebelle à la signification, le pôle d'attrait et de répulsion, demeure de la sexualité"). In the *Chemin de long estude* we see this escalation from Object to Thing when mourning for her husband's death precipitates Christine's feeling that the whole world is out of joint: the loss of a specific individual object triggers the more absolute and catastrophic absence of the Thing. The libidinal core of melancholy persists, however, in its dream remedy when Christine's widowhood is imaginatively compensated by her personifications. All female figures, they take her back in time through motherhood and nursing (La Terre) to being offered as a bride (Sagece), while Sagece also tenders a wider hope of order restored.

As it extends outward from the libidinal, Kristeva's Thing takes on metaphysical implications. Aware of the philosophical history of the term (notably in Heidegger), Kristeva sees the Thing as that which is not knowable in itself but which corresponds with what Heidegger calls the "pre-ontological." It is "the indeterminate, the undifferentiated, the ungraspable" (*Soleil noir*, 22 n. 10, "l'indéterminé, l'inséparé, l'insaisissable"), known to us only through the Object, which is what the Thing becomes once it is caught up (and thereby "ontologized") in the universal order of language. The Thing is thus resistant to signification ("rebelle à la signification") not just by virtue of its unacknowledged sexual origins but also constitutively.[30] When Kristeva describes melancholia as grief for the Thing rather than for the Object, she also has in mind this radical unavailability of reality to the speaking subject. Although her theory is Heideggerian rather than Aristotelian, it is remarkably appropriate to the metaphysical impasse inherited from Aristotle by medieval thinkers and confronted by Christine in the *Chemin de long estude*. The absence of her husband and of a sense of order are not so radical as her incapacity directly to experience that absence, given that the particular always remains unknown. I have already quoted Cathelineau's formulation whereby "the core of Aristotelian ontology remains essentially that of the individual uncognizable in itself and known only through the language of knowledge as expressed through genera and species,"[31] and this is very much what Kristeva understands by the Thing as opposed to the Object.

Kristeva sees allegory as a means by which the melancholic processes and transforms loss. She calls it a "hyper-sign," a term which she does not explicitly define but in which we can discern at least three meanings. Most obviously, the hyper-sign relies on another absent (lost or lacking) sign. For example, if I say, "Venus does this" as a way of meaning "Love does this," then as a sign "Venus" is "hyper" because it stands over and above another sign rather than signifying something directly; it acknowledges that there is something ("love") that is absent and must be sought, and that we find difficult or impossible to speak about. The hyper-sign thus, first, always comes accompanied by a gap or pause that is infused with desire for what is missing. Surrounded by it as by an aura, the allegorical sign is thus, second, hyper in the sense of appearing superior to other signs, transfigured or sublime. But third, the allegorical sign, in signaling the absence around it, acknowledges the inexpressibility of the Thing that haunts all language. It is hyper in the sense of drawing attention to the constitutive failure of *all* signs to designate the singular realities that constitute the world. Its aura of the sublime stems from its reconfiguring this radical lack, as opposed to the mere absence of some object. This at least is how I understand Kristeva's difficult prose, itself illustrative of the elusive beauty of which she speaks:

The dynamic of sublimation mobilizes the primary processes and those of idealization in order to weave, from and with the emptiness of depression, a *hyper-sign*. This is *allegory* as the splendor of that which *no longer is*, but which takes on a higher meaning because I am able to recreate nothingness in an improved form, in an immutable harmony, here and now and for eternity, for the benefit of a third party [e.g., a reader]. A sublime meaning instead of and in place of implied underlying non-being, allegory is artifice substituted for the ephemeral. Beauty is intrinsic to it. Like feminine adornments veiling persistent depressive states, beauty manifests itself as the admired face of loss and transforms it in order to give it life.[32]

In the *Chemin de long estude* Christine's allegory could be said explicitly to constitute itself as a hyper-sign. All three figures I have just proposed as identifications of Christine are transcendent figures that stand over and above her, abstracting from her a universal form: that of Poet, Earth Mother, or Wisdom incarnate. While transfiguring her into something sublime and knowable they also acknowledge the possibility that she herself is melancholic and unknown. All three problematize the relation to the body, Calliope by not appearing, La Terre by being represented only by a text, and Sagece by having at best a metaphorical body. Their names are thus hyper-signs that declare the lack of the individual-corporeal in language. And all three, likewise, are depicted as relating to the rational faculty but as not subsumed by it, and thus as pointing to something (or Thing) that escapes rational understanding. Ovid's Calliope talks to Pallas, and in the *Chemin de long estude* the Muse inspires both poets and philosophers, which suggests that poetry addresses the framework of intellectual reflection but is not the same as it. Loquence delivers the Earth's letter to Raison (the resulting exchange between a mother and reason, however mediated, is certainly a rarity in medieval poetry!), implying that while her grief can be rationally understood, it is not itself a product of reasoning. According to Sagece, the reason she failed to govern human behavior is that Raison had absented herself from the world, and yet Raison appeals to Sagece to account for the world's plight. Sagece, it appears, depends on the exercise of Raison, but she also does more than Raison can alone—there is more to wisdom than rationality.[33]

Thus, in all three personifications there is a surplus of something that escapes the purely intellectual faculty but is instead located in some aspect of praxis: a chord of artistic, emotional, moral, or practical experience. This surplus of experience over reason in Christine's personifications corresponds with the lack of congruence between the unexpressed Thing and the rationalized Object, and is both lost and found in her sublime allegorical figures. More broadly, and finally, Christine's allegory can be read as a hyper-sign in Kristeva's widest, metaphysical sense: as a place of mourning for the inevitably *dis*placed Thing. The poetic form in which she has chosen to write draws attention to the crucial Aristotelian epistemic impasse: to the way individual experience is both vital to and elided from the process of making sense. In short, the allegorical gap in the *Chemin de long estude* might be supplemented by autobiography, or the body, or praxis, were it not that the cognizability of all of these individual things is forfeit by their being compromised in *the* Thing.

But as Kristeva points out, allegory also compensates for the loss of the Thing, for readers as well as the writer: "When we have passed through our melancholic states to the point of interesting ourselves in the life of signs, we may be seized by beauty that bears witness to how someone has magnificently found the royal road by means of which man transcends the grief of separation: the way of the word made over to suffering. . . . The magnificent would be the impossible dream, even, the other world of the depressive realized here on earth."[34] Kristeva's "royal road" was, for Christine, a more modest, pedestrian pathway made, as we have seen, from the study of learned poetry. Yet Kristeva's invocation here of "an other world" ("l'autre monde") is intriguingly the same as the Sybil's invitation to Christine to follow her "en autre monde plus parfaict," while Christine's "impossible dream," as both reader and dream-vision poet, is identical to Kristeva's: that her personal melancholia can be transcended in universal magnificence and translated into a new world order.

As an instance of how this *chemin* leads Christine's dream self to an *autre monde* in which allegory turns melancholy into splendor, I shall look briefly at a passage from Sagece's speech about the transformative powers of knowledge. It begins as a tribute to Alan of Lille, learned allegory acclaiming learned allegory. Christine recognizes *De Planctu* as a model for transforming grief into serenity by means of a metaphysical reflection:[35]

In his *De Planctu Naturae* Alan [of Lille] plainly says that possessing the noble quality of learning is more desirable than any other thing that is loved or that ought to be esteemed. For the more you spread learning far and wide, the more of it you have; and the more it is shared out, the better everyone's share is; so the more it is broadcast, the more intimately it is owned. Through it the great boon of conscience, more precious than gold, is conceived in our heart, and its fruit soothes all ills. Learning is the sun whose light brings daylight flooding into the shadows of our thoughts. It is the eye of our soul in reflection, it is the garden of delights where everything is good for us. It is what has the authority, in its own right and through its beneficial powers of conversion, to transform the workings of an imperfect worldly creature into celestial perfection, change mortal into immortal, and transitory human life into perfect and utter glory.

> En son livre le dit Alain
> *De Plainte de Nature* a plain
> que la noble possession
> de scïence a l'eleccion
> sur toutes les choses amees
> qui doivent estre renommees;
> laquelle plus est espandue,
> plus est aux respendans rendue,
> et plus est par tout deppartie,
> plus en vault chacune partie;
> tant plus est partout publïee,
> plus l'a chacun en soy lïee;
> par la quelle le grant tresor
> de conscïence, meillor qu'or,
> est conceu en nostre courage,
> dont le fruit tous maulx assouage.
> C'est le souleil par quel lumiere
> ajourne o sa lueur plainiere
> es tenebres de la pensee.
> C'est l'œil de nostre ame appensee,
> c'est le paradis des delices
> ou toutes choses sont propices.
> C'est celle qui l'auctorité
> a de droite proprieté
> par sa bonne conversion
> de müer l'opperacion
> de l'œuvre imparfaicte et terrestre
> a la perfeccïon celestre.
> C'est celle qui peut le mortel

faire müer en inmortel,
l'umaine et transitoire vie
en gloire parfaicte, assouvie. (*CLE*, 5207–38)

This is indeed an "impossible dream," from which Christine's mother un-
fortunately jolts her, but is a fabulous hymn to the power of the intellect
to transform melancholy at the loss of the ephemeral and mutable Thing
into a celebration of eternal beauty from which all will benefit.

Conclusion

Christine is the French medieval author most consistently preoccupied by
her uniqueness, a preoccupation seized upon by her modern critics. Upon
her, the philosophical conviction that only particulars exist is impressed
with unusual force. Yet knowing Aristotle's *Metaphysics* as she does, she is
also familiar with the teaching that only universals are available to be
known. The *Chemin de long estude* is a didactic poem that aspires to discover a universal moral and political order from the experience of individuals like herself. This is its ambition, but by the same token, this is the
intellectual problem that it has to resolve. In her waking life Christine's
"place of thought" is her study, where she finds herself melancholy and
alone. But in her dream, this study transforms into a living world of authors and thinkers, clustered round the fountain of the Muses and enact-
ing before her very eyes the drama of the one and the many. By drawing
from the fountain a series of female figures—Calliope, the Earth personified, and the Destinies, especially Sagece—Christine combines autobiography and didacticism by abstracting universal forms of herself. Although
the particular is acknowledged as lacking in the universal order, her mood
passes from mourning to exaltation as, beginning with an inevitable attachment to an individual female body, she experiments with sublime dis-
embodiment. The complex balancing act her personifications perform
between intellect and its practical application—all are both more and less
than either—acts as a way of binding together the poles of reasoning and
individual sensory experience. Through them Christine finds a way of ad-
dressing and progressively embodying the tensions at the heart of her
philosophico-poetic concerns. Indeed, allegory turns the alienation of language from things to advantage: by displaying itself in aesthetic splendor,
the gap severing knowledge from being becomes poetry, which enacts as
well as it displays the eternal glories of *science*.

As the conclusion to the *dit* allows, however, the fact that the universal alone is known does not mean that everyone knows things in the same
way. It remains difficult to see how unity, including and especially political
unity, can ever be attained. Christine dreams of overriding seemingly in-
transigent differences such as those between pagan and Christian. Yet she
also concedes that unity may ultimately depend only on force. Sagece may
have a better understanding than the other Destinies of practical politics,
but she doesn't control them—force, wealth, and power are a significant
part of human behavior and are recalcitrant to Wisdom's efforts to dominate them; they all command significant support in Raison's court. When
at the end of the *dit* human history is thrown back on its own resources,
this chimes with Christine's intellectual recognition that, while all knowledge is universal knowledge, it is always delimited by an individual's capacity to know. For all the splendor and luminosity that infuse her heavenly
visions, the "place of thought" that is the fountain remains unenvis-
ageable in its entirety. Everyone has to follow his or her own path and
stream and define his or her own place there. Similarly, in the heavenly
debate, the never-ending enumeration of *sententiae* and *exempla* betrays
the way the unity of human history consists in endless multiplicity from
which we might draw endlessly different lessons. Although Christine's
own particularity is resplendently transfigured, it still determines the form
taken by the personifications in the *dit*—another author/reader would
have done it differently. In reworking Boethius, Christine contrives her
own "consolation of philosophy," which (much like Machaut in the *Jugement dou roy de Navarre*) misdoubts the Boethian One. In its place she
views the universal as a mental construct that indefinitely many minds,
some better than hers, are engaged in constructing.

The libidinal character of Christine's melancholy differentiates it from
the saturnine mood afflicting Froissart at the start of the *Joli buisson de
Jonece* or even Machaut's initial melancholia in the *Navarre*, although Machaut's humor does of course become caught up in sexual difference as
the *dit* progresses. However, just as the Sybil's summons to the *autre
monde* of the didactic poem illumines the ambitions of all of the works
studied in this book, so Christine's shift from melancholy to allegory illumines the "complexity of one" for many of these poets as they pine for
the singular one that is essential, yet lacking, in the conceptual one of the
universal. These are the issues that Christine raises with her pen/banner,
and that she leads us to reflect on.

Conclusion

Monologism Reconsidered

I HAVE SET OUT TO ILLUSTRATE how didacticism in late medieval poetry involves "placing" thought. Place in this poetry, I have argued, can be understood in Aristotle's terms as what bounds or circumscribes a body. This definition of place was illuminating to a period of thought that, under Aristotle's influence, took visual perception as the model of how we know things, and that saw being as pertaining primarily to individuals that are typically embodied and thus in place. Nevertheless, the visual model and with it the shaping role of place run up against the limitation that these individual things, however bodily they appear to us, may not be cognizable as such; according to Aristotle, the intellect knows only universal ideas, which do not belong in place. As the "long fourteenth century" advances it becomes ever clearer that the issues faced by didactic poets have affinities with the preoccupations of philosophers in the same period, who are tussling with questions of whether singulars are intellectually cognizable, and how far the perceptions of the individual subject of knowledge condition what it is that is known. Albeit at a respectful distance from the dazzling heights that academic philosophy reached in this period, the oneness of meaning on which didacticism relies becomes caught up in comparable reflections on unity and singularity, and the difficulty of working from one to the other. As a result, the *loci* in which poets place their thought are often difficult or impossible to visualize.

From a literary standpoint, the most important conclusion to draw from this study is that what Bakhtin called "monologism" is not a simple butt or foil to the more complex and intriguing concept of dialogism. On the contrary, I have argued that didacticism, while it is undoubtedly a monologist mode, involves medieval poets in highly complex negotiations between unity and uniqueness. The religious poets discussed in Chapters 1 to 3 believe that it *is* possible for the individual to be united with the divine One, but conceiving how this can come about leads to the "places" of its thinking being contorted, unstable, and paradoxical, the more so as

the divine One with whom unity is sought is so far removed from what
human beings can conceptualize. The poets discussed in Chapters 4 to 6,
whose outlook is at least partly secular, do not share this faith in the individual's potential for inclusion within a higher unity. They do not deny
the priority of universality, but they regard the individual's relation to it
as one of exclusion (Machaut), eclipse (Froissart), or dissonant partiality
(Christine de Pizan). There is a consequent tension in all these poems
between unity of meaning—the didactic purport of the text—and awareness of the singularity of the poet's own perception.

This singularity often emerges with most force in the confrontation
with a "common place." Both Matfre Ermengaud and Jean Froissart
"place" their thought in an adaptation of one of the most widely read
textbooks of the Middle Ages, Porphyry's *Isagoge*, and yet, despite their
common location in a tree, their poems record utterly different encounters
with the "complexity of one." Machaut, Froissart, and Christine de Pizan
all rewrite Boethius's *Consolation of Philosophy*, but with very diverse out-
comes. Machaut uses it to talk ironically about the possibility of a universal
good of happiness in a world split by sexual difference. Froissart's personification of Philozophie and the "maistre en philozophie" are both viewed
askance as Froissart rallies instead to the common places offered by the
Ovide moralisé. Christine ambitiously combines Boethius with as many
literary places as she can muster, including the *Moralisé*. The role of Philosophy is distributed among various characters, one of whom, Sagece, is
the *dit*'s major spokesperson, but we are left in doubt whether her insights
will ever be realized in day-to-day politics. A further common place in
which Froissart and Christine de Pizan both meet and diverge is the *Ovide
moralisé*, Froissart imitating its trope of Christian metamorphosis, Christine absorbing Christian allegoresis into a wider, humanistic perspective.
Finally, the *Roman de la rose*, which, like Boethius, serves as model
throughout the period, is also used in a diversity of ways. The *Chemin de
long estude* theorizes the diversity of potential responses to the *Rose* when
it emphasizes that the fountain comprises a multitude of ducts and is surrounded by many paths. Froissart upgrades the rose bush to a cosmic *buisson* but then repudiates the love allegory that unfolds in its branches.
Rebuttal of the *Rose* is most explicit in the *Pèlerinage de vie humaine*,
which reorients the entire dream vision around mankind's need for salvation.

In my Introduction I suggested that the *Rose* may have influenced
the continuing use of verse throughout this period despite the much-

trumpeted rise of prose. Jean de Meun had demonstrated that verse was not just a possible vehicle for thought but actually a highly appropriate one. The twin themes of the *Rose*, desire and knowledge, are dialectically intertwined so that desire for knowledge generates knowledge of desire, and vice versa. By using a verse form associated with vernacular romance, and adorning it with features associated with courtly lyric, the *Rose* implies that poetic genres are directly relevant to philosophical and theological reflection. In the fourteenth century, as the study of metaphysics became more psychological, this relevance may have seemed even more assured. The *Rose*, itself a recasting of Boethius, may have influenced the way the *Consolation of Philosophy* was rewritten in this period, when melancholy runs so deep in the human heart that philosophy no longer seems consoling. Boethius's fourteenth-century avatars seek enlightenment but recognize a need for more personal forms of comfort. The result is that, when they embrace affective themes of love, desire, and mourning, they revitalize the lyric qualities of their model in line with contemporary vernacular poetry. Knowledge, emotion, and poetry become ever more intimately associated.[1]

Another aspect of the *Rose* that lent itself to fourteenth-century imitators was its use of place. Guillaume de Deguileville, Froissart, and Christine de Pizan all allude to and rework its *loci*. But this aspect of the *Rose*'s influence also poses a problem for my central thesis, given the poem's much-debated relation to monologism. For some critics, the *Rose* certainly does possess unity of meaning. Indeed, the patristic-inspired exegetical criticism of D. W. Robertson and John Fleming has been the most potent and vocal promoter of monologism in medieval literature, to the extent that it has positively recruited adherents to dialogism. Critics dissatisfied with the exegetical approach have acclaimed the *Rose* as one of the most dialogic possible of all texts, applauded its gutsy disrespect toward the authority of oneness and detailed its elaborate flirtations with duality and multiplicity. I myself have argued that the *Rose* is not just dialectical but infinitely slippery, its approach to meaning having much in common with what Derrida would later term "dissemination." I cannot conclude this book about place, thought, and the monologic without some brief consideration of the way the *Rose* seems to be at once the model of almost all the texts I have examined here and a counterexample to their practice. Does the *Rose* assume any convergence between place, thought, and interpretation, and if not, how, under its influence, can placing thought have become a prop of didacticism, or of reflection on what I have been calling the complexity of one? Is there any way in which the placing of thought in the *Rose* prepares the way for the didactic poetry that follows in its wake?

From the outset the *Rose* associates place and thought. Every major speaker both has a view to expound and is strongly associated with a particular *locus*: Amor with his garden, Raison her tower, Nature her forge. The outlines of a place are sometimes explicitly identified as the outline of a concept, so that, for example, Raison's description of the house of Fortune is a means of presenting the contradictions and uncertainties of chance itself. Perhaps one reason why I see the *Rose* as refractory to monologism is simply that there are too many places in it for oneness to be reckoned among its priorities, or for any unified thought to emerge. However, I do not want simply to assert that each "place" in the *Rose* is used to circumscribe a "one" and that it is merely the multiplicity of places that makes for there being, as it were, too many "ones." It seems to me that the poem's attitude toward "placing thought" is already playful at the level of the individual scene. Given that I cannot analyze all of its *loci* (that would require a whole book), I shall concentrate here on Genius's sermon, since it aspires to a summative role in the text, dismissing all of its previous places and relocating their thought instead in the "park of the Lamb."

Genius's address to Love's army is one of the most problematic parts of the *Rose*. Dressed by Amor in bishop's robes, with a lighted candle given him by Venus, mounted on a scaffold, and speaking in the name of Nature, Genius conjures his congregation of miscellaneous barons to fulfill their sacred obligation to have reproductive sex or be damned to hell. The upside is that, if they carry out his bawdy exhortations, they will enjoy eternal bliss in contemplation of the Trinity. Genius has unerringly identified what will prove the principal foci of oneness for the didactic authors that follow: the one of the universal (the species, man); that of the singular (the individual man); the One of the divine; and the community of believers with that One. The way he combines them is, however, intellectually preposterous. There is outrageous miscegenation of sex and theology in the promise that the individual can achieve union with the Godhead through reproduction. In addition, there is quite egregious confusion of the particular with the universal. Immortality is the concern of the individual, whereas reproductive sex enables the perpetuation of the species. Genius is oblivious to the most elementary distinctions within what I have been calling "the complexity of one."

Despite his intellectual deficiencies, Genius's command of the mechanisms of didactic poetry is impressive. His sermon reads like a fulfillment of the Sybil's assurance that the "place of thought" to which we are summoned is "another and more perfect world." He exhorts his listeners to commit every word of his sermon to heart, repeat it wherever they may be, and practice what it preaches, so that

[they] will never be prevented . . . from entering the park of the merry field where the son of the Virgin, that ewe with her white fleece, bouncing ahead over the pastureland, leads the sheep with him.

> ja ne seeroiz anpeeschiez . . .
> d'antrer ou parc du champ joli,
> ou les berbiz conduit o li
> saillant devant par les herbiz
> li filz de la Vierge, berbiz
> o toute sa blanche toison. (*RR*, 19902, 19905–9)

If they all subscribe to the *bonne escole*, the multitude of disparate places where they may be—suburbs, castles, cities, towns (*RR*, 19985–86)—will give way to a single place, the "parc du champ joli." A common understanding, that is, will take them all to a common place. The conjunction of thought with location is reiterated in the helpful digest of his sermon (*RR*, 20601–29) where Genius again assures his listeners that if they think and act as instructed they will be admitted to the *parc* and drink at its fountain. Further to underline their future unanimity in this place of thought, within the parc they will all look exactly alike. Led by the Lamb, son of the Virgin ewe who doubles as shepherd, they will all be ewes together, since "it pleases him that his robe resembles theirs" (*RR*, 19969–70, "bon li samble / que sa robe la leur resemble"). Although the images of Christ as Lamb and shepherd are familiar enough, the way Genius herds his listeners into uniformity has a comic side—he is rounding them up like sheep—and a ludicrous ambition, since his audience, in addition to the Lover and nameless barons, includes the pagan gods Amor and Venus: scarcely promising material for admission to this Christian idyll.

The Sybil uses the pun on *penon* to insinuate the possibility of didacticism being backed by force, and Genius's sermon similarly resorts to the stick as much as the carrot. We learn a lot about the misery of the black sheep that are condemned to a pagan hell and that the shepherd vigilantly excludes from the *parc* (*RR*, 20213–16). Somewhat surprisingly, we are also told that there are extremely few white sheep (*RR*, 20212, "de tex bestes n'i a guieres"). Presumably Genius is echoing Nature's complaints against humanity for being so dilatory at reproducing. Whatever the reason, the *parc* is a place of privilege reserved for the happy few, and those excluded from it suffer.

As Genius continues to define his thinking in relation to the *parc*, the dissonant conjunction of sex and theology from which he started develops into a broader conflation of the physical and the metaphysical. The *parc* is a reward for physical activity (reproductive sex) but is itself defined by its denial of natural laws. Its sheep eat grass that never runs out, and the more they eat the more it grows; the sheep themselves are never sheared, slaughtered, or sick (*RR*, 19945–62). It is avowedly a place removed from the world of corruption and change, outside time and basking in eternity, which, it emerges, is a single, perpetual, glorious spring day (*RR*, 19971–20000). Genius uses the *parc* as a textual *locus* in which to clash together the mutest of mute bodies (grazing sheep) and metaphysical ideas. More alert readers may be provoked into recognizing that, while it might be helpful to visualize or "place" thought, ideas are actually very different from place. The very thoroughness with which Genius treats the traditional pious metaphor of Christ with his flock pushes it to absurdity, confronting his listeners with the misfit between animal bodies and the theological burden placed upon them.

Genius also seems to suggest that this place, on which so much description has been lavished, while it may be a place of thought, is actually a *non*-place. This idea emerges when, in the course of comparing his *parc* with the garden described by Guillaume de Lorris, he explicitly removes the *parc* from everything that is or can be known. Excluded from Guillaume's *jardin* are the "ten ugly little statues" (*RR*, 20273, ".x. ledes ymagetes") depicting vices on its outer wall. But anyone looking at the *parc* would see represented outside it, and thereby be excluded from it, every imaginable fault and all material reality too: so he would see the whole earth with its riches, the sea and all sea creatures, fresh water and its inhabitants, the air and all that flies in it, and the fire and stars surrounding the earth (*RR*, 20282–300):

If he were to be outside it, he would see all these things excluded from this fine park painted in as much evidence as they appear in their actual reality.

> Qui la seroit, toutes ces choses
> verroit de ce biau parc forcloses
> ausint apertement portretes
> con proprement aperent fetes. (*RR*, 20301–4)

Many of the didactic texts studied in this book have an encyclopedic impulse, but the *parc* is, as it were, an antiencyclopedia, defined by the fact that the whole world is absent from it. The *parc* is surrounded by the natural order and yet outside it, just as thought is shaped by physical reality yet not part of it. (The *parc* is also defined negatively in the long digression on the age of Jupiter, which, with its physical pleasure, labor, and suffering, is everything the *parc* is not.) The rationale behind Genius's method of exposition may stem from negative theology, but the effect is to concede that, while place as what circumscribes individual bodies is the condition of thought, it is also excluded from it.

As a didactic text, Genius's sermon is very different from the rest of the poem in which it occurs, and from which he sets out to differentiate it. He had earlier referred his listeners to the *Roman de la rose* as if it were a completely separate work. There is no need for him to sully himself by expatiating on the vices Nature has condemned, Genius claims, because they are quite adequately expounded in the *Roman de la rose*, which thereby enables us to avoid them (*RR*, 19849–54). At this point in his sermon, Genius is assuming distance from the *Rose* in order to underline a more positive message: lead the good life, love, reproduce, confess, and thereby enter the *parc*. But when he proceeds to detailed comparison between his *parc* and Guillaume de Lorris's *jardin*, Genius seems rather to be contrasting two different approaches to didacticism. Stigmatizing Guillaume's text as *corrompable*, Genius sets about dismantling and scrapping every aspect of his garden and substituting in its place a counterbalancing feature of the *parc*. Although he postulates the *parc* as prior, he seems to infer its qualities by contrast with those of the *jardin*. Where the garden circumscribes a world that is impure, bodily, and shifting, the *parc* announces one that is pure, metaphysical, and unchanging. For Genius, then, the *Rose* is didactic in a negative (and potentially counterproductive) way, in that it depicts everything we should choose to avoid. There is a risk that, rather than warning its readers away from vice, the *Rose* might lead them astray. Genius's own didacticism makes this negativity explicit: if his listeners shun all the vicious places in the *Rose*, they can follow him to the virtuous non-place of the *parc*.

Genius's metaphysical utopia presents a different kind of totality from the *jardin*. It includes all things that are delightful and true and enduring (20353–54). It is the realm of a Trinitarian One, with all three ducts of its fountain distinct yet unified (20444–48). This contrasts with the pagan threesomes—the Furies, the Fates, the Kings of the underworld—from earlier in his sermon, whose identities within each trio remain distinct. The *parc*'s divine nature is also manifest in the fact that the fountain does not rely on a spring but generates its own water (*RR*, 20450), while the carbuncle within it doesn't need the sun but gleams with its own light (*RR*, 20524–25). When people gaze into the mirroring surface of the fountain,

> always, wherever they are, they can see all every thing in the park and know its true nature and themselves likewise, and once they have seen themselves there become such wise masters that they will never again be deceived about anything that is.

> toujours, de quelque part qu'ils soient,
> toutes les choses du parc voient
> et les connoissent proprement,
> et eus meïsmes ansement;
> et puis que la se sunt vëu,
> ja mes ne seront deceü
> de nule chose que puisse estre,
> tant i devienent sage mestre. (*RR*, 20541–48)

Genius's *parc* is a metaphysician's paradise from which all physical reality is excluded but where all true knowledge is simultaneously available (unlike the *jardin,* where only half is ever visible at once). He thus seems thoroughly aware that thought does not belong in place, even though it helps us envisage it to place it. It is all the more shocking that, immediately following this lofty realization, he reiterates his sermon's principal theme of "reproduce or be damned," and we see that this whole metaphysical construction depends entirely on the body.

   In conclusion, then, Genius exhibits a virtuoso command of didacticism together with the utmost confusion as to its intellectual bases. Looked at alongside its successors of the long fourteenth century, his sermon seems to be an instance of that uncanny phenomenon in medieval poetry: the parody that is consubstantive with its model.[2] Genius's sermon is an exemplary instance of didacticism in all respects except the crucial one, that it is impossible to take seriously the thought he places in the *parc*. The reason it seems parodic or self-undermining is that he wants to keep in play, and blur together, so many kinds of oneness all at once; and that he treats the place of thought both as entirely bodily and as entirely excluded from physical place, so that the distinction between the physical and the metaphysical is sometimes affirmed and sometimes negated. The outcome is that the reader/listener stumbles, disoriented, from one form of oneness to another, which all seem to merge (or disseminate) one into the next.

Alastair Minnis sees Genius's discourse as harking back to older forms of allegory that Jean de Meun otherwise eschews.[3] In my view, however, it is quite forward-looking, in that the didactic texts I have studied rely on Genius's techniques. They also take up several of his themes, but in a way that conforms to their (better) understanding of how oneness is complex. Genius's sermon, that is, seems to have been read as a text about didacticism, if not as a didactic text. So, for example, Genius's emphasis on the union of creation with the Creator and of the individual creature with God is the central concern of the *Breviari*. Like Genius, the *Ovide moralisé* sets out to forge a community of resemblance between Christ and his people in a paradise landscape, and to subdue pagan polytheism to the framework of Christian thought. The analogy between the divine nature and that of mankind is a preoccupation of the *Pèlerinage de vie humaine*, which, like Genius's sermon, draws attention to a paradoxical internal limit between the physical and the metaphysical such that the realm of grace is "excluded within" that of nature. The connection that Genius establishes between sex and salvation surfaces explicitly in the *Joli buisson de Jonece*, where Froissart reverses Genius's contention in favor of the more orthodox view that sex imperils the immortal soul. In the *Jugement dou roy de Navarre*, sex is used more obliquely to question the existence of a single human "good." Christine de Pizan not only repeats Genius's summons to a place of thought but also responds, in her fountain of the Muses, to the way he repudiates Guillaume de Lorris's fountain. With the *Ovide moralisé* as her intermediary, she recuperates the fountain as a *locus* of enlightenment, seriously reflecting on it as a metaphysical spectacle instead of a burlesque one.[4]

"No text is homogeneous," says Derrida.[5] But texts can address what it might mean to confront oneness of meaning rather than retreat into endlessly deferred and indefinite meanings. Indeed, when he says "No text is homogeneous," Derrida is affirming just such a one truth, or a truth of one, about texts. A "one" can be ineffable, elusive, or enigmatic; it is certainly no less intellectually demanding than a "many." Genius's sermon sports with the placing of a complex one of thought, but the didactic poetry of the long fourteenth century develops its intellectual and aesthetic potential.

Notes

Introduction

1. Quintilian, *Institutio*, V, 10, 20–21, cited Carruthers, *Book of Memory*, 173.

2. Carruthers, *Book of Memory*, 182.

3. On medieval *florilegia*, ibid., 178–84; on their role as precursors to the Renaissance, Moss, *Printed Commonplace-Books*, 24–50.

4. Bakhtin, "On the Pre history of Novelistic Discourse."

5. Cave, *Cornucopian Text*, 96.

6. Aristotle, *On Memory*, 450a1 (also *De anima*, 431a15–19); Coleman, *Ancient and Medieval Memories*, 423. The Latin text of *On Memory* most probably used by Aquinas, and edited together with his commentary on it by Spiazzi, reads "intelligere non est sine phantasmate" and points out that the same line is found in the *De Anima*.

7. See, for example, Cowling, *Building the Text*; Cornelius, *The Figurative Castle*; Piehler, *The Visionary Landscape*; Robertson, "The Doctrine of Charity in Medieval Gardens"; Whitehead, *Castles of the Mind*. I explore the figure of the city in Christine de Pizan's *Cité des dames* in "The Didactic Space."

8. The oldest Latin translation of Aristotle's *Physics* (*Aristoteles Latinus, Physica, translatio vetus*) runs: "Dicit [Ysiodus] igitur . . . propter id quod opinati sunt, quemadmodum multi, omnia esse ubique et in loco. Si autem huius modi est, mirabilis quedam utique erit potentia loci et prima omnium et prior omnibus." Cited henceforth as *Physica vetus*.

9. See Lang, *Order of Nature in Aristotle's Physics*, 69: "The notions of nature as orderly and place as determinate clearly contrast with the modern concept of 'space,' which is by definition indeterminate."

10. See Casey, *Fate of Place*. For a historical overview, see Malpas, *Place and Experience*, 19–43.

11. *Physica vetus*: "inpossibile autem est corpus esse locum; in eodem enim utique essent duo corpora."

12. *Physica vetus*: "necesse est locum esse . . . terminum continentis corporis. Quare continentis terminus immobilis primum, hoc est locus."

13. Morison, *On Location*, 56.

14. Ibid. Future page references to this work are in the text.

15. My study therefore presents similarities with Suzanne Conklin Akbari's *Seeing Through the Veil*, which is about the visibility or invisibility of meaning in dream-vision poetry, though her book appeared as mine was nearing completion.

16. *Physics*, 210a14–24; summary adapted from Morison, *On Location*, 73.

17. At the beginning of the *Chemin de long estude*, and again in the *Cité des dames*.

18. "L'Un n'est donc pas un concept simple," Green, *Narcissisme*, 25.

19. My translation; "la croyance en la vérité universelle et définitive de la foi chrétienne, faite pour tout assimiler et tout réunir en le transformant," de Lubac, *Exégèse médiévale*, part II, vol. ii, 221, cited Demats, *Fabula*, 2.

20. Compagnon, *La Seconde main*, part IV. The term *monographie* is first used on pages 157 and 158.

21. Compagnon, *La Seconde main*, 227.

22. See Adams, "Universals in the Early Fourteenth Century," 411.

23. Notably between the *Categories,* the *De Interpretatione*, *Metaphysics*, *De Anima,* and *Posterior Analytics*. See de Libera, *Querelle des universaux,* 29–33, 48–49.

24. Adams, "Universals in the Early Fourteenth Century," 412–17.

25. Ibid., 415–16.

26. Lest "esset quodlibet universale purum figmentum intellectus," cited Owen, "Faith, Ideas, Illumination and Experience," 456 n. 63. The implications of this problem in Ockham have been explored by de Looze, *Pseudo-Autobiography*, 12–14.

27. Adams, "Universals in the Early Fourteenth Century," 434.

28. Bolar, "Intuitive and Abstractive Cognition," 474.

29. My translation; "le processus aboutissant à la formation de l'image devient ainsi le modèle structurel du processus allant de l'image au concept," de Libera, *Querelle des universaux*, 273.

30. Ibid., 141–42.

31. Bérubé, *Connaissance de l'individuel*.

32. Bolar, "Intuitive and Abstractive Cognition," 461.

33. Adams, "Universals in the Early Fourteenth Century," 412–15. See also Wippel, "Essence and Existence," 405–7, and Owens, "Faith, Ideas, Illumination, and Experience," 455–57.

Chapter 1. Book-Trees

1. See the excursus "Baumsymbolik und Baumschematik" in Kamber, *Arbor Amoris*, 129–40.

2. "L'arbre a dominé la réalité occidentale et toute la pensée occidentale, de la botanique à la biologie, l'anatomie, mais aussi la gnoséologie, la théologie, l'ontologie, toute la philosophie" (Deleuze and Guattari, *Mille plateaux*, 27–28; trans. Massumi, *A Thousand Plateaus*, 18).

3. Trans. Massumi, 16; "Les systèmes arborescents sont des systèmes hiérarchiques qui comportent des centres de signifiance et de subjectification, des automates centraux comme des mémoires organisées" (*Mille plateaux*, 25).

4. Trans. Massumi; "Un premier type de livre, c'est le livre racine. L'arbre est déjà l'image du monde, ou bien la racine est l'image de l'arbre-monde. C'est le livre classique, comme belle intériorité organique, signifiante et subjective (les

strates du livre). Le livre imite le monde, comme l'art, la nature: par des procédés qui lui sont propres, et qui mènent à bien ce que la nature ne peut pas ou ne peut plus faire. La loi du livre, c'est celle de la réflexion, le Un qui devient deux. Comment la loi du livre serait-elle dans la nature, puisqu'elle préside à la division même entre monde et livre, nature et art? Un devient deux: chaque fois que nous rencontrons cette formule . . . nous nous trouvons devant la pensée la plus classique et la plus réfléchie, la plus vieille, la plus fatiguée" (*Mille plateaux*, 11).

5. Alain de Libera (*Querelle des universaux*, 14–17) credits Porphyry with inflecting Aristotelian thought toward the medieval conception of "universal." Although the *Isagoge* docs not speak of "universals" but continues Aristotle's term "predicable," the way Porphyry questions the scope and implications of this term laid the groundwork for the "universals debate" to which the *Isagoge* gave rise in its commentators.

6. "Sit autem in uno praedicamento manifestum quod dicitur. Substantia est quidem ipsa genus, sub hac autem est corpus, sub corpore vero animatum corpus sub quo animal, sub animali vero rationale animal sub quo homo, sub homine vero Socrates et Plato et qui sunt particulares homines. Sed horum, substantia quidem generalissimum est et quod genus sit solum, homo vero specialissimum et quod species solum sit; corpus vero species quidem est substantiae, genus vero corporis animati; et animatum corpus species quidem est corporis, genus vero animalis; animal autem species quidem est corporis animati; genus vero rationalis; sed rationalis animal species quidem est animalis, genus autem hominis; homo vero species quidemen est rationalis animalis, non autem etiam genus particularium hominum, sed solum species; et omne quod ante individua proximum est, species erit solum, non etiam genus," "Porphyrii Isagoge, translatio Boethii," 4.21–5.1, pp. 9–10. The English translation is from Spade, *Five Texts on the Medieval Problem of Universals*, 4. I have also consulted *Porphyre:* Isagoge, trad. Tricot.

7. Trans. Dinneen, 11; "Et hec omnia patent in figura, que dicitur arbor Porphirii," *Tractatus*, ed. De Rijk, 20. Also known as the *Summulae logicales*, the *Tractatus* was composed in the 1230s. Avicenna (eleventh century) would seem to have used the term "Porphyrian tree" (cf. Prantl, *Geschichte der Logik im Abendlande*, II, 345 n. 132), and indeed "tree-like representations of Porphyry's scheme of genera and species are certainly found in medieval manuscripts, even in some of the earliest medieval logical manuscripts—that is to say, those from the ninth century" (John Marenbon, personal communication). Other terms used by medieval philosophers to refer to the tree are "hierarchy" and "categorial line."

8. For early modern representations, see Blum, "Dio e gli individui."

9. De Libera, *Querelle des universaux*, 34–46.

10. Thus "Porphyry bequeathed the problem he was seeking to avoid, but did not himself transmit any of the elements that would have enabled it to be considered from every point of view" (my translation; de Libera, *Querelle des universaux*, 41; "Porphyre a légué le problème qu'il aurait voulu éviter et il n'a transmis lui-même aucun des éléments qui eussent permis de le construire dans toute son ampleur").

11. *Isagoge*, §4, pp. 1–2; "sic enim, Oresten quidem dicimus a Tantalo habere

genus, Illum autem ab Hercule, et rursus Pindarem quidem Thebanum esse genere, Platonem vero Atheniensem" (2.2–2.4, p. 6).

12. Trans. Massumi, 4; "Il n'y a pas de différence entre ce dont un livre parle et la manière dont it est fait" (*Mille plateaux*, 10).

13. My translation; "L'arbre est à la fois l'amour et le livre," Galent-Fasseur, "La dame de l'arbre," 36. In fact the program is only unevenly carried out, and the text ends so abruptly as to appear unfinished. For an overview of the contents of the *Breviari*, see Meyer, "Matfre Ermengaud de Béziers, troubadour."

14. Meyer, "Matfre Ermengaud de Béziers, troubadour," 18, reiterated by Ricketts, "The Hispanic Tradition of the *Breviari d'Amor*," 228.

15. On which, see for example Picone, *L'Enciclopedismo medievale*.

16. Meyer, "Matfre Ermengaud de Béziers, troubadour," suggests various sources for different parts of the *Breviari*. Segre, "Le forme et le tradizione didattiche," 139, opts for a tension between ancient scientific schemata ("vecchi schemi scientifici") and recent Victorine allegories ("le nuove allegorie dei Vittorini"). Cherchi, "L'enciclopedia nel mondo dei trovatori," suggests possible debts to Hugh of Saint Victor (282) and Bartholomeus Anglicus (286). Galent-Fasseur argues that the *Breviari* is Christocentric and promotes belief in the incarnation specifically in order to convert the Jews, who were numerous in the Midi at the time ("La dame de l'arbre," 37–38). This view overestimates the importance of the anti-Jewish polemic that occupies a relatively small part of the work (approximately 11770–12465, though with intercalated passages of prose). See also Blumenkranz, "Ecriture et image dans la polémique anti-juife de Matfré Ermengaud."

17. Kamber, *Arbor Amoris*. Here the tree is essentially a variant on the ladder, inspired by Dionysius's *Celestial Hierarchies* via Hugh of Saint Victor. See Kamber's detailed study of ways of representing this mystical ascent.

18. For example, the section devoted to the theological virtues expatiates on faith to the neglect of charity and hope.

19. A late contemporary of Matfre's, the Catalan Ramón Llull likewise drew on the traditions of both the "tree of love" and the "tree of knowledge." His *Arbre de Philosophia de Amor* was written in 1298, in both Catalan and Latin versions (see Llull, *Tree of Love*, trans. Allison Peers, 1); it was subsequently translated into French, though the French text does not survive (Langlois, *La Vie spirituelle*, 337). Llull also wrote a Latin encyclopedia entitled the *Arbor Scientiae*, and he makes use of the Porphyrian tree in his *Logica Nova* of 1303. On the latter, see Sowa, *Knowledge Representation*, 4–7, and Figure 1.

20. The opening illustration in most of the illuminated manuscripts shows Matfre reading his work to assembled lovers and troubadours. Cherchi, "L'enciclopedia nel mondo dei trovatori," 289, says the *Breviari* is the earliest encyclopedia to be written with a particular social group in mind—a practice later associated with the Renaissance.

21. The most thorough study (with edition) of these is Richter, *Die Troubadourzizate im* Breviari d'amor.

22. Evidence for Matfre's life derives almost entirely from his works. The phrase "senhers en leis" is taken to mean "doctor of law" by Segre, "Le forme et le tradizione didattiche," 138. Although in the rubric to his epistle to "Sister Suau"

("Gentle Sister"; see edition of this text in the appendix to vol. V of the *Breviari*) Matfre is designated a Fraire Menres, the *Breviari* is not typical of Franciscan spirituality; but he may nevertheless have been a friar, or indeed have become one at a later date.

23. See Collison, *Encyclopaedias*, 32, 47.

24. Levy, *Petit dictionnaire*, s.v. *generologia*.

25. Cf. Hesketh's notes to the *Lumiere as lais* at 651ff., a passage that (as Hesketh points out) invokes the Porphyrian headings of genus, species, difference, property, and accident. Hesketh points to his glossary to attest the frequency of the terms *general, generaument, generauté, especial, especiaument, especiauté, difference, propreté, propre,* and *proprement* in the *Lumiere*.

26. The form *lunh* is a metathesized form of *nulh* found throughout the *Breviari*.

27. These points are also expanded later with reference to the creed, and the coming of the Holy Spirit (*BA*, 25510ff.).

28. "AISSI MOSTRA QUE L'EXPOSITIOS DEL ALBRE D'AMOR SE DEU FAR DI CHENDEN QUAR AMORS DICHEN" (*BA* 846T). The rubrics are consistent across the manuscript tradition.

29. This distinction between "natural" and "human" law is fundamental to Roman law; see Meyer, "Matfre Ermengaud, troubadour," 20, who quotes the *Institutes* of Justinian, Lib. I.ii: "Jus naturale est quod natura omnia animalia docuit. Nam jus istud non humani generis proprium est, sed omnium animalium quae in caelo, quae in terra, quae in mari nascuntur . . . jus autem gentium omni humano generi commune est." ("Natural law is that which nature taught to all animals. For this law is not a property just of the human race but of all animals whether they are born in the air, on the earth or in the sea . . . and the law of men is common to the whole human race.")

30. Trans. Spade, 5. The Latin text runs: "familiis quidem plerumque ad unum reducuntur principium, verbi gratia Iovem, in generibus autem et speciebus non se sic habet; neque enim est commune unum genus omnium ens, nec omnia eiusdem generis sunt secundum unum supremum genus, quemadmodum dicit Aristoteles, sed sint posita (quemadmodum in Preadicamentis) prima decem genera quasi prima decem principia. Vel, si omnia quis entia vocet, aequivoce (inquit) nuncupabit, non univoce; si enim unum esset commune omnium genus ens, univoce entia dicerentur, cum autem decem sint prima, communio secundum nomen est solum, non etiam secundum definitionis rationem que secundum nomen est" (6.3–6.12, pp. 11–12).

31. For elaboration of this point see Tricot's note to this passage in *Porphyre: Isagoge*, 21 n. 2.

32. The influence of Porphyry or Plotinus or both on Augustine's thinking in this regard has long been commented upon; see Smith, "Porphyrian Studies Since 1913," 768–71.

33. This was chiefly effected by contending that Aristotle's *Categories* offer a logician's tool for dissecting our arguments about the world, not an ontological tool for analyzing its makeup. By this means the Organon was divorced from Aristotle's writings on physics and metaphysics, which could then be read in such a

way as to bring out their compatibility with Christian belief (and with Plato). See the essays on Porphyry in Haase, ed., *Aufstieg und Niedergang*, especially Strange, "Plotinus, Porphyry and the Neoplatonic Interpretation of the Categories"; or, more recently, Girgente, "La metafisica de Porforio."

34. Cf. the argument about Aquinas's *De ente et essentia* in Blum, "Dio e gli individui," 23, esp. n. 17.

35. *Summa theologiae*, Ia. 65.1, quoted Davis, *Thought of Thomas Aquinas*, 31. The original runs: "Si enim diversa in aliquot uniantur, necesse est hujus unionis causam esse aliquam; nam enim diversa secundum se uniuntur. Et inde est quod, quandocumque in diversis invenitur aliquid unum, oportet quod illa diversa illud unum ab aliqua una causa recipient, sicut diversa corpora calida habent calorem ab igne. Hoc autem quod est esse, communiter invenitur in omnibus rebus quantcumque diversis. Necesse est ergo esse unum essendi principium, a quo esse habeant quaecumque sunt quocumque modo, sive sint invisibilia et spiritualia, sive sint visibilia et corporalia."

36. The shift from the Aristotelian term "substance" to "being" goes back to Augustine's treatise *On the Trinity*, V, ii, §3, where Augustine says that "essence" (*ousía*) is a better term than "substance" because God has "being" in the highest degree, and his essence involves his not having any accidents: "Est tamen sine dubitatione substantia uel si melius hoc appellatur essencia, quam graeci οὐσίαυ uocant."

37. Quoted Davis, *Thought of Thomas Aquinas*, 54; *Summa theologiae*, Ia. 44.1; "Dicendum quod necesse est dicere omne quod quocumque modo est a Deo est."

38. Davis, *Thought of Thomas Aquinas*, 44–57.

39. Matfre returns to the Trinity later (*BA*, 21520ff.) in his exposition of the creed.

40. "Introductiones breves ad fidem sancte Trinitatis pro rudibus instruendis" (fols. 78–108v).

41. "Deus autem est substantia spiritualis rationalis benignissima simplex" (fol. 78). "Simplex est deus quod non est in deo aliud qualitas."

42. *Etymologies* II, xxv.

43. Thus if Matfre privileges any person of the Trinity, it is not the Son (*pace* Galent-Fasseur) but the Holy Spirit as manifestation of divine love.

44. For *la us* as "the one," cf. *BA*, 502.

45. "La dame de l'arbre," 44–45.

46. The rubric of the prose text in Ricketts's edition runs "L'ENTENDEMENS DEL ALBRE D'AMOR ABREUJATZ E SENES RIMAS" (528 T, p. 28). His base manuscript is Madrid Escurial, S.I.3, also used as a base by Richter.

47. See Laske-Fix, *Der Bildzyklus des Breviari d'Amor*, for a reproduction of the whole cycle in Madrid Escurial S.I.3 (ascribed the *siglum M*) together with description and analysis. This manuscript is very decorative. Jaunty little birds are drawn sitting on the enlarged initials. Some of the initials sport faces, and the decorative bars extending from them up and down the margins also incorporate human or animal figures. It is as though the pulse of divine love through creation has enthused the scribe and transmitted itself to the page.

48. The image from *M* is reproduced (together with the other illuminations from this manuscript) in Laske-Fix. The image from BL Yates Thompson 31 (*T*) is reproduced in Ricketts, "Hispanic Tradition." Meyer, "Matfre Ermengaud," and Ricketts in the frontispiece to vol. II of his edition of the *Breviari* both reproduce the image from BL Royal 19.C. I (*L*), but Meyer misidentifies it as BL Harley 4940 (*K*). The image from BNF esp. 353, a Catalan prose version (*E*), is reproduced in Galent-Fasseur, "La dame de l'arbre," from the edition of the *Breviari* by Azaïs. The illumination of the "albre d'amor" in *L* is the one that most scholars choose to reproduce. Ricketts uses it as frontispiece to his edition, even though his text is based on *M*. This may be because it is the image that corresponds most faithfully to the text(s).

49. See Kay, "Grafting the Knowledge Community," and Nicholson, "Branches of Knowledge," for more on the imagery of grafting in the *Breviari*.

50. For Galent-Fasseur ("La dame de l'arbre," 40), this combination of ascending and descending movements in the tree represents the processes of illumination and response that are necessary to conversion. I agree, provided conversion is understood in the broad Augustinian sense of turning one's will toward God.

51. The "albre d'amor" in BNF fr. 858 (*C*) presents in an extreme form of this drift into symmetrical replication. Like *K* it is incomplete, lacking the inscriptions. The medallions disposed around the tree contain only heads, and they are all portrayed three-quarters face, except for the one at the center of the roots, presumably representing God, which is full face. Consequently the illumination replicates a series of identical images rather than articulating the complex structure of the accompanying text(s). It presents the further peculiarity that the medallions on the right-hand descending branch are not linked to one another, unlike those on the left. If this is the side of "nature," then not only does humanity not depend on natural law, as according to the text it should, but the other parts of nature do not either.

52. The left-right division is significant in the paintings given that they introduce "the word of the angel" and "the word of the devil" at the top of the left and right sides of the painting, respectively. The angel warns humanity against carnal delights, while the devil threatens those who take insufficient care for their souls. Their confrontation anticipates Matfre's exposé, in the concluding review of troubadour poetry, of the risk posed by *fin' amor* when it isn't *fina* enough. The painting upsets the relation between human and natural law established in the texts in order to affirm the need for moral and religious control over "natural" sexual conduct.

53. Prose and verse texts both comment on the way the dame unifies the tree. However, again the illuminations vary in the consistency with which they locate the different aspects of love within the figure of *amor general*. In several manuscripts, including the Royal one, two key forms of love—sexual love and love of temporal goods—are located under her feet, not within her, and so are not repeated.

54. BNF esp. 205 (*siglum X*).

55. Thus Figure 4; other images with completed inscriptions present merely orthographic variants.

56. Trans. Massumi, 21. "Le rhizome ne se laisse ramener ni à l'Un ni au multiple. Il n'est pas l'Un qui devient deux, ni même qui deviendrait directement trois, quatre ou cinq, etc. Il n'est pas un multiple qui dérive de l'Un, ni auquel l'Un s'ajouterait (n + 1). Il n'est pas fait d'unités mais de dimensions, ou plutôt de directions mouvantes. Il n'a pas de commencement ni fin, mais toujours un milieu, par lequel il pousse et déborde" (*Mille plateaux*, 31).

57. For Deleuze and Guattari the rhizome is arrived at by taking away a singular: "The multiple must be made, not by always adding a higher dimension, but rather in the simplest of ways. . . . Subtract the unique from the multiplicity to be constituted; write *n* − 1 dimensions. A system of this kind could be called a rhizome" (trans. Massumi, 6; "Le multiple, *il faut le faire*, non pas en ajoutant toujours une dimension supérieure, mais au contraire le plus simplement. . . . Soustraire l'unique de la multiplicité à constituer; écrire à n − 1. Un tel système pourrait être nommé rhizome," *Mille plateaux*, 13).

58. Cf. the beginning of this chapter and note 3.

Chapter 2. Form in Anamorphosis in the Ovide Moralisé

1. Demats, *Fabula*, chap. 3.

2. Demats, *Fabula*, 143–56.

3. Cf. also Blumenfeld-Kosinski's review of interpretations of the story of Myrrha, *Reading Myth*, 91–98.

4. Engels, *Etudes sur l'*Ovide moralisé, 46–62; Jung, "Les Editions manuscrites," 254–55.

5. Previous commentators tended to summarize rather than translate Ovid's text: see Blumenfeld-Kosinski, *Reading Myth*, 94. The *Ovide moralisé* poet's determination to replace Ovid in the role of author has been acutely analyzed by Copeland in *Rhetoric, Hermeneutics and Translation*, 107–26.

6. Demats, *Fabula*, chap. 2. The main principles of expansion that she identifies are mythic coverage, respect for chronology, and the desire to reconstitute and complete mythographic cycles. Copeland (*Rhetoric, Hermeneutics and Translation*, 120–22) points out that some of the poet's expansions derive from vernacular poems like the *Roman de la rose*. Demats (*Fabula*, 61) reckons that translations/adaptations of Ovid occupy some 36,000 lines and existing glosses ca. 8,000 (*Fabula*, 63), which means that the poet's own moralizations/interpretations account for the remaining ca. 28,000.

7. Modern scholars' view of the *Ovide moralisé* has been decisively influenced by De Boer's choice of MS Rouen Bibliothèque Municipale o.4 as the base for his edition, a preference inscribed in his awarding it the *siglum A*. While this is the oldest extant manuscript, it is also without doubt the most Christian and orthodox version of the text and accords the most value to the moralizations, of which it includes a prefatory Table. The manuscript that, at the other end of the scale, accords most prominence to Ovid's original and contains virtually no moralizations is Lyon Bibliothèque Municipale 742 (*B*). Manuscripts of the *y* group, of which more below, present a different edition again, which repositions and re-

shapes some of the moralizations and incorporates some features directly from Ovid. See Jung, "Les Editions manuscrites," and Lord, "Three Manuscripts."

8. Blumenfeld-Kosinski, *Reading Myth*, 94.

9. Demats, *Fabula*, esp. 107–12; Copeland, *Rhetoric, Hermeneutics and Translation*, 124–25.

10. The moralist includes this story in order to link this Theban episode to the later adventure of Jason in Book VII; see Demats, *Fabula*, 79–81.

11. The concept of community is thus related to Agamben's concept of "bare life" in his *Homo Sacer*. See *Coming Community*, trans. Hardt, 67, 85–87, *La Comunità che viene*, 55, 67–69.

12. Trans. Hardt, *Coming Community*, 48; "né generico né individuale, né immagine della divinità né forma animale, il corpo diventava ora veramente *qualunque*," *La Comunità che viene*, 42.

13. Trans. Hardt, *Coming Community*, 1; "La singolarità si scoglie dal falso dilemma che obbliga la conoscenza a scegliere fra l'ineffabilità dell'individuo e l'intelligibilità dell' universale," *La Comunità che viene*, 9.

14. Trans. Hardt, *Coming Community*, 10; "Esso è una singolarità fra le altre, che sta però in luogo di ciascuna di esse, vale per tutte," *La Comunità che viene*, 14. Note that, in the original Italian, Agemben assigns the *qualunque* to a "place"; this concern to "place" his thinking will be considered below.

15. Trans. Hardt, *Coming Community*, 16–20; *La Comunità che viene*, 19–22.

16. See my Introduction.

17. See Lacan's *Seminar*, Book VII (*Ethics of Psychoanalysis*), sessions x–xi, and Book XI (*Four Fundamental Concepts*), session vii; and Žižek, *Looking Awry*, passim.

18. Simpson, *Fantasy, Identity and Misrecognition in Medieval French Narrative*, chap. 3; the term "anamorphic" is used on p. 135. The term is also used by Croizy-Naquet, "L'*Ovide moralisé* ou Ovide revisité," 50, to refer to the combination of history and mythography in the *Moralisé* that fold into one another thanks to their shared potential for allegory.

19. See Copeland, *Rhetoric, Hermeneutics and Translation*, 107–26; Demats, *Fabula*, 173–77; Blumenfeld-Kosinski, *Reading Myth*, 98–100. The entire last chapter of Engels's book is devoted to a running commentary on the sources and analogues of Book I of the *Ovide moralisé*.

20. On this word in the sense of "matter, building matter," cf. *OM*, XV, 665–66, where the four elements are described as "li naturel merrien / de tout le monde." Its usual meaning is "wood (for construction)," see *OM*, XIV, 400.

21. My translation; "en substituant à la métamorphose l'union primordiale de la forme et de la matière, il élimine en fait le sujet même de l'oeuvre" (Demats, *Fabula*, 173).

22. Demats, *Fabula*, 91–94.

23. My translation; "Tria esse semper dixerunt, scilicet Deum et IIII elementa insimul comixta et formas omnium rerum in mente Dei existentes id est ideas hoc est differentias, sicut rationalitatem et caliditatem et frigiditatem et caetera, per quae Deus ipse res futuras constiturus erat" (Demats, *Fabula*, 114 n. 30, and her Appendix 1, 179).

24. "Study of this central text as a way of explaining the relationship of God, the eternal ideas of things, and the material expression of these ideas, was the chief project of these [early twelfth-century] Platonists. That the visible universe is a coherent cosmos, informed by soul and modelled on an ideal exemplar, was fundamental, and to the extent that the world-soul and the archetype were seen as manifestations of God, expressions of his goodness and wisdom, they could render his activity accessible to reason through the visible universe" (Wetherbee, "Philosophy, Cosmology, and the Twelfth-Century Renaissance," 25; see also Gregory, "The Platonic Inheritance").

25. My translation; "Et potest dici cum per efficientem intelligatur Deus Pater qui creando visibilia et invisibilia humane consuluit nature, per formalem vero sapientia i.e. Filius Dei, per finalem vero Spiritus Sanctus," Demats, *Fabula*, 183.

26. As attested, for example, by John of Salisbury in his *Policraticus*, cited by Gregory, "The Platonic Inheritance," 56–57: "In the books of Plato we find many things consonant with the words of the prophets. In the *Timaeus*, for example, during his subtle investigation of the causes of the world, he seems clearly to express the Trinity which is God, when he locates the efficient cause in the power of God, the formal cause in his wisdom, and the final cause in his goodness, which alone induced him to make all creatures sharers in his goodness."

27. Which is not to say that mortals cannot represent Christ: for example, Hero drowning for love of Leander represents *devine sapience* (*OM*, IV, 3666).

28. Jung, "Les Editions manuscrites," 259; cf. Blumenfeld-Kosinski, "Illustrations et interprétations," 71–72. The manuscripts in question are BNF fr. 373 (*G¹*); Geneva, Bibliothèque publique et universitaire, fr. 176 (*E¹*); Vatican, Biblioteca Apostolica Vaticana, Vat. Reg. Lat. 1480 (*E²*); and London, BL Cotton Julius F.VII (*E³*).

29. For example, the description of Arachne's weaving in Ovid's Book VI includes mention of the rape of Europa, but the moralist declines to comment on the myth on the grounds that he has already done so (OM, VI, 739–41)—even though this was way back in Book II, 5103ff. Many references are less explicit but convey the same expectation that the reader will have read the whole poem, such as the way Book VII opens with a flashback to Book IV.

30. Blumenfeld-Kosinski, *Reading Myth*, 116.

31. See Hardie, "Ovid's Theban History," which argues that Ovid shapes his Theban material as an anti-*Aeneid*.

32. See Demats, *Fabula*, 71–80, for a comparative study of Book IV in Ovid and the *Moralisé*.

33. Blumenfeld-Kosinski, *Reading Myth*, 111–13, offers a reading of Book X, contrasting its procedures with those of earlier books.

34. This creation of place is another theme of commentaries on Ovid, such as the one summarized by Demats: "Appealing to 'reason,' the commentator defines *hyle* (as distinct from chaos) as a mere receptacle or place (*locus*) in which the forms of things change; it is neither eternal nor assimilable to a 'creature'; it is the 'material cause' of the world, together with the four elements" ("En s'appuyant sur 'la raison,' l'auteur définit *hyle* comme distincte du chaos, pur réceptacle, lieu

(*locus*) où varient les formes des choses; elle n'est ni éternelle, ni assimilable à une 'créature'; c'est la 'cause matérielle' du monde, avec les quatre elements," 153–54). The *accessus* in question is printed in her Appendix 1 (ll. 150–59, p. 182).

35. De Boer assigns this manuscript the *siglum* Υ^2. The *y* group comprises, in addition, BNF fr. 871, BL Add. 10342, and Rouen, Bibliothèque Municipale, o.11 bis.

36. Trans. Hardt, *Coming Community*, 48; "poiché lo 'a immagine e somiglianza' della Genesi, che radicava in Dio la figura humana, la vincolava però, in questo modo, a un archetipo invisibile e fondava, con ciò, il concetto paradossale di una somiglianza assolutamente immateriale," *La Communità que viene*, 42.

37. Bynum, *Metamorphosis and Identity*, 168–69, and see also her helpful n. 10 on p. 268.

38. On these shared components compare the gloss material quoted earlier on the meaning of "form": "They said that there had always been three things, namely God and the four elements mixed together and the forms of all things existing in the mind of God, that is to say Ideas or Differences, such as rationality and heat and cold, etc., by means of which God would constitute the things that were to come."

39. See Wippel, "Essence and Existence," 390–91, and *Metaphysical Thought of Thomas Aquinas*, chap. 4.

40. See my Introduction.

41. Trans. Hardt, *Coming Community*, 17; "Il limito di Scoto è che egli sembra qui pensare la natura commune come une realtà anteriore, cui compete la proprietà di essere indifferente a qualsivoglia singolarità, e alla quale la singolarità verrebbe ad agguingere soltanti l'ecceità," *La Communità che viene*, 19.

42. De Libera, *Querelle des universaux*, 330–35, here 330–31; the quotation is from Duns Scotus, *Ordinatio*, II, dist. 3, §39.

43. De Libera, *Querelle des universaux*, 333.

44. According to Agamben it is not until Spinoza that community ceases to depend on "an essence or a concept" (trans. Hardt, *Coming Community*, 18; *La Comunità che viene*, 19), on the singular being possessing some kind of common nature with others. With Spinoza, community "takes place" as "*the communication of singularities in the attribute of extension* [which] *does not unite them in essence, but scatters them in existence*," trans. Hardt, *Coming Community*, 19, emphasis in original; "*L'aver-luogo, il communicare delle singolarità nell'attributo dell'estensione, non le unisce nell'essenza, ma le sparpaglia nell'esistenza*," *La Communità che viene*, 20.

45. Cf. Bynum, *Metamorphosis and Identity*, 169–70.

46. Quoted Simpson, *Fantasy, Identity and Misrecognition*, 165.

47. Cf. Hardie, "Ovid's Theban History," 224.

48. Cf. Agamben, trans. Hardt, *Coming Community*, 13–15, 23; *La Comunità che viene*, 15–17, 23.

49. See Lord, "Three Manuscripts of the *Ovide moralisé*," for a comparative study of the Arsenal, Lyon, and Rouen manuscripts.

50. Several narrative episodes of the *Metamorphoses* function metatextually, gathering together and reflecting on the wider work, and thereby assuming a sig-

nificance comparable with that of the opening and closing books. One such episode is the Fountain of the Muses in Book V, discussed in Chapter 6 below.

51. Trans. Hardt, *Coming Community*, 48; *La Comunità que viene*, 42,
"*Qualunque* è una somiglianza senza archetipo, cioè un' Idea."

Chapter 3. The Divided Path in Guillaume de Deguileville's
Pèlerinage de Vie Humaine

1. Sturzinger's introduction to his edition of the *Pèlerinage de vie humaine*
surveys the manuscript tradition. Illuminated manuscripts of the various *Pèlerinage*
poems have been studied by Michael Camille in both "The Illustrated Manuscripts" and the later *Master of Death*; Tuve devotes a lengthy study to them too
in her *Allegorical Imagery* (chap. 3). On the *Pèlerinage* trilogy as a whole, see
Boulton, "Digulleville's *Pèlerinage de Jésus Christ*: A Poem of Courtly Devotion."
Spellings of the name Deguileville vary; many modern scholars adopting the form
Degulleville, which is the modern name of the village near Cherbourg from which
the poet came. Deguileville, the spelling used by Sturzinger, has the merit of being
supported by the acrostic signature GVJLLERMVS DE DEGUJLEVJLLA provided by the author himself in (among other places) the *Pèlerinage de l'âme*.

2. This fourteenth-century manuscript, which belonged to Jean duc de
Berri, contains the second version of the *Vie humaine* together with the *Pèlerinage
de l'âme*, the two works being titled "Pilgrimage of the Body and of the Soul"
("le rommant du pelerinage du corps et de l'ame").

3. On Deguileville's debt to the *Rose*, see Badel, *Le* Roman de la Rose *au
XIVe siècle*, 362–76; Wright, "Deguileville's *Pèlerinage de Vie humaine* as 'Contrepartie Edifiante' of the *Roman de la Rose*," and Huot, *The Romance of the Rose
and Its Medieval Readers*, 207–38. On the theme of life as a pilgrimage, and Deguileville as the initiator of a whole genre devoted to this theme, see Wenzel, "The
Pilgrimage of Human Life as a Late Medieval Genre." The relation of this theme
to other conceptions of pilgrimage is explored in Dyas, *Pilgrimage in Medieval
English Literature*.

4. Philips, "Chaucer and Deguileville," notes that "this is an allegory of
faith rather than works" (6); its inset documents "convey the message that the
important truths—calm, fixed and unchanging—are always *there*, ever accessible in
the midst of the turmoil of temporal experience" (10); "the message behind all
this is a quietist and pietistic one . . . for all the plot's violence, its message is a
fugitive and cloistered virtue" (11). See also Wenzel, "Pilgrimage," 384.

5. Dyas, *Pilgrimage*, 207–8, considers the theme of monasticism as pilgrimage.

6. See most recently Whitehead, *Castles of the Mind*, 71–76, for the figure of
the *castel* on the Ship of Religion as an image of the cloister. Wenzel identifies the
preoccupation with aging as an inherent part of the "pilgrimage of life" genre,
"Pilgrimage," 377.

7. This summary holds true of the second recension, except that (i) Degu-

ileville redefines his relationship to the *Rose*, condemning it instead of recognizing it as his inspiration, and (ii) he assumes a religious rather than a lay audience, keying the poem to monasticism more explicitly in the second redaction. It will be helpful to summarize here the main differences of detail between the different versions in the episodes with which this chapter is concerned. Divergences begin when Grace Dieu has presented the pilgrim with his staff and stole; she returns to and amplifies the discussion of the role of the various senses that took place in the first encounter with Penitence. The presentation of his staff and stole is accompanied by long hymns in Latin. After the pilgrim has been given armor but then taken it off again, Grace Dieu gives him five stones by which to remember key Christian tenets; this is in addition to Memoire, who carries the discarded armor as in the first redaction. This leads straight into the conversation about why Memoire can bear their weight and he can't, whether he is single or double, and the experience of being released from his body; in all this, Grace Dieu takes the place of Raison in version 1. Grace Dieu then vanishes from view and we have the meeting with Rude Entendement (Crude Understanding) and Raison, which in the earlier version precedes this discussion; at the end of this episode Raison withdraws. Another episode to be relocated is the encounter with Jeunesse (Youth), which in the first version comes after the pilgrim has left the divided path, but which here follows next after the meeting with Rude Entendement. The approach to the divided path is handled differently as a result. In version 2, the pilgrim sets out down the path of Occupation, but he gets discouraged when he meets with the figure of Vertu (Virtue) and a pilgrim whose body has been mortified by its soul. Some of the material about the relation between body and soul in version 1 is moved into the *Pèlerinage de l'âme*. Grace Dieu describes his duality in terms of a double wheel, the two parts of which are turning in different directions. She then withdraws again, and the pilgrim is transported over the Hedge and onto the path of Huiseuse by the flying figure of Jeunesse. The meeting with the sins follows immediately after this, and they are ordered differently from their order in version 1, the list being now headed by Luxure (Lust) and Gloutonnie (Gluttony). In general, the changes reduce the role of Raison and the space given to dilemma in order to focus more centrally on the opposition between Grace and the sensual (and youthful) body.

8. Its importance is, if anything, enhanced in the revised *Vie humaine* where Raison's part in this conversation is made over to Grace Dieu; see preceding note.

9. The same motif of a division adumbrated but not yet realized is also found in BNF fr. 823, fol. 46 (the manuscript whose illuminations, attributed to Remiet, are the focus of Camille's *Master of Death*), where again the pilgrim stands just before the fork in the path, while a female figure (Raison or Grace Dieu) stands just beyond its farther branch; and in BNF fr. 1818, fol. 57v., where again one sees the pilgrim just before the fork, and it is not clear yet which path he will take.

10. Foucault, *Order of Things*, 354; "Que faut-il que je sois, moi qui pense et qui suis ma pensée, pour que je sois ce que je ne pense pas, pour que ma pensée soit ce que je ne suis pas?" (Foucault, *Les Mots et les choses*, 335–36). Foucault is referring here to Lacan's revision of the *cogito*, "I think where I am not, therefore

I am where I do not think," in *Ecrits: A Selection*, trans. Sheridan, 166. The original French is: "Je pense où je ne suis pas, donc je suis où je ne pense pas," *Ecrits*, 517.

11. See, for example, Taylor, *Sources of the Self*, 113, and, for more extended studies, Menn, *Descartes and Augustine*, and Matthews, *Thought's Ego in August-ine and Descartes*, passim, but especially chap. 3. The similarity between some of Descartes' formulations and Augustine's *De libero arbitrio* was recognized by An-toine Arnaud, see Menn, *Descartes and Augustine*, 4–5. For an essay placing Des-cartes in the wider sweep of thought from Augustine to Lacan, see Moriarty, *Early Modern French Thought: The Age of Suspicion*, chap. 2.

12. This reading differs sharply from that of Wenzel, who sees the *Pèlerinage* and related poems as no more than "versified religious handbooks which present catechetical material in allegorical shapes, both by images and by expository speeches coming from allegorical figures, and which structure this catechetical ma-terial with the help of the pilgrimage metaphor," "Pilgrimage," 378.

13. On the theme of pilgrimage in Augustine and its subsequent influence, see Dyas, *Pilgrimage*, 32–36.

14. "Et ideo rectarum voluntatum conexio iter est quoddam ascendentium ad beatitudinem quod certis velut passibus agitur; prauarum autem atque distort-arum voluntatum implicatio vinculum est quo alligabitur qui hoc agit ut proiciatur *in tenebras exteriores*."

15. In a reversal of usual practice, round brackets are used by Sturzinger to signal editorial additions, square ones to signal what should, he thinks, be sup-pressed.

16. See Augustine, *On the Trinity*, XIII, 2, §5, and XIII, 4, §7.

17. In quoting Sturzinger's edition I have added acute accents in accordance with modern editorial practice.

18. BNF fr. 829, fol. 27v., col. a: "l'escharpe et le bourdon que veulz / ont tel condition en eulz / que veoir tu ne les pourras / se les yeulx es oreilles nas / et croy que se tu les veoyes/ que trop petit les priseroyes / si ques les yeulx je t'osteray / de la ou sont et les mettray / en tes oreilles par dehors / si ques veoir les pouras lors" ("the scrip and staff that you want are of such a nature that you cannot see them unless you have your eyes in your ears; and I think that if you were to see them you would fail to value them properly and so I shall take your eyes away from where they are and put them on the outside of your ears so that you will be able to see them then").

19. In the second recension of the *Vie humaine*, Nature's subordination to Grace Dieu is emphasized by her stopping remonstrating as soon as Grace Dieu asserts her authority; in the earlier version Nature continues to grumble and let off steam even though she knows she has lost the argument.

20. On Aristotle's philosophy of place and its importance in medieval didac-tic poetry see my Introduction.

21. *Sic*, rather than expected *trestout* agreeing with *pain*.

22. In the subsequent *mise en prose* of the *Pèlerinage de vie humaine* this *exemplum* is altered to dispel anxiety about Sapience's culpability, the apprentice becoming a worthless figure involved in crime. I am grateful to Stephanie Gibbs for this note.

23. "Age nunc videamus ubi sit quasi quoddam hominis exterioris interiorisque confinium . . . non enim solum corpus homo exterior deputabitur sed adiuncta quadam uita sua qua compages corporis et omnes sensus uigent quibus instructus est ad exteriora sentienda."

24. Huot, *The Romance of the Rose and Its Medieval Readers*, 213, points out that this fountain is a reworking of the Fountain of Narcissus in the *Rose*: "By transforming the crucial fountain from a locus of bewitching vision to one of self-knowledge, penance and tears, Deguilleville reminds us of the dangers of the senses and of the importance of inner, rather than outer, vision."

25. For example, in *On Christian Teaching*, Book I, already referred to, or throughout the *City of God*. The Augustinian image of the exiled soul is pervasive in subsequent writing. See Wenzel, "Pilgrimage," 372, for its use by St. Bernard, whose importance for Deguileville is also brought out by Helen Philips, "Chaucer and Deguileville," 4–6.

26. The importance of this oblique self-identification, and its parallel with the way Jean de Meun has himself named by Amor in the *Rose*, has been brought out by Gibbs in "Allegories of Authorship."

27. "Ita duae voluntates meae, una vetus, alia nova, illa carnalis, illa spiritualis, confligebant inter se."

28. Cf. Augustine, *On the Trinity*, X, 5 and 6. The second redaction of the *Vie humaine* tries to simplify matters by placing greater emphasis on the body and less on inner division throughout the episode of the Hedge.

29. There is lengthy discussion of memory as liminal between senses and soul in *On the Trinity*, XI, viii–xi.

30. On the treatment of the sins in vernacular writings see Delumeau, *Le Péché et la peur*, 229ff. In identifying Paresse as the initial sin, Deguilleville is underlining the need for mental rather than physical activity, an emphasis that changes in the second redaction, where the onslaught of the sins is headed by Luxure.

31. "Vtquid ergo ei praeceptum est ut se ipsa cognoscat? Credo ut se cogitet et secundum naturam suam uiuat, id est ut secundum suam naturam ordinari appetat, sub eo scilicet cui subdenda est, supra ea quibus praeponenda est."

32. "Viuere se tamen et meminisse et intellegere et uelle et cogitare et scire et iudicare quis dubitet? Quandoquidem etiam si dubitat, uiuit; si dubitat, unde dubitat meminit; si dubitat, dubitare se intellegit; si dubitat, certus esse uult; si dubitat, cogitat; si dubitat, scit se nescire; si dubitat, iudicat non se temere consentire oportere."

33. Augustine, *City of God*, XI, xxvi. This passage, and its wider context, are cited and discussed by Matthews, *Thought's Ego in Augustine and Descartes*, 29–30. Here is the original Latin of the passage I have quoted: "Quid si falleris? Si enim fallor, sum. Nam qui non est, utique nec falli potest."

34. Foucault, *Order of Things*, 352, translation modified by me; "Mais comment peut-il se faire que l'homme pense ce qu'il ne pense pas, habite ce qui lui échappe sur le mode d'une occupation muette, anime, d'une sorte de mouvement figé, cette figure de lui-même qui se présente à lui sous la forme d'une extériorité têtue?" *Les Mots et les choses*, 334.

35. Quoted by Matthews, *Thought's Ego in Augustine and Descartes*, 73.

36. Ibid., 192–96, cf. 73.

37. Freud, *Neue Folge der Vorlesungen*, 86; "where id was, there ego shall be," *New Introductory Lectures*, 80.

38. The most famous passage is the one quoted by Foucault; see my note 10 to this chapter. See also Lacan, *Four Fundamental Concepts of Psychoanalysis*, trans. Sheridan, 35–37, 220–21, 203–15. For discussion of this theme in this seminar, see the two "Alienation and Separation" essays by Laurent and the two "The Subject and the Other" essays by Soler.

39. Lacan, *Four Fundamental Concepts of Psychoanalysis*, trans. Sheridan, 36; "D'une façon exactement analogique, Freud, là où il doute . . . est assuré qu'une pensée est là, qui est inconsciente, ce qui veut dire qu'elle se révèle comme absente. C'est à cette place qu'il appelle . . . le *je pense* par où va se révéler le sujet. En somme, cette pensée, il est sûr qu'elle est là toute seule de tout son *je suis*, si on peut dire,—pour peu que, c'est là le saut, quelqu'un pense à sa place," *Quatre concepts*, 44.

40. For more on Lacan's reflections on the *cogito* see Dolar, "*Cogito* as the Subject of the Unconscious," and several of the essays in Rabaté, ed., *The Cambridge Companion to Lacan*, especially Shepherdson, "Lacan and Philosophy."

Chapter 4. Universality on Trial in Machaut's Jugement *Poems*

1. The pioneering study is Calin, *Poet at the Fountain*, followed by such major critical works as Brownlee, *Poetic Identity in Guillaume de Machaut*; Cerquiglini, *"Un engin si soutil"*; and de Looze, *Pseudo-Autobiography*, Introduction and chap. 3.

2. Calin, *Poet at the Fountain*, 57–62; Huot, "Consolation of Poetry"; Cerquiglini, *"Un engin si soutil,"* 75–76.

3. "For [Machaut], the *Rose* provided a vernacular poetic model of supreme importance," Huot, *Romance of the Rose and Its Medieval Readers*, 241 and the whole of chap. 7, from which that quotation is taken. For the influence of the *Rose* on the *Jugement* poems in particular, see Palmer, "Metafictional Machaut." The rubrics of the illuminations of the *Jugement dou Roi de Navarre* in BNF fr. 1587, fols. 79 and 86v, go so far as to identify Guillaume de Machaut as "guillaume de loris"! For the influence of the *Rose* more generally on Machaut, see Badel, *Le "Roman de la rose" au XIVe siècle*, 82–94; Brownlee, *Poetic Identity*, 20.

4. My translation; "les conditions de possibilité de l'écriture lyrique," Cerquiglini-Toulet, "Lyrisme de désir et lyrisme d'espérance dans la poésie de Machaut," 46.

5. Cf. de Looze, *Pseudo-Autobiography*, 79, who sees the *Jugement* poems in particular as both creating and negating "an experimental Machaldian 'I'" and as "a first experiment in the ordonnance of a textualized self."

6. See Earp, *Guillaume de Machau: A Guide to Research*, 33.

7. Cerquiglini, *"Un engin si soutil,"* 61. On the *Jugement dou Roy de Navarre* as "a key text in the codification of Machaut's oeuvre," see Huot, *From Song to Book*, 247.

8. According to Earp, some manuscripts originally intended to place the *Lay de Plour* after the *Jugement dou roy de Navarre* but then placed it with Machaut's other *lais* in a gesture that seems to distance its composition even further from the gesture of atonement it is alleged to be. See *Guillaume de Machaut: A Guide to Research*, 209, 365.

9. Machaut's self-portrayal is the main subject of Brownlee, *Poetic Identity*, though Brownlee's emphasis lies more on Machaut's self-awareness as a poet.

10. Although Machaut's comic persona has been widely remarked on, I owe the idea that it represents the public's disdain for a poet to a former student, Judith Bottomley.

11. Cf. Calin, *Poet at the Fountain*, 111–23.

12. The fullest study of the *Navarre* from this perspective is Ehrhart, "Machaut and the Duties of Rulers Tradition." For valuable insights into Machaut's political poetry and complex relations with his various patrons, see Gauvard, "Portrait du Prince d'après l'oeuvre de Guillaume de Machaut." Whereas Jean de Luxembourg was already an established figure at the time of the *Behaigne*, Charles of Navarre was still a boy when the *Navarre* was written. He was to become the spearhead of a reformist movement that opposed political developments under the monarchy in fourteenth-century France, favoring a return to aristocratic interest, and it seems that Machaut was largely in sympathy with these aims (Gauvard, "Portrait du Prince," 27–31). Machaut's *Confort d'ami* was also written for Charles of Navarre.

13. I have been able to consult MSS BNF fr. 843, 1584, 1585, 1587, and 22545. In BNF fr. 9221, the *Remède de Fortune* (under the title *L'Ecu bleu*) is inserted between *Vergier* and *Behaigne*, and there are several blank folios between *Behaigne* and *Navarre*. The *Navarre* has many fewer MS attestations than the *Behaigne* and never occurs without it, while clearly the obverse is quite common.

14. The verdict is delivered as from Amor in *JRN*, 3805–7, where Raison says: "Or de ce meffait premerain / vous di de par le souverain / Amours" ("On behalf of the sovereign god of Love, regarding this first crime, I tell you").

15. Calin (*Poet at the Fountain*, 35) observes a comparable swapping and doubling of the personifications in the *Dit du Vergier*.

16. Where the edition has *setisme* ("seventh") referring to Foy, BNF fr. 1587 has *.vi.ᶜ*.

17. The relationship between these two is explained by Cognoissance, *JRN*, 3467–74.

18. Cf. the lines from Machaut's *Complainte a Henri*, "Mais j'aim trop miex franchise et po d'avoir / que grant richesse et servitude avoir," cited Gauvard, "Portrait du Prince," 36.

19. For example, in the *Joli buisson de Jonece* Froissart deliberately renames personifications (see my next chapter).

20. Gauvard, "Portrait du Prince," 38 n. 61, observes that during the considerable political unrest that marked the middle of the fourteenth century the genre of the "mirror for princes" declined in favor of more practical "advice to rulers."

21. See Thomas Bradwardine, "De memoria artificiali" (Carruthers, *Book of Memory*, Appendix C, 282–83): "And if you can, make for the image a right hand

and a left hand, and constitute the image that comes next in order on the right hand of the first, then position it so that the first image with its right hand holds, drags, strikes the following image, or does something of this nature to it, or the second holds itself opposed to the first; thus the procedure should be like gluing together the order of them."

22. The most-studied illuminated manuscript of Machaut, BNF fr. 1586, lacks the *Navarre*, though it does contain the *Behaigne*. See Huot, *From Song to Book*, chap. 8, and Avril, "Les Manuscrits enluminŕes de Guillaume de Machaut."

23. Fol. 58v (*incipit* of *Behaigne*), poet in garden with knight, lady, pucele, and little dog; fol. 67v (between *Behaigne* lines 1184 and 1185), poet in garden with knight and lady; fol. 69 (between *Behaigne* 1380 and 1381), poet indicates to knight and lady a castle on a hill; fol. 70 (between *Behaigne* 1464 and 1465) the entry into the court room of the castle; fol. 74v (the beginning of *Navarre*, but not signaled as such), interior of house with melancholy poet; fol. 78 (between *Navarre* 465 and 466), view of wedding party observed by poet; fol. 79 (between *Navarre* 548 and 549), hunting scene, with poet observed by Dame Bonneürté and her retinue; fol. 86 (between *Navarre* 1474 and 1475), reproduced as Figure 9, the king of Navarre and Dame Bonneürté sit in judgment on the left, the figure of Machaut in the center has been defaced, and the damsels acting as his accusers cluster on the right.

24. Calin, *Poet at the Fountain,* 128. I thus disagree with Cerquiglini (*"Un engin si soutil,"* 87–88, 185), who sees Machaut as rallying to the One as the index (if not the content) of truth.

25. The history of Aristotle's *Nicomachean Ethics* in the medieval period is fascinating. Initially only the first three books were known, often circulated appended to Aristotle's works on logic (Dod, "Aristoteles Latinus," 47–52). The earliest surviving student syllabus from Paris University, from about 1215, prescribes the *Ethics* (Marenbon, *Later Medieval Philosophy*, 16), and it continued to be required reading throughout the century (Dod, "Aristoteles Latinus," 72–73). The figure who most shaped medieval reception of the *Ethics* was Robert Grosseteste, whose translation of the complete text, dating from c. 1246–47, survives in thirty-three manuscripts, while its subsequent revision (by William of Moerbeke?) survives in a staggering 246 (Dod, "Aristoteles Latinus," 71). Grosseteste's *Ethics* "became in its original or a revised form the standard version in the Middle Ages" (Dod, "Aristoteles Latinus," 61). If, as he is believed to have done, Machaut had a university education (Earp, *Guillaume de Machaut*, 3), he would have read Grosseteste's translation in one form or the other. All quotations from the *Ethics* in this chapter are accordingly from Grosseteste's text as edited in the *Aristoteles Latinus*.

26. In Grosseteste's text: "Proprium enim unicuique natura, optimum et delectabilissimum est unicuique; et homini utique que secundum intellectum vita, si quidem maxime hoc homo. Iste ergo felicissimus."

27. Mesure's reasons for condemning Guillaume include his outrage at the madness (*forcenerie*, 3685) of the behavior of the clerk of Orléans, who cut off his finger in a display of passion for his lady. Does the figure of Mesure allude to the moderation between extremes that Aristotle sees as the guiding principle behind all of the moral virtues?

28. The only figure among the witnesses who is an intellectual virtue is Prudence, whose strange effacement in favor of Franchise I have talked about. Moreover, the poem presents her not in her sapiential guise but as versed in practical understanding of the world.

29. Grosseteste's text: "Cercius agere autem videbitur utique unumquodque, propria cura facta; magis enim conveniente potitur unusquisque. Set curabit quidem optime, secundum quod et medicus et exercitativus et omnis alius universale sciens quoniam omnibus vel talibus autem congruit."

30. Grosseteste's term; "state" or *habitus* is one of Aristotles's categories in the *Categories*.

31. For example, in *Looking Awry*, 86, Žižek uses Hitchcock's film *Vertigo* to explain how an object can be made sublime and then be lost; the "loss of loss" ensues when it is learned that the object was never as she was believed to be. See the use of Žižek's term made by Huot with reference to the *Navarre* in *Madness in Medieval Literature*, 148–49.

32. Lacan, Seminar XX, *Encore*, trans. Fisk, 34; "il n'y a pas de rapport sexuel," *Encore*, 35.

33. Butler, *Psychic Life of Power*, 132–50.

34. Huot, "Consolation of Poetry," 180: "The masculine response is to stage one's suffering through some kind of grand gesture such as that of the knight who cut off his finger when asked to return his lady's ring, to sublimate it into heroic activity, or indeed to escape it entirely through the amnesia of madness, as in the tale of the clerk of Orléans who was reduced to abject insanity upon learning that the lady he loved had gotten married. The feminine response, in turn, is characterized by bodily reactions of illness or death, whether by suicide or simply from the effects of grief and emotional trauma. The relative qualities and merits of these two modes are debated at length by the allegorical court of Navarre, which determines ultimately that women's experience of suffering is more profound than that of men." See also her *Madness in Medieval French Literature*, 146, 172, 178–79, which likewise maintains that gender difference lies at the heart of the *Navarre*'s treatment of suffering.

35. Lacan, Seminar XX, *Encore*, 73; trans. Fink, 78.

36. Wright, *Lacan and Postfeminism*, 41–42

37. See the brilliant reading of this story and the ensuing discussion in Huot, *Madness in Medieval French Literature*, 146–51.

38. A worthy antecedent of Lacan's "bone in the throat," as Žižek (*Contingency, Hegemony, Universality*, 310) puts it: "The Lacanian Real is that traumatic 'bone in the throat' that contaminates every ideality of the symbolic, rendering it contingent and inconsistent."

39. My translation. Cathelineau, *Lacan, lecteur d'Aristote*, 263: "Le noyau de l'ontologie aristotélicienne demeure essentiellement *l'individu inconnaissable en lui-même* et seulement connu par le discours scientifique qui s'exprime à travers le genre et l'espèce"; original emphasis.

40. But it does confirm that there is a vital kinship, long recognized by Lacan, between medieval poetic expression and psychoanalytic logic. See Shepherdson, "Lacan and Philosophy," 137, for how the psychoanalytic approach to

sexual difference has ethical implications, since it situates masculinity and femininity differently with regard to law.

41. Cerquiglini, *"Un engin si soutil,"* 162, takes a similar line when she attributes Machaut's concept of the sign as inherently fictional to the influence of
Ockham.

Chapter 5. Understanding, Remembering, and Forgetting in Froissart's Le Joli Buisson de Jonece

1. See Zink, *Froissart et le temps*; Bennett, *"Ut pictura memoria."*

2. *Le Joli buisson de Jonece* is transmitted in the two manuscripts that contain
Froissart's poetical works, BNF fr. 830 and 831. In both the *Buisson* follows the
Espinette but is separated from it by a collection of short lyric works; the *Buisson* is
followed in 830 by the *Dit dou florin* and in 831 by the *Plaidoirie de la rose et de la
violette.*

3. See de Libera, *Querelle*, chap. 6; Coleman, *Ancient and Medieval Memories*, helpfully dissects late medieval thinkers' theories of memory in relation to the
wider field of epistemology; Marenbon, *Later Medieval Philosophy*, 167, provides a
useful table of the interrelations between intelligible and sensible species in the act
of remembering according to John Duns Scotus.

4. Cf. Chapter 3, where memory is seen as liminal between body and soul.

5. See Carruthers, *Book of Memory*, 46ff.

6. Aristotle, *On Memory*, 450a1. The Latin text most probably used by Aquinas, and edited, together with Aquinas's commentary on it, by Spiazzi, reads "intelligere non est sine phantasmate." The same line is found in the *De Anima*.

7. BNF fr. 831 is slightly more ornate than 830. Neither has pictures, except
for the opening fol. of 831 (clerical author reading to an audience). Both have
decorations of foliage in gold, pink, red, and blue, and in 831 these are quite luxuri-
ant and invasive. The idea, found in both the *Espinette* and the *Buisson*, that the
bush of the title is in some way double, may be given expression in the branching
out of foliage from right and left, top and bottom, of uprights running the height
of the page. The title page of fr. 831 is a spectacular mass of vines; see also the
incipits of both the *Espinette* and the *Buisson* in fr. 830 (fols. 43r and 170r) and fr.
831 (fols. 104r and 155r).

8. The rhyme *brance* : *ramembrance* recurs at 4409–10, again with memorial function. On the use of the tree as a mnemonic design in Hugh of St. Victor,
see Carruthers, *Book of Memory*, 209–10, 238–40, and on numerical grids, 80ff.

9. See Marenbon, *Later Medieval Philosophy*, 139–42; de Libera, *Querelle*,
273–304.

10. The meaning of "comprehend" as "possessing exhaustive knowledge"
is given in the index in the final volume of the Blackfriars edition of Aquinas's
Summa theologiae.

11. Except for this passage, which is quoted by both Tobler-Lommatzsch
and Godefroy, I have not found the verb in any of the Old or Middle French

dictionaries, or in any of the Medieval Latin dictionaries, or in Walther von Wartburg, *Französisches etmologisches Wörterbuch: Eine Darstallung des galloromanischen Sprachshatzes* (Bonn: Schroeder, 1922–). The closest extant form is *unversaliser*, not used until much later.

12. "It is impossible for our intellect, in its present state of being joined to a body capable of receiving impressions, actually to understand anything without turning itself over to sense images" (*Summa theologiae*, Ia, 84, 7: "Impossibile est intellectum nostrum, secundum praesentis vitae statum quo passibili corpori conjungitur, aliquid intelligere in actu, nisi convertendo se ad phantasmata").

13. See Henry, "Predicables and Categories," 130–31.

14. Bardell, "Allegorical Landscape," 151.

15. This confirms Bennett's suggestion ("Mirage of Fiction," 288) that the bush represents the conceptual world inside Froissart's own head; as Bennett says, it is this status, poised between truth and fiction, that lends it to poetic elaboration.

16. On the use of the concept of "form" in the *Ovide moralisé* to justify Christian interpretations of Ovid see Chapter 2. The same book of the *Ovide moralisé* offers a double reading of Venus, who plays a vital role in the *Joli buisson*. In the gloss on the story of Ino, Venus is first said to be the goddess of love who sets fire to the heart of man, while the sea in which Ino drowns represents "the vain desire for love" ("vaine volenté d'amer," *OM*, IV, 4791). But then Venus can, it is claimed, also represent charity, which sets fire to the heart of man when in the grip of penance. This progression from the fire of sensual passion to that of religious devotion structures the second half of the *Joli buisson* (see below).

17. In corroboration of this conclusion, note the resemblance between Froissart's description of the *joli buisson* and the way, thirty years later, Christine de Pizan represents Opinion in the *Avision* (109–10) as a floating, amorphous cloud made up of innumerable particles and shimmering with all the colors. In this mysterious prose vision, Opinion is the middle of three queens with whom Christine's dream persona dialogues, coming between Libera and Philosophie. The section of the *Avision* devoted to her is conceived as an encounter with secular thought, specifically Scholastic philosophy. Dame Opinion retails to Christine all the errors, as well as the achievements, of human thinking, giving pride of place to Aristotle as the best producer of mere "opinions," since he gives the most cogent account of the nature and origin of being. Although capable of intellectual advances, Opinion, the structure of the work implies, is subordinate to true Philosophy, which, for Christine, involves personal revelation and reevaluation on the Boethian model. Christine does not mention Froissart, but the position she accords Scholastic philosophy presents similarities with the *Joli buisson*, where the merry bush of youthful experience (including the experience of university education) is likewise superseded by personal religious commitment. (The Boethian element in Froissart's *dit* calls for a different interpretation, however; see below.) Whether or not Christine is responding to Froissart, reading the *joli buisson* through her *Avision* confirms that, as a place of thought, it serves to locate "the means whereby one thinks" (the mental operations that form one's opinions) rather than "the object of one's thoughts" (the reality of things, whatever that may be).

18. Carruthers, *Book of Memory*, 33–43; for the image of memory as an *arca*

or strongbox, 42; the term *tresor* or its equivalent is used in the title of medieval poems that preserve and transmit memories; see, for example, Bardell, "Allegorical Landscape." Froissart's *coffret* is later equated with a *tresor*, *JBJ*, 600. Aquinas uses this image to describe the imagination: "For the imagination is like a storehouse of forms received through the senses" (*Summa theologiae* Ia, 78, 4; "est enim phantasia sive imaginatio quasi thesaurus quidam formarum per sensum acceptarum").

19. Aquinas's Latin Aristotle reads: "Manifestum enim quoniam oportet intelligere talem aliquam passionem factam per sensum in anima et in parte corporis habente ipsam, velut picturam quamdam, ciuis dicimus habitum esse memoriam."

20. Cf. Carruthers, *Book of Memory*, 23.

21. On books stored in a strongbox as an image of memory, see Carruthers, *Book of Memory*, 42; for a book store as an image of memory, 36; for the collapsing together of the metaphors of box and book, 45.

22. Marenbon, *Later Medieval Philosophy*, 128–29; Coleman, *Ancient and Medieval Memories*, 434.

23. Coleman, *Ancient and Medieval Memories*, 497. I also found Marenbon's account of memory in Duns Scotus very helpful: *Later Medieval Philosophy*, 160–68.

24. Quoted Marenbon, *Later Medieval Philosophy*, 163.

25. Coleman, *Ancient and Medieval Memories*, 524.

26. *Recorder* (*Joli buisson*, 477), glossed by Fourrier as "dire, déclarer, exposer," can also mean "remember," "recall"; see Freeman, "Froissart's *Le Joli Buisson de Jonece*," p. 244, n. 3.

27. Cf. Archambault, "Froissart and the Ockhamist Movement"; Thiry, "Allégorie et histoire." Scholastic influence on Froissart is also discerned by Pioche, *Le Vocabulaire psychologique dans les* Chroniques *de Froissart*.

28. My translation; Zink, *Froissart et le temps*, 152: "Les poèmes [de Froissart] construisent une représentation du moi structurée par le processus de la réminiscence, par la présence du souvenir à la conscience, cette conscience qui n'est que dans le reflet du souvenir." Cf. Marenbon, *Later Medieval Philosophy*, 168.

29. Cf. Carruthers, *Book of Memory*, 58, on the unfettered imagination of dreams.

30. For more extended study of the relations between the *Espinette* and the *Buisson*, see Zink, *Froissart et le temps*, 149–68; Kay, "*Le Moment de conclure*."

31. If a boy went to university aged fourteen or fifteen and studied for four years before progressing to the *quadrivium*, he would have been eighteen or nineteen at the very least before studying astronomy. See Marenbon, *Later Medieval Philosophy*, 21. The chronology of the *Joli buisson* and the age of the poet are anyway unclear; see Zink, *Froissart et le temps*, 164–65, and Kay, "*Le Moment de conclure*," 156.

32. "Because the past as past means something that is determined within time, it pertains to the realm of the particular and, therefore, to sense memory alone. . . . The past as past, as unique, as particular, is not capable of being understood. The past preserved as past in the mind is an irrational, sense memory with no meaning because meaning requires abstract and universal ideas, a processed

past which makes it, of necessity, present and generally meaningful in an exemplary way" (Coleman, *Ancient and Medieval Memories*, 433).

33. Bennett, "*Ut pictura memoria.*"

34. The *exempla* in *Le Joli buisson* have been extensively studied. See Kelly "Les Inventions ovidiennes de Froissart"; Huot, *From Song to Book*, 319–22; Kay, "Mémoire et imagination."

35. Freud, *Traumdeutung*, 513–14, 538–39, 555–56, 576–77; *Interpretation of Dreams*, 509–10, 533–34, 550, 570–71.

36. Trans. Sheridan, *Four Fundamental Concepts*, 58, 59, 69, 70; *Les Quatre concepts fondamentaux de la psychanalyse*, 68, 70, 81, 83.

37. Trans. Sheridan, *Four Fundamental Concepts*, 49; "Le réel est ici ce qui revient toujours à la même place—à cette place où le sujet en tant qu'il cogite, où la *res cogitans* ne le rencontre pas," *Les Quatre concepts fondamentaux de la psychanalyse*, 59. For more on this distinction see Fink, "Real Cause of Repetition," 225, and Cathelineau, *Lacan, lecteur d'Aristote*, 291–304.

38. "Only a rite, an endlessly repeated act, can commemorate this not very memorable encounter," trans. Sheridan, *Four Fundamental Concepts*, 59; "Seul un rite, un acte toujours répété, peut commémorer cette rencontre immémorable," *Les Quatre concepts fondamentaux de la psychanalyse*, 69.

39. The potential for universality in *automaton* is not in Aristotle, but in Lacan it is a consequence of the way arbitrariness inheres in the symbolic order.

40. Such a memory, I have argued elsewhere, is found in the inset lyrics in this *dit*: the trauma of finding himself on fire is seared into the *formes fixes* as though implanted in the signifying system; the repetition of vocabulary and rhyme that occurs within and between poems transmits Froissart's agony more than it represents it, eventually transmuting it from the register of physical desire to that of spiritual adoration. See my "Mémoire et imagination" and "*Le Moment de conclure.*"

41. Heller-Roazen, *Fortune's Faces*, 81–82.

42. *Physica vetus*: "Manifestum itaque est quod fortuna causa sit secundum accidens in his que in minori sunt secundum propositum eorum que propter hoc sunt. Unde circa idem intellectus et fortuna est; propositum enim non sine intellectu est." Confusingly, in the English translation *automaton* is rendered by "spontaneity" and *tuché* by "chance."

43. *Physica vetus*: "Fortuna . . . omnino actus est."

44. *Physica vetus*: "Ratio est enim aut eorum que sunt semper aut eorum que sicut frequenter."

45. *Physica vetus*: "Per se quidem igitur causa finita est, secundum accidens autem infinita; infinite enim uni utique accidunt."

46. Aquinas, *Summa theologiae* Ia, 78, 4; cf. Duns Scotus, *fit collatio ex tali recordatione*, "a comparison is drawn from such recollection," cited Marenbon, *Later Medieval Philosophy*, 165; Coleman, *Ancient and Medieval Memories*, 340.

47. "Pueritia quippe mea, qua iam non est, in tempore praeterito est, quod ima non est; imaginem uero eius, cum eam recolo et narro, in praesenti tempore intueor, qui est adhuc in memoria mea."

*Chapter 6. Melancholia, Allegory, and the Metaphysical Fountain in
Christine de Pizan's* Le Livre du Chemin de Long Estude

1. On the integration of political events with personal experience in the
Mutacion and *Avision* see Blumenfeld-Kosinski, "Christine de Pizan and the Political Life in Late Medieval France," 11–13, which also summarizes the political turmoil Christine is responding to. The relation of the personal and the political in
the *Avision* is discussed by Brown-Grant, "*L'Avision Christine*: Autobiographical
Narrative or Mirror for the Prince?" and again in *Christine de Pizan and the Moral
Defence of Women*, chap. 3; see also the response to this article by Tarnowski, "Perspectives on the *Advision*," which argues that allegory is a device by means of
which Christine can superimpose personal, political, and theological insights.

2. Richards, "French Cultural Nationalism and Christian Universalism in
the Works of Christine de Pizan." The question of universalism is also interestingly
discussed by Brabant and Brint, "Identity and Difference in Christine de Pizan's
Cité des Dames."

3. Richards, "Somewhere Between Destructive Glosses and Chaos," 46
(with reference to the *Avision* and the *Cité de dames*).

4. Aquinas, *Commentary on the Metaphysics of Aristotle*. For more on the
texts of Aristotle used by Aquinas, see James C. Doig, *Aquinas on Metaphysics*,
3–11. On Christine's use of Aquinas's *Commentary*, see Dulac and Reno, "Traduction et adaptation dans *L'Advision-Cristine*."

5. "Omnes homines natura scire desiderant. Alia quidem igitur imagina-
tionibus et memoriis vivunt, experimenti autem parum participant: hominum
autem genus arte et rationibus." I quote from the Latin text probably used by
Aquinas and included by the editor in the edition of Aquinas's commentary on the
Metaphysics, *In duodecim libros Metaphysicorum Aristotelis expositio*, 5.

6. On the importance of experience in the *Chemin de long estude* see Tarnowski, "The Lessons of Experience and the *Chemin de long estude*."

7. Trans. Rowan, Aquinas, *Commentary on the Metaphysics of Aristotle*, 5;
Metaphysics, 981a1ff. The Latin text runs: "Fit autem ex memoria hominibus experimentum. Eiusdem namque rei multae memoriae unius experientiae potentiam
faciunt. Et fere videtur scientiae simile experimentum esse, et arti. Hominibus
autem scientia et ars per experientiam evenit. . . . Fit autem ars cum ex multis
experimentibus conceptionibus una fit universalis, velut de similibus, acceptio."
Aquinas, *In duodecim libros Metaphysicorum Aristotelis expositio*, 5.

8. Trans. Rowan, Aquinas, *Commentary on the Metaphysics of Aristotle*, 68;
Aquinas, *In duodecim libros Metaphysicorum Aristotelis expositio*, §166, "Cum enim
aliquid generatur accipit formam quidem, quae forma eadem numero non potest
alteri generatio advenire, sed esse desinit generatio corruptio. In quo manifeste
apparet quod una materia ad multas formas se habet, et non e converso une forma
ad multas materias se habet. Et sic videtur rationabilius ponere ex parte materiae
unitatem, sed dualitatem sive contrarietatem ex parte formae, sicut posuerunt na-
turales, quam e converso sicut posuit Plato."

9. De Libera, *Querelle des universaux*, 272.

10. Bernard Ribémont has studied the relation between the space of knowledge and psychological space in this *dit* in his "Christine de Pizan: Entre espace scientifique et espace imaginé."

11. On Christine's use of Dante see in particular Brownlee, "Literary Genealogy and the Problem of the Father," and De Rentiis, " 'Sequere me': 'Imitatio' dans la *Divine Comédie* et dans le *Livre du chemin de long estude*."

12. Their scrutiny of MS BNF fr. 1643 of the *Chemin de long estude* leads Ouy and Reno ("Où mène le *Chemin de long estude*?") to reconstruct in detail the circumstances of some of the individuals surrounding Christine at the time of composition of this poem. Noting the similarities between her portrait of the ideal ruler and the political poetry of Abrogio Migli, secretary of Louis d'Orléans, they conclude that the favored candidate for the position of universal monarch in the *Chemin de long estude* is not Charles VI but Louis, his brother.

13. Her various appearances have been studied by Fenster, "Who's a Heroine?" 116–21; see also McGinn, "*Teste David cum Sibylla*."

14. Dulac gives an excellent account of Christine's use of *exempla* in "Poétique de l'exemple dans le *Corps de policie*." Rather than the moral-homiletic intent associated with medieval usage, Christine returns to the classical oratorical use of exempla as simultaneously forensic (their purpose is to *prove*) and emotive (96).

15. In the *Aeneid* Aeneas visits the underworld accompanied by the Sybil, so in recasting Dante's journey with Virgil, Christine is also returning it to its source.

16. Thus Philosophy to Boethius: "In all the care with which they toil at countless enterprises, mortal men travel by different paths, though all are striving to reach one and the same goal" (*Consolation of Philosophy*, III, prose 2; "Omnis mortalium cura, quam multiplicium studiorum labor exercit, diverso quidem calle procedit, sed ad unum . . . finem nititur pervenire"). In this (as in other) respects the *Chemin de long estude* shares common ground with Machaut's *Jugement* poems. See further Altmann, "Reopening the Case: Machaut's *Jugement* Poems as a Source in Christine de Pizan."

17. Hult, *Self-fulfilling Prophecies*, 283. In the *Mutation de Fortune*, 211–338, Christine's father similarly procures the precious gems of his learning from the fountain of the Muses.

18. See Tarnowski, "Maternity," 119–20, on this alteration from the *Rose*.

19. "Torvis inflammata luminibus: Quis, inquit, has scenicas meretriculas ad hunc aegrum permisit accedere. . . . Hae sunt enim, quae infructuosis affectuum spinis uberem fructibus rationis segetem necant."

20. Krueger, "Christine's Anxious Lessons," 22.

21. There is a detailed description of the illustrations in the Harley manuscript in Tarnowski's edition of the *Chemin de long estude*, 45–51. See also Gibbons, "Visual Allegory," which analyzes depictions of the fountain across all the manuscripts and points out that its stylized portrayal as a bath, while ignoring some aspects of the textual context, also provides it with new associations of healing and baptism.

22. Christine's laments at the beginning of the *Chemin* also stand out metri-

cally, being in heptasyllabic rather than octosyllabic couplets. The song of the Earth echoes this metrical isolation.

23. Cf. the opening section of the *Mutation de Fortune*, in which Nature is also figured as mother.

24. E.g., *Consolation of Philosophy* III, prose 3.

25. Ceres's quest for Proserpine involves an underworld journey similar to that of Aeneas, but the father-son relation is replaced by one of mother and daughter. Similarly, and more obviously, Christine and the Sybil form a mother-daughter pair.

26. Many of them, apparently, conveniently assembled for her in John of Wales's *Communiloquium*; see Beltran, "Christine de Pizan, Jacques Legrand et le *Communiloquium* de Jean de Galles."

27. And see also, e.g., her description of the ideal prince, 3389–448.

28. Christine's embrace of autocracy marks her difference from John of Salisbury's *Policraticus*, as shown by Forhan, "Polycracy, Obligation, and Revolt." Forhan is writing primarily about Christine's *Livre du corps de policie*, but her remarks apply equally to the *Chemin de long estude*, which cites the *Policraticus* several times.

29. In line with her euhumerist thinking, Christine interprets pagan gods as human qualities.

30. Kristeva sees this as a point of contrast between her view of the Thing and Lacan's. See *Soleil noir*, 23 n. 13, where she cites Lacan saying explicitly that for him the Thing does not call into question the way reality is taken up in language.

31. My translation; Cathelineau, *Lacan, lecteur d'Aristote*, 263: "Mais le noyau de l'ontologie aristotélicienne demeure essentiellement *l'individu inconnaissable en lui-même* et seulement connu par le discours scientifique qui s'exprime à travers le genre et l'espèce," *Lacan, lecteur d'Aristote*; emphasis in the original.

32. My translation; Kristeva, *Soleil noir*, 111: "La dynamique de la sublimation, en mobilisant les processus primaires et l'idéalisation, tisse autour du vide dépressif et avec lui un *hyper-signe*. C'est *l'allégorie* comme magnificence de ce qui *n'est plus*, mais qui re-prend pour moi une signification supérieure parce que je suis apte à refaire le néant, en mieux et dans une harmonie inaltérable, ici et maintenant et pour l'éternité, en vue d'un tiers. Signification sublime en lieu et place du non-être sous-jacent et implicite, c'est l'artifice qui remplace l'éphémère. La beauté lui est consubstantielle. Telles les parures féminines voilant des dépressions tenaces, la beauté se manifeste comme le visage admirable de la perte, elle la métamorphose pour la faire vivre."

33. See Griffin, "Material and Poetic Knowledge."

34. My translation; Kristeva, *Soleil noir*, 111: "Lorsque nous avons pu traverser nos mélancolies au point de nous intéresser aux vies des signes, la beauté peut aussi nous saisir pour témoigner de quelqu'un qui a magnifiquement trouvé la voie royale par laquelle l'homme transcende la douleur d'être séparé: la voie de la parole donnée à la souffrance. . . . Le magnifique serait même le rêve impossible, l'autre monde du dépressif, réalisé ici-bas."

35. Tarnowski's note in her edition to these lines identifies the passage in question as *De Planctu* 1128–203.

Conclusion. Monologism Reconsidered

1. See Huot, "Guillaume de Machaut and the Consolation of Poetry."

2. Such a practice of "inaugural parody" is especially rife among the troubadours, when early poets seem to parody texts that in fact come later.

3. Minnis, *Magister Amoris*, 108–13.

4. Huot's study of *Rose* manuscripts suggests that Genius's sermon was one of the parts of the text that was most often reworked by fourteenth-century scribes and editors, and that the way they responded to it was either to strengthen the bodily-individual axis or the universal-theological one, that is, they registered Genius's failure to engage with the complexity of one as I have argued for it here. See, for example, *The Romance of the Rose and Its Medieval Readers*, 186–89, 194–95. I have not worked on these texts and am certainly not claiming that these reworkings produced superior versions of the *Rose*, only that they transformed Genius's speech from being *about* didacticism to being an *instance* of it.

5. Derrida and Roudinesco, *For What Tomorrow*, 171.

Bibliography

For how works in this Bibliography are cited in the text and notes, please see "Abbreviations, References, and Other Conventions" on page ix. Where there is more than one way of naming an author or work, names are entered in the form to which I refer to them in this book even if this is not the form used in the printed source in this Bibliography.

MEDIEVAL FRENCH AND OCCITAN WORKS

Christine de Pizan. *Avision: Lavision-Christine. Introduction and Text*. Ed. Sister Mary Louis Towner. Catholic University of America Studies in Romance Languages and Literatures, 6. Washington, D.C.: Catholic University of America, 1932.

———. *La Cité des dames: La Città delle dame*. Ed. E. J. Richards, trans. Patrizia Caraffi. Milan: Luni, 1997.

———. *Le (livre du) Chemin de long estude: Le Chemin de longue étude*. Ed. Andrea Tarnowski. Lettres gothiques. Paris: Librarie Générale Française, 2000.

———. *Le Livre des Fais et bonnes meurs du sage roy Charles V*. Ed. Suzanne Solente. 2 vols. Paris: Champion, 1936–40.

Deguileville, Guillaume de. *Le Pèlerinage de vie humaine*. Ed. J. J. Stürzinger. Roxburghe Club. London: Nichols, 1893.

———. *Le Pèlerinage de l'âme*. Ed. J. J. Stürzinger. Roxburghe Club. London: Nichols, 1895.

Froissart, Jehan. *L'Espinette amoureuse*. Ed. Anthime Fourrier. Paris: Klincksieck, 1963.

———. *Le Joli buisson de Jonece*. Ed. Anthime Fourrier. TLF. Geneva: Droz, 1975.

Guillaume de Lorris and Jean de Meun. *Le Roman de la rose*. Ed. Félix Lecoy. 3 vols., CFMA. Paris: Champion, 1967–70.

La Lumiere as lais *by Pierre d'Abernon of Fetcham*. Ed. Glynn Hesketh. 3 vols. London: ANTS, 1996–2000.

Machaut, Guillaume de. *Le Jugement dou roy de Navarre*. Ed. and trans. R. Barton Palmer. New York: Garland, 1988.

———. *Le Jugement du roy de Behaigne*. Ed. and trans. James J. Wimsatt and William W. Kibler. Athens: University of Georgia Press, 1988.

Matfre Ermengaud. *Le Breviari d'amor*. Ed. Peter T. Ricketts. 5 vols. Vol. V, Leiden: Brill, 1976. Vols. II and III, London: Publications de l'AIEO, 1989, 1998. Vol. IV, Turnhout: Brepols, Publications de l'AIEO, 2004. A revised edition of vol. V is forthcoming, Turnhout: Brepols, Publications de l'AIEO.

Ovide moralisé: Poème du commencement du quatorzième siècle. Ed. C. de Boer and others. *Verhandelingen der Koninklijke Akademie van Wetenschapen te Amsterdam, Afdeeling Letterkunde.* T. I (Books I–III), ed. C. de Boer, Nieuwe Reeks XV (1915). T. 2 (Books IV–VI), ed. C. de Boer, Niuewe Reeks XXI (1920). T. 3 (Books VII–IX), ed. C. de Boer, Martina G. de Boer, and Jeannette Th. M. van't Sant, Niuewe Reeks XXX (1931). T. 4 (Books X–XIII), ed. C. de Boer, Martina G. de Boer, and Jeannette Th. M. van't Sant, Niuewe Reeks XXXVII (1936). T. 5 (Books XIV and XV and Appendices), ed. C. de Boer, Niuewe Reeks XLIII (1938).

PHILOSOPHICAL, CRITICAL, AND OTHER SECONDARY WORKS

Adams, Marilyn McCord. "Universals in the Early Fourteenth Century." In *The Cambridge History of Later Medieval Philosophy.* Ed. Norman Kretzman, Anthony Kenny, and Jan Pinborg. Cambridge: Cambridge University Press, 1982. 411–39.

Agamben, Giorgio. *La Comunità che viene.* Turin: Bollati Boringhieri, 2001; first published Turin: Einaudi, 1990. Trans. Michael Hardt, *The Coming Community.* Minneapolis: University of Minnesota Press, 1993.

Akbari, Suzanne Conklin. *Seeing Through the Veil: Optical Theory and Medieval Allegory.* Toronto: University of Toronto Press, 2004.

Altmann, Barbara K. "Reopening the Case: Machaut's *Jugement* Poems as a Source in Christine de Pizan." In *Reinterpreting Christine de Pizan.* Ed. E. J. Richards. Athens: University of Georgia Press, 1992. 137–56.

Altmann, Barbara K., and Deborah McGrady, eds. *Christine de Pizan: A Casebook.* New York: Routledge, 2003.

Aquinas, Thomas, Saint. Commentary on *Metaphysics. In duodecim libros Metaphysicorum Aristotelis expositio.* Ed. M. R. Cathale, O.P., and R. M. Spiazzi, O.P. Turin: Marietti, 1950. Trans. John P. Rowan, *Commentary on the Metaphysics of Aristotle.* 2 vols. Chicago: Regnery, 1961.

———. Commentary on *On Memory. In Aristotelis libros "De sensu et sensato" "De memoria et reminiscentia" commentarium.* Ed. Raymund M. Spiazzi, O.P. Turin: Marietti, 1949.

———. *Summa theologiae.* Latin text and English translation, Introduction, Notes, Appendices, and Glossaries. Blackfriars edition. London: Eyre and Spottiswoode, 1964–80.

Archambault, P. J. "Froissart and the Ockhamist Movement: Philosophy and Its Impact on Historiography." *Symposium* 28 (1974): 197–211.

Aristotle. *The Complete Works of Aristotle.* The Revised Oxford Translation. Ed. Jonathan Barnes. 2 vols. Bollingen Series LXXI.2. Princeton: Princeton University Press, 1984.

———. *Categories.* In *Complete Works,* I, 3–24.

———. *De Interpretatione.* In *Complete Works,* I, 25–38.

———. *Metaphysics.* In *Complete Works,* II, 1552–728.

———. *Nicomachean Ethics.* In *Complete Works,* II, 1729–867.

———. *On Memory* (*De Memoria et reminiscentia*). In *Complete Works*, I, 714–20.

———. *On the Soul* (*De Anima*). In *Complete Works*, I, 641–92.

———. *Physics.* In *Complete Works* I, 315–446.

Aristoteles Latinus.

———. *Metaphysics.* See Aquinas, Commentary on the *Metaphysics.*

———. *On Memory.* See Aquinas, Commentary *On Memory.*

———. *Nicomachean Ethics.* Ed. Robert Grosseteste. *Aristotelis Moralium ad Nicomachum*, Lincoln text. In *Aristoteles Latinus* XXVI, 1–3, fasc. 3. Ed. R. A. Gauthier. Leiden: Brill, and Brussels: Desclée de Brouwer, 1972.

———. *Physics. Physica: Translatio vetus.* In *Aristoteles Latinus* VII, 1–2, fasc. 1.2. Ed. Fernand Bossier and Josef Brams. Leiden: Brill, 1990.

———. Porphyry, *Isagoge.* "Porphyrii Isagoge, translatio Boethii." In *Aristoteles Latinus* I, 6–7, *Categoriarum Supplementa*, ed. L. Minio-Paluello and B. G. Dod. Bruges: Desclée de Brouwer, 1966. 5–31.

Augustine, Saint, Bishop of Hippo. Cited from the editions in the Corpus Christianorum Series Latina. Turnhout: Brepols, 1954–, abbreviated below as CCSL.

———. *City of God. De Civitate Dei contra paganos.* Ed. Bernard Dombart and Alphonse Kalb. CCSL 47, 48 (1955). Trans. Henry Bettenson, *Concerning the City of God Against the Pagans.* Introduction by John O'Meara. Harmondsworth: Penguin, 1984.

———. *Confessions. Confessionum libri XIII.* Ed. Luc Verheijen, CCSL 27, 1981. Trans. with an Introduction and Notes by Henry Chadwick, *Confessions.* Oxford: Oxford University Press, 1991.

———. *On Christian Teaching.* Ed. Joseph Martin. CCSL, 32 (1962). Trans. with an Introduction and Notes by R. P. H. Green, *On Christian Teaching.* World's Classics. Oxford: Oxford University Press, 1997.

———. *On the Trinity. De Trinitate libri XV.* Ed. W. J. Mountain. CCSL 50, 50A. Trans. Stephen McKenna, *On the Trinity.* The Fathers of the Church 45. Washington, D.C.: Fathers of the Church, 1970.

Avril, François. "Les Manuscripts enluminées de Guillaume de Machaut: Essai de chronologie." In *Guillaume de Machaut poète et compositeur: Colloque— Table ronde, Reims (19–22 avril 1978).* Paris: Klincksieck, 1982. 117–33.

Badel, Pierre-Yves. *Le* Roman de la Rose *au XIVe siècle: Etude de la réception de l'oeuvre.* Geneva: Droz, 1980.

Bakhtin, Mikhail M. "On the Pre-history of Novelistic Discourse." In *The Dialogic Imagination: Four Essays.* Ed. Michael Holquist, trans. Caryl Emerson and Michael Holquist. Austin: University of Texas Press, 1981. 41–83.

Bardell, Matthew. "The Allegorical Landscape: Peire Vidal's *Ric Thesaur.*" *French Studies* 55 (2001): 151–65.

Bennett, Philip E. "The Mirage of Fiction: Narration, Narrator, and Narrative in Froissart's Lyrico-Narrative *dits.*" *Modern Language Review* 86 (1991): 285–97.

———. "*Ut pictura memoria*: Froissart's Quest for Lost Time." Unpublished conference paper, University of Edinburgh, 2001.

Bérubé, Camille. *La Connaissance de l'individuel au moyen âge.* Montreal: Presses de l'Université de Montréal and Paris: PUF, 1964.

Betran, Evancio. "Christine de Pizan, Jacques Legrand et le *Communiloquium* de Jean de Galles." *Romania* 104 (1983): 208–28.

Blum, Paul Richard. "Dio e gli individui: l'«arbor porphyriana» nei secoli XVII e XVIII." *Rivista di filosofia neoscolastica* 91 (1999): 18–49.

Blumenfeld-Kosinski, Renate. *Reading Myth: Classical Mythology and Its Interpretation in Medieval French Literature*. Stanford, Calif.: Stanford University Press, 1997.

———. "Illustrations et interprétations dans un manuscrit de l'*Ovide moralisé* (Arsenal 5069)." In *Lectures et usages d'Ovide (XIIIe–XVe siècles)*. Ed. Emmanuèle Baumgartner. Cahiers de Recherches Médiévales (XIIIe–XVe siècles) 9. Paris: Champion, 2002. 71–82.

———. "Christine de Pizan and the Political Life in Late Medieval France." In *Christine de Pizan: A Casebook*. Ed. Barbara K. Altmann and Deborah McGrady. New York: Routledge, 2003. 9–24.

Blumenkranz, Bernhard. "Ecriture et image dans la polémique anti-juife de Matfré Ermengaud." In *Juifs et Judaïsme en Languedoc, Cahiers de Fanjeaux* 12 (1977): 295–317.

Boethius. *Consolation of Philosophy. Philosophiae consolationis libri quinque*. Ed. Walter Berschin and Walther Bulst. Editiones Heidelbergenses. Heidelberg: Winter, 1977. *The Consolation of Philosophy*. Trans. with an Introduction by V. E. Watts. Harmondsworth: Penguin, 1969.

Boler, John F. "Intuitive and Abstractive Cognition." In *The Cambridge History of Later Medieval Philosophy*. Ed. Norman Kretzman, Anthony Kenny, and Jan Pinborg. Cambridge: Cambridge University Press, 1982. 460–78.

Boulton, Maureen. "Digulleville's *Pèlerinage de Jésus Christ*: A Poem of Courtly Devotion." In *The Vernacular Spirit: Essays on Medieval Religious Literature*. Ed. Renate Blumenfeld-Kosinski, Duncan Robertson, and Nancy Bradley Warren. New Middle Ages Series. New York: Palgrave Macmillan, 2002. 125–44.

Brabant, Margaret, ed. *Politics, Gender and Genre: The Political Thought of Christine de Pizan*. Boulder, Colo.: Westview Press, 1992.

Brabant, Margaret, and Michael Brint. "Identity and Difference in Christine de Pizan's *Cité des Dames*." In *Politics, Gender and Genre: The Political Thought of Christine de Pizan*. Ed. Margaret Brabant. Boulder, Colo.: Westview Press, 1992. 207–22.

Brown-Grant, Rosalind. "*L'Avision Christine*: Autobiographical Narrative or Mirror for the Prince?" In *Politics, Gender and Genre: The Political Thought of Christine de Pizan*. Ed. Margaret Brabant. Boulder, Colo.: Westview Press, 1992. 95–111.

———. *Christine de Pizan and the Moral Defence of Women*. Cambridge: Cambridge University Press, 1999.

Brownlee, Kevin. *Poetic Identity in Guillaume de Machaut*. Madison: University of Wisconsin Press, 1984.

———. "Literary Genealogy and the Problem of the Father: Christine de Pizan and Dante." In *Dante Now: Current Trends in Dante Studies*. Ed. Theodore J. Cachey, Jr. Notre Dame: University of Notre Dame Press, 1995. 205–35.

Butler, Judith. *The Psychic Life of Power: Theories in Subjection.* Stanford: Stanford University Press, 1997.

Bynum, Caroline Walker. *Metamorphosis and Identity.* New York: Zone Books, 2001.

Calin, William C. "A Reading of Machaut's *Jugement dou roy de Navarre.*" *Modern Language Review* 66 (1971): 294–97.

———. *A Poet at the Fountain.* Lexington: University Press of Kentucky, 1974.

Camille, Michael. "The Illustrated Manuscripts of Guillaume de Deguileville's *Pèlerinages*, 1330–1426." Ph.D. thesis, University of Cambridge, 1985.

———. *The* Master of Death: The Lifeless Art of Pierre Remiet, Illuminator. New Haven: Yale University Press, 1996.

Campbell, John, and Nadia Margolis, eds. *Christine de Pizan 2000: Studies on Christine de Pizan in Honour of Angus J. Kennedy.* Amsterdam: Rodopi, 2000.

Carruthers, Mary. *The Book of Memory: A Study of Memory in Medieval Culture.* Cambridge: Cambridge University Press, 1990.

Casey, Edward. *The Fate of Place.* Berkeley: University of California Press, 1997.

Cathelineau, Pierre-Christophe. *Lacan, lecteur d'Aristote: Politique, métaphysique, logique.* Paris: Editions de l'Association Freudienne Internationale, 1998.

Cave, Terence. *The Cornucopian Text.* Oxford: Clarendon, 1979.

Cerquiglini, J. *"Un engin si soutil": Guillaume de Machaut et l'écriture au XIVe siècle.* Paris: Champion, 1985.

Cerquiligni-Toulet, J. "Lyrisme de désir et lyrisme d'espérance dans la poésie de Machaut." In *Guillaume de Machaut 1300–2000.* Ed. Jacqueline Cerquiglini-Toulet and Nigel Wilkins. Paris: Presses de l'Université de Paris-Sorbonne, 2002. 41–51.

Cherchi, Paolo. "L'enciclopedia nel mondo dei trovatori: Il *Breviari d'amor* di Matfre Ermengau." In *L'enciclopedismo medievale.* Ed. Michelangelo Picone. Ravenna: Longo, 1994. 277–91.

Coleman, Janet. *Ancient and Medieval Memories: Studies in the Reconstruction of the Past.* Cambridge: Cambridge University Press, 1992.

Collison, Robert. *Encyclopaedias: Their History Throughout the Ages.* New York: Hafner, 1966.

Compagnon, Antoine. *La Seconde main ou le travail de la citation.* Paris: Seuil, 1979.

Copeland, Rita. *Rhetoric, Hermeneutics and Translation in the Middle Ages: Academic Traditions and Vernacular Texts.* Cambridge: Cambridge University Press, 1991.

Cornelius, Roberta D. *The Figurative Castle: A Study in the Mediaeval Allegory of the Edifice with Especial Reference to Religious Writings.* Bryn Mawr, Pa.: Bryn Mawr College, 1930.

Cowling, David. *Building the Text: Architecture as Metaphor in Late Medieval and Early Modern France.* Oxford: Clarendon, 1998.

Croizy-Naquet, Catherine. "L'*Ovide moralisé* ou Ovide revisité: De métamorphose en anamorphose." In *Lectures et usages d'Ovide (XIIIe–XVe siècles).*

Ed. Emmanuèle Baumgartner. Cahiers de Recherches Médiévales (XIIIe–XVe siècles) 9. Paris: Champion, 2002. 39–51.

Davis, Brian. *The Thought of Thomas Aquinas*. Oxford: Clarendon, 1992.

Deleuze, Gilles, and Félix Guattari. *Capitalisme et schizophrénie 2: Mille plateaux.* Paris: Minuit, 1980. Trans. Brian Massumi, *A Thousand Plateaus: Capitalism and Schizophrenia*. Minneapolis: University of Minnesota Press, 1987.

De Libera, Alain. *La Querelle des universaux de Platon à la fin du Moyen Age.* Paris: Seuil, 1996.

De Looze, Lawrence. *Pseudo-Autobiography in Fourteenth-Century France.* Gainesville: University of Florida Press, 1997.

Delumeau, Jean. *Le Péché et la peur: La culpabilisation en Occident XIII–XVIIIe siècles*. Paris: Fayard, 1983.

Demats, Paule. *Fabula: Trois Etudes de mythographie antique et médiévale*. Geneva: Droz, 1973.

De Rentiis, Dina. " 'Sequere me': 'Imitatio' dans la *Divine Comédie* et dans le *Livre du chemin de long estude*." In *The City of Scholars: New Approaches to Christine de Pizan*. Ed. Margarete Zimmermann and Dina De Rentiis. Berlin: De Gruyter, 1994. 31–42.

Derrida, Jacques, and Elisabeth Roudinesco. *For What Tomorrow? A Dialogue.* Trans. Jeff Fort. Stanford, Calif.: Stanford University Press, 2004.

Desmond, Marilynn. ed. *Christine de Pizan and the Categories of Difference*. Minneapolis: University of Minnesota Press, 1998.

Dod, Bernard G. "Aristoteles Latinus." In *The Cambridge History of Later Medieval Philosophy*. Ed. Norman Kretzman, Anthony Kenny, and Jan Pinborg. Cambridge: Cambridge University Press, 1982. 45–79.

Doig, James C. *Aquinas on Metaphysics: A Historico-doctrinal Study of the "Commentary on the Metaphysics."* The Hague: Nijhoff, 1972.

Dolar, Mladen. "*Cogito* as the Subject of the Unconscious." In *Cogito and the Unconscious*. Ed. Slavoj Žižek and Renate Salecl. Durham, N.C.: Duke University Press, 1998. 11–40.

Dulac, Liliane. "Poétique de l'exemple dans le *Corps de policie*." In *Christine de Pizan 2000: Studies on Christine de Pizan in Honour of Angus J. Kennedy*. Ed. John Campbell and Nadia Margolis. Amsterdam: Rodopi, 2000. 91–104.

Dulac, Liliane, and Christine Reno. "Traduction et adaptation dans *L'Advision-Cristine* de Christine de Pizan." In *Traduction et adaptation en France à la fin du Moyen Age et à la Renaissance*. Ed. Charles Brucker. Paris: Champion, 1997. 121–31.

Dyas, Dee. *Pilgrimage in Medieval English Literature, 700–1500*. Woodbridge: D. S. Brewer, 2001.

Earp, Lawrence. *Guillaume de Machaut: A Guide to Research*. New York: Garland, 1995.

Ehrhart, Margaret. "Guillaume de Machaut's *Jugement dou roy de Navarre* and Medieval Treatments of the Virtues." *Annuale Medievale* 19 (1979): 46–67.

———. "Machaut and the Duties of Rulers Tradition." *French Forum* 17 (1992): 5–22.

Engels, Joseph. *Etudes sur l'*Ovide moralisé. Groningen: J. B. Wolters, 1943.

Feldstein, Richard, Bruce Fink, and Maire Jaanus, eds. *Reading Seminar XI: Lacan's Four Fundamental Concepts of Psychoanalysis*. Albany: SUNY Press, 1995.

Fenster, Thelma. "Who's a Heroine?" In *Christine de Pizan: A Casebook*. Ed. Barbara K. Altmann and Deborah McGrady. New York: Routledge, 2003. 115–28.

Forhan, Kate Langdon. "Polycracy, Obligation, and Revolt: The Body Politic in John of Salisbury and Christine de Pizan." In *Politics, Gender and Genre: The Political Thought of Christine de Pizan*. Ed. Margaret Brabant. Boulder, Colo.: Westview Press, 1992. 33–52.

Foucault, Michel. *Les Mots et les choses: Une archéologie des sciences humaines*. Paris: Gallimard, 1966. Trans. as *The Order of Things: An Archaeology of the Human Sciences*. London: Routledge, 1989.

Freeman, Michelle. "Froissart's *Le Joli Buisson de Jonece*: A Farewell to Poetry?" In *Machaut's World: Science and Art in the Fourteenth Century*. Ed. Madeleine Pelner Cosman and Bruce Chandler. New York: New York Academy of Sciences, 1978. 235–47.

Freud, Sigmund. *Gesammelter Werke, chronologisch geordnet*. Ed. Marie Bonaparte, Anna Freud, Edward Bibring, and Ernst Kris. 17 vols. London: Imago, 1940–52, abbreviated as *GW*. Trans. under the editorship of James Strachey as *The Standard Edition of the Complete Psychological Works of Sigmund Freud*. 24 vols. London: Hogarth Press, 1953–74, abbreviated as *SE*.

———. *Die Traumdeutung* [1900]. *GW* II–III, 1942; *The Interpretation of Dreams, SE* IV–V, 1953.

———. *Neue Folge der Vorlesungen zur Enführung in die Pychanalyse* [1933]. *GW*, XV, 1940; *New Introductory Lectures on Psycho-Analysis, SE* XXII, 1964, 5–182.

Galent-Fasseur, Valérie. "La dame de l'arbre: Rôle de la «vue» structurale dans le *Bréviaire d'amour* de Matfre Ermengaud." *Romania* 117 (1997): 32–50.

Gauvard, Claude "Portrait du Prince d'après l'oeuvre de Guillaume de Machaut: Etude sur les idées politiques du poète." In *Guillaume de Machaut poète et compositeur. Colloque—Table ronde, Reims (19–22 avril 1978)*. Paris: Klincksieck, 1982. 23–39.

Gibbons, Mary Wetzel. "Visual Allegory in the *Chemin de long estude*." In *Christine de Pizan and the Categories of Difference*. Ed. Marilynn Desmond. Minneapolis: University of Minnesota Press, 1998. 128–45.

Gibbs, Stephanie. "Allegories of Authorship in the *Roman de la rose* and the *Pèlerinage de la vie humaine*." Unpublished seminar paper, Cambridge University, 2005.

Girgente, Giuseppe. "La metafisica de Porforio como mediacion entre la «henologia» platonica y la «ontologia» aristotelica." *Anuario filosofico* 33 (2000): 151–63.

Godefroy, F. *Dictionnaire de l'ancienne langue française et de tous ses dialectes du IXe au XVe siècle*. 10 vols. Paris: Vieweg and Bouillon, 1880–1902.

Green, André. *Narcissisme de vie, narcissisme de mort*. Paris: Minuit, 1983.

Gregory, Tullio. "The Platonic Inheritance." In *A History of Twelfth-Century*

Western Philosophy. Ed. Peter Dronke. Cambridge: Cambridge University Press, 1988. 54–80.

Griffin, Miranda. "Material and Poetic Knowledge in Christine de Pizan." Forthcoming.

Hardie, Philip. "Ovid's Theban History." *Classical Quarterly* n.s. 40 (1990): 224–35.

Heller-Roazen, Daniel. *Fortune's Faces: The* Roman de la Rose *and the Poetics of Contingency.* Baltimore: Johns Hopkins University Press, 2003.

Henry, D. P. "Predicables and Categories." In *The Cambridge History of Later Medieval Philosophy.* Ed. Norman Kretzmann, Anthony Kenny, and Jane Pinborg. Cambridge: Cambridge University Press, 1982. 128–42.

Hult, David. *Self-fulfilling Prophecies: Readership and Authority in the First* Roman de la rose. Cambridge: Cambridge University Press, 1986.

Huot, Sylvia. *From Song to Book: The Poetics of Writing in Old French Lyric and Lyrical Narrative Poetry.* Ithaca, N.Y.: Cornell University Press, 1987.

———. *The Romance of the Rose and Its Medieval Readers.* Cambridge: Cambridge University Press, 1993.

———. "Guillaume de Machaut and the Consolation of Poetry." *Modern Philology* 100 (2002): 169–95.

———. *Madness in Medieval French Literature: Identities Found and Lost.* Oxford: Oxford University Press, 2003.

Isidore, Saint, Bishop of Seville. *Etymologies.* Isidori Hispalensis Episcopi, *Etymologiarum sive originum libri xx.* Ed. W. M. Lindsay. 2 vols. Oxford: Clarendon, 1911.

Jung, Marc René. "Les Editions manuscrites de l'*Ovide moralisé.*" *Cahiers d'Histoire des Littératures Romanes* 20 (1996): 251–74.

Kamber, Urs. *Arbor Amoris: Der Minnebaum: Ein Pseudo-Bonaventura-Traktat.* Philosophische Studien und Quellen 20. Berlin: Erich Schmidt, 1964.

Kay, Sarah. "The Didactic Space: The City in Christine de Pizan, Augustine, and Irigaray." In *Text und Kultur. Mittelalterliche Literatur 1150–1450.* Ed. Ursula Peters. Stuttgart: Metzler: 2001. 438–66.

———. "Mémoire et imagination dans *Le Joli buisson de Jonece* de Jean Froissart: La fiction entre philosophie et poétique." *Francofonia* 45 (2003): 179–97.

———. "Flayed Skin as *objet a*: Representation and Materiality in Guillaume de Deguileville's *Pèlerinage de vie humaine.*" In *Medieval Fabrications: Dress, Textiles, Cloth Work, and Other Cultural Imaginings.* Ed. E. Jane Burns. New Middle Ages Series. New York: Palgrave Macmillan, 2004. 193–205 and 249–51.

———. "*Le Moment de conclure*: Initiation as Retrospection in Froissart's *dits.*" In *Rites of Passage.* Ed. Nicola McDonald and Mark Ormrod. Woodbridge: Boydell and Brewer, 2004. 153–71.

———. "Grafting the Knowledge Community: The Purposes of Verse in the *Breviari d'amor* of Matfre Ermengaud." *Neophilologus,* forthcoming.

Kelly, Douglas. *Medieval Imagination: Rhetoric and the Poetry of Courtly Love.* Madison: University of Wisconsin Press, 1978.

————. "Les Inventions ovidiennes de Froissart: Réflexions intertextuelles comme imagination." *Littérature* 41 (1981): 82–92.

Kretzmann, Norman, Anthony Kenny, and Jan Pinborg, eds. *The Cambridge History of Later Medieval Philosophy.* Cambridge: Cambridge University Press, 1982.

Kristeva, Julia. *Soleil noir: Dépression et mélancolie.* Paris: Gallimard, 1987. Trans. Leon S. Roudiez, *Black Sun: Depression and Melancholia.* New York: Columbia University Press, 1989.

Krueger, R. L. "Christine's Anxious Lessons: Gender, Morality, and the Social Order from the *Enseignements* to the *Avision.*" In *Christine de Pizan and the Categories of Difference.* Ed. Marilynn Desmond. Minneapolis: University of Minnesota Press, 1998. 16–40.

Lacan, Jacques. *Ecrits.* Paris: Seuil, 1966. Trans. Alan Sheridan. *Ecrits. A Selection.* London: Tavistock, 1977.

————. *Le Séminaire de Jacques Lacan,* ed. Jacques-Alain Miller. Paris: Seuil, 1973–. Containing:

————. *Le Séminaire, Livre VII, L'Éthique de la psychanalyse. 1959–60.* Paris: Seuil, 1986. Trans. with notes by Dennis Porter.

————. *Book VII. The Ethics of Psychoanalysis. 1959–60.* London: Routledge, 1992.

————. [Book XI] *Les Quatre concepts fondamentaux de la psychanalyse.* Paris, Seuil, 1973. Trans. Alan Sheridan. *The Four Fundamental Concepts of Psychoanalysis.* Introduction by David Macey. London: Penguin, 1994.

————. *Le Séminaire Livre XX, Encore. 1972–3.* Paris: Seuil, 1975. Trans. Bruce Fink. *Book XX. Encore. On Feminine Sexuality, the Limits of Love and Knowledge.* London: Norton, 1998.

Lang, Helen. *The Order of Nature in Aristotle's Physics.* Cambridge: Cambridge University Press, 1998.

Langlois, Charles-Victor. *La Vie en France au Moyen Age du XIIe au milieu du XIVe siècle.* T. IV, *La Vie spirituelle: Enseignements, méditations et controverses.* Paris: Hachette, 1928.

Laske-Fix, Katja. *Der Bildzyklus des Breviari d'Amor.* Munich: Schnell and Steiner, 1973.

Laurent, Eric. "Alienation and Separation I" and "Alienation and Separation II." In *Reading Seminar XI: Lacan's Four Fundamental Concepts of Psychoanalysis.* Ed. Richard Feldstein, Bruce Fink, and Maire Jaanus. Albany: SUNY Press, 1995.19–28, 29–38.

Levy, Emil. *Petit dictionnaire provençal-français.* 3rd edition. Heidelberg: Winter, 1961.

Llull, Ramón. *Arbor Scientiae.* Ed. Pere Villalba Varneda. 3 vols. Corpus Christianorum. Continuatio Medievalis 180A, B, & C. Turnhout: Brepols, 2000.

————. *Logica Nova.* In *Raimundi Lulli Opera Latina.* Ed. Walter Euler. Corpus Christianorum. Continuatio Medievalis 115. Turnhout: Brepols, 1998.

————. *The* Tree of Love *translated from the Catalan of Ramón Lull; with an introductory essay* by E. Allison Peers. London: SPCK, 1926.

Lord, Carla. "Three Manuscripts of the *Ovide moralisé.*" *Art Bulletin* 57 (1975): 161–75.

Malpas, J. E. *Place and Experience: A Philosophical Topography*. Cambridge: Cambridge University Press, 1999.

Marenbon, John. *Later Medieval Philosophy*. London: Routledge, 1987.

Matthews, Gareth B. *Thought's Ego in Augustine and Descartes*. Ithaca, N.Y.: Cornell University Press, 1992.

McGinn, Bernard. "*Teste David cum Sibylla*: The Significance of the Sibylline Tradition in the Middle Ages." In *Women in the Medieval World: Essays in Honor of John H. Mundy*. Ed. Julius Kirshner and Suzanne Wemple. Oxford: Blackwell, 1985. 7–35.

Menn, Stephen. *Descartes and Augustine*. Cambridge: Cambridge University Press, 1998.

Meyer, Paul. "Matfre Ermengaud de Béziers, troubadour." *Histoire Littéraire de la France* 32 (1898): 16–56.

Minnis, Alastair. *Magister Amoris. The* Roman de la rose *and Vernacular Hermeneutics*. Oxford: Oxford University Press, 2001.

Moriarty, Michael. *Early Modern French Thought: The Age of Suspicion*. Oxford: Oxford University Press, 2003.

Morison, Benjamin. *On Location: Aristotle's Concept of Place*. Oxford: Clarendon Press, 2002.

Moss, Ann. *Printed Commonplace-Books and the Structuring of Renaissance Thought*. Oxford: Clarendon Press, 1996.

Nicholson, Francesca M. "Branches of Knowledge: The Purposes of Citation in the *Breviari d'amor* of Matfre Ermengaud." *Neophilologus*, forthcoming.

Ouy, Gilbert, and Christine M. Reno. "Où mène le *Chemin de long estude*? Christine de Pizan, Ambroglio Migli, et les ambitions impériales de Louis d'Orléans." In *Christine de Pizan 2000: Studies in Honour of Angus J. Kennedy*. Ed. John Campbell and Nadia Margolis. Amsterdam: Rodopi, 2000. 177–95.

Owens, Joseph. "Faith, Ideas, Illumination, and Experience." In *The Cambridge History of Later Medieval Philosophy*. Ed. Norman Kretzman, Anthony Kenny, and Jan Pinborg. Cambridge: Cambridge University Press, 1982. 440–59.

Palmer, R. Barton. "The Metafictional Machaut: Self-Reflexivity and Self-Mediation in the Two Judgment Poems." *Studies in the Literary Imagination* 20 (1987): 23–39.

Peter of Spain. *Tractatus*. Ed. L. M. de Rijk. Assen: van Gorcum, 1972. Trans. Francis P. Dinneen, *Peter of Spain: Language in Dispute*. Studies in the History of the Language Sciences 39. Amsterdam: Benjamin, 1990.

Philips, Helen. "Chaucer and Deguileville: The *ABC* in Context." *Medium Aevum* 62, no. 1 (1993): 1–19.

Picherit, Jean Louis. "Les Exemples dans le *Jugement dou roy de Navarre*." *Lettres Romanes* 36 (1982): 103–16.

Picoche, J. *Le Vocabulaire psychologique dans les* Chroniques de Froissart. Vol. 1, Paris: Kleincksieck, 1976 ; vol. 2, Amiens: Publications du Centre d'Etudes picardes, 1984.

Picone, Michelangelo. *L'Enciclopedismo medievale*. Ravenna: Longo, 1994.

Piehler, Paul. *The Visionary Landscape: A Study in Medieval Allegory.* London: Arnold, 1971.

Porphyry. *Isagoge.* Porphyre: *Isagoge.* French trans. and notes J. Tricot. Bibliothèque des textes philosophiques. Paris: Vrin, 1947. English translation in Paul Vincent Spade, *Five Texts on the Medieval Problem of Universals: Porphyry, Boethius, Abelard, Duns Scotus, Ockham.* Indianapolis: Hackett, 1994. See also *Aristoteles Latinus.*

Prantl, Carl. *Geschichte der Logik im Abendlande,* II. Leipzig: Hirzel, 1885.

Quintilian, *Institutio oratoria.* Ed. M. Winterbottom. 2 vols. Oxford: Clarendon Press, 1970. Trans. H. E. Butler. 4 vols. Loeb Classical Library. London: Heinemann, 1922.

Rabaté, Jean-Michel, ed. *The Cambridge Companion to Lacan.* Cambridge: Cambridge University Press, 2003.

Ribémont, Bernard. "Christine de Pizan: Entre espace scientifique et espace imaginé." In *Une femme de Lettres au Moyen Age: Etudes autour de Christine de Pizan.* Ed. Liliane Dulac and Bernard Ribémont. Medievalia 16. Série Etudes Christiniennes. Orléans: Paradigme, 1995. 245–61.

Richards, Earl Jeffrey. "French Cultural Nationalism and Christian Universalism in the Works of Christine de Pizan." In *Politics, Gender and Genre: The Political Thought of Christine de Pizan.* Ed. Margaret Brabant. Boulder, Colo.: Westview Press, 1992. 75–94.

———. "Rejecting Essentialism and Gendered Writing: The Case of Christine de Pizan." In *Gender and Text in the Later Middle Ages.* Ed. Jane Chance. Gainesville: University of Florida Press, 1996. 96–131.

———. "Somewhere Between Destructive Glosses and Chaos: Christine de Pizan and Medieval Theology." In *Christine de Pizan: A Casebook.* Ed. Barbara K. Altmann and Deborah McGrady. New York: Routledge, 2003. 43–55.

Richter, Reinhilt. *Die Troubadourzizate im* Breviari d'amor. Modena: Mucchi, 1976.

Ricketts, Peter T. "The Hispanic Tradition of the *Breviari d'Amor* by Matfre Ermengaud of Béziers." In *Hispanic Studies in Honour of Joseph Manson.* Ed. Dorothy M. Atkinson and Anthony Hedley Clarke. Oxford: Dolphin Books, 1972. 227–53.

Robertson, D. W. Jr. "The Doctrine of Charity in Medieval Gardens: A Topical Approach Through Symbolism and Allegory." *Speculum* 26 (1951): 24–49.

Rorty, Amélie Oksenberg, ed. *Essays on Aristotle's Ethics.* Berkeley: University of California Press, 1980.

Segre, Cesare. "Le forme et le tradizione didattiche." In *Grundriss der Romanischen Literturen des Mittelalters,* Vol. VI, fasc. i, *La Littérature allégorique et satirique.* Dir. Hans Robert Jauss. Heidelberg: Winter, 1966. 58–146.

Shepherdson, Charles. "Lacan and Philosophy." In *The Cambridge Companion to Lacan.* Ed. Jean-Michel Rabaté. Cambridge: Cambridge University Press, 2003. 116–52.

Simpson, James R. *Fantasy, Identity and Misrecognition in Medieval French Narrative.* Bern: Lang, 2000.

Smith, Andrew. "Porphyrian Studies Since 1913." In *Aufstieg und Niedergang der Römischen Welt: Geschichte und Kultur Roms im Spiegel des neueren For-schung.* Ed. Wolfgang Haase. Berlin: De Gruyter. Teil II, vol. 36, no. 2 (1987): 717–73.

Soler, Colette. "The Subject and the Other I" and "The Subject and the Other II." In *Reading Seminar XI: Lacan's Four Fundamental Concepts of Psycho-analysis.* Ed. Richard Feldstein, Bruce Fink, and Maire Jaanus. Albany: SUNY Press, 1995. 39–44 and 44–54.

Solterer, Helen. *The Master and Minerva: Disputing Women in French Medieval Culture.* Berkeley: University of California Press, 1995.

Sowa, John F. *Knowledge Representation: Logical, Philosophical, and Computa-tional Foundations.* Pacific Grove, Calif.: Brooks Cole, 2000.

Spade, Paul Vincent, trans. *Five Texts on the Medieval Problem of Universals: Por-phyry, Boethius, Abelard, Duns Scotus, Ockham.* Indianapolis: Hackett, 1994.

Strange, S. K. "Plotinus, Porphyry and the Neoplatonic Interpretation of the *Cat-egories.*" In *Aufstieg und Niedergang der Römischen Welt: Geschichte und Kultur Roms im Spiegel des neueren Forschung.* Ed. Wolfgang Haase. Berlin: De Gruyter. Teil II, vol. 36, no. 2 (1987): 955–74.

Tarnowski, Andrea W. "Maternity and Paternity in *La Mutation de Fortune.*" In *The City of Scholars: New Approaches to Christine de Pizan.* Ed. Margareta Zimmermann and Dina de Rentiis. Berlin: De Gruyter, 1994. 116–26.

———. "Perspectives on the *Advision.*" In *Christine de Pizan 2000: Studies on Christine de Pizan in Honour of Angus J. Kennedy.* Ed. John Campbell and Nadia Margolis. Amsterdam: Rodopi, 2000. 105–14.

———. "The Lessons of Experience and the *Chemin de long estude.*" In *Christine de Pizan: A Casebook.* Ed. Barbara Altmann and Deborah McGrady. New York: Routledge, 2003. 181–97.

Taylor, Charles. *Sources of the Self: The Making of the Modern Identity.* Cambridge: Cambridge University Press, 1989.

Thiry, Claude. "Allégorie et histoire dans la *Prison amoureuse* de Froissart." *Studi Francesi* 61 (1977): 15–29.

Tobler-Lommatzsch. Tobler, Adolf, and E. Lommatzsch. *Altfranzösisches Wörter-buch.* 14 vols. Stuttgart: Steiner, 1925–2002.

Tuve, Rosamund. *Allegorical Imagery: Some Medieval Books and Their Posterity.* Princeton: Princeton University Press, 1966.

Wenzel, Siegfried. "The Pilgrimage of Human Life as a Late Medieval Genre." *Medieval Studies* 35 (1973): 371–88.

Wetherbee, Winthrop. "Philosophy, Cosmology, and the Twelfth-Century Renais-sance." In *A History of Twelfth-Century Western Philosophy.* Ed. Peter Dronke. Cambridge: Cambridge University Press, 1988. 21–53.

Whitehead, Christiana. Castles of the Mind: A Study of Medieval Architectural Allegory. Cardiff: University of Wales Press, 2003.

Wippel, John F. "Essence and Existence." In *The Cambridge History of Later Medieval Philosophy.* Ed. Norman Kretzman, Anthony Kenny, and Jan Pin-borg. Cambridge: Cambridge University Press, 1982. 385–410.

———. *The Metaphysical Thought of Thomas Aquinas: From Finite Being to Uncre-ated Being.* Washington, D.C.: Catholic University of America Press, 2000.

Wright, Elizabeth. *Lacan and Postfeminism*. Duxford: Icon Books, 2000.

Wright, Steven. "Deguileville's *Pèlerinage de Vie humaine* as 'Contrepartie Edifiante' of the *Roman de la Rose*." *Philological Quarterly* 68 (1989): 399–422.

Zimmermann, Margareta, and Dina de Rentiis, eds. *The City of Scholars: New Approaches to Christine de Pizan*. Berlin: De Gruyter, 1994.

Zink, M. *Froissart et le temps*. Paris: Presses Universitaires de France, 1998.

Žižek, Slavoj. *Looking Awry: An Introduction to Jacques Lacan Through Popular Culture*. Cambridge, Mass.: MIT Press, 1991.

———. *Did Somebody Say Totalitarianism? Five Interventions in the (Mis)use of a Notion*. London: Verso, 2001.

Žižek, Slavoj, with Judith Butler and Ernesto Laclau. *Contingency, Hegemony, Universality: Contemporary Dialogues in the Left*. London: Verso, 2000.

Index

Acknowledgments

I should begin by thanking Nicolette Zeeman, whose chance remark many years ago that monologism might be more challenging than dialogism sowed the seed of this undertaking. The book assumed its final shape within the context of a research project entitled "Poetic Knowledge in Late Medieval France" funded by the Arts and Humanities Research Council at the Universities of Cambridge and Manchester. I wish to acknowledge both the support of the AHRC and the high-octane intellectual input of my colleagues on the project: Adrian Armstrong, Miranda Griffin, Sylvia Huot, Francesca Nicholson, and Finn Sinclair. All of them read and commented on several draft chapters, providing invaluable guidance, friendship, and support. Parts of the book were researched and written during periods of leave funded by the University of Cambridge and Girton College, for which I am extremely grateful.

Various colleagues have been generous with their expertise. I want to thank Renate Blumenfeld-Kosinski for commenting so insightfully on a very early version of the book proposal. I am extremely grateful to Peter Ricketts for making available to me in electronic form volumes of his edition of the *Breviari d'amor* prior to their publication, and for reviewing and commenting on Chapter 1. Also with reference to Chapter 1, John Marenbon responded very helpfully to my inquiry about Porphyrian trees. Rega Wood read and thoroughly disliked Chapter 2, resulting in a stimulating exchange. Stephanie Gibbs responded to an early draft of Chapter 3 and kindly shared with me her astonishing knowledge of Deguileville. Maureen Boulton and Philip Bennett were kind enough to give me copies of, respectively, "Digulleville's *Pèlerinage de Jésus Christ*: A Poem of Courtly Devotion" and "*Ut pictura memoria*: Froissart's Quest for Lost Time" before they were published, and I thank them for their trust and friendship in doing so.

Material from various chapters was presented as papers at the following institutions: Boston University, the University of California (Berkeley, Santa Barbara), Girton College Cambridge, Johns Hopkins University, the University of Kansas (Lawrence), King's College London, the University of Manchester, Princeton University, the University of Southern Denmark (Odense), and Stanford University. Other versions of eventual chapters were test-driven at seminars or conferences at the University of Cambridge, Kalamazoo, the Society for French Studies, and the British Occitan Conference. I cannot thank individually all of the people who commented constructively on these papers but I should like gratefully to acknowledge the contributions made by Marianne Børcht, Cynthia Brown, Mathilda Bruckner, Jodie Enders, John Fleming, Noah Gwynn, David Hult, Caroline Jewers, Stephen G. Nichols, Linda Paterson, Vance Smith, and Zrinka Stahuljak.

Most important but hardest to quantify is the debt I owe to friends and colleagues who formed such a vital part of my intellectual life during the writing of this book, in particular Bill Burgwinkle, Christopher Canon, Simon Gaunt, and Colin Davis, with whom I was in dialogue through most of its genesis, and from whose brilliance I have greatly benefited.